Rhythms of Faithfulness

Rhythms of Faithfulness

Essays in Honor of John E. Colwell

Edited by
ANDY GOODLIFF
& PAUL W. GOODLIFF

Foreword by Stanley Hauerwas

◦PICKWICK *Publications* · Eugene, Oregon

RHYTHMS OF FAITHFULNESS
Essays in Honor of John E. Colwell

Copyright © 2018 Wipf and Stock Publishers. All rights reserved. Except for brief quotations in critical publications or reviews, no part of this book may be reproduced in any manner without prior written permission from the publisher. Write: Permissions, Wipf and Stock Publishers, 199 W. 8th Ave., Suite 3, Eugene, OR 97401.

Pickwick Publications
An Imprint of Wipf and Stock Publishers
199 W. 8th Ave., Suite 3
Eugene, OR 97401

www.wipfandstock.com

PAPERBACK ISBN: 978-1-5326-3350-8
HARDCOVER ISBN: 978-1-5326-3352-2
EBOOK ISBN: 978-1-5326-3351-5

Cataloguing-in-Publication data:

Names: Goodliff, Andy, editor. | Goodliff, Paul W., editor | Hauerwas, Stanley, 1940–, foreword writer

Title: Rhythms of faithfulness : essays in honor of John E. Colwell / edited by Andy Goodliff and Paul W. Goodliff, with a foreword by Stanley Hauerwas.

Description: Eugene, OR: Pickwick Publications, 2018 | Includes bibliographical references.

Identifiers: ISBN 978-1-5326-3350-8 (paperback) | ISBN 978-1-5326-3352-2 (hardcover) | ISBN 978-1-5326-3351-5 (ebook)

Subjects: LCSH: Church calendar | Liturgics | Theology, Doctrinal | Worship | Theology

Classification: BV30 G662 2018 (paperback) | BV30 (ebook)

Manufactured in the U.S.A.   10/01/18

Contents

Foreword by Stanley Hauerwas | vii
Contributors | ix
Introduction | xi
 —Andy Goodliff and Paul Goodliff

PART ONE

1. Becoming Present to God | 3
  —Paul Goodliff
2. Celebrating the Presence of God—Spirituality and the Arts | 16
  —Geoff Colmer
3. Acknowledging Our Humanity: Confessing Our Sins Together | 28
  —Christopher J. Ellis
4. Listening for the Word of God: Divine Speech, Scripture, and the Task of Interpretation | 44
  —Sean F. Winter
5. Bringing Our Concerns | 55
  —Richard Kidd
6. Going to Love and Serve: As the Father Sends Me . . . | 69
  —Margaret Gibbs

PART TWO

7. Advent: The Light Who Dawns | 87
  —Joseph Haward
8. Christmas: Eternal Humanity at the Heart of God | 100
  —E. Anne Clements
9. Epiphany: The One Who Is Revealed | 112
  —Ian Randall

10 Annunciation: Behold, a Virgin Shall Conceive | 128
—Paul Goodliff

11 Lent and Dissent: Discovering the "Poor" | 140
—Sally Nelson

12 Passiontide: Soteriology and the Prayers of Passiontide | 155
—Stephen R. Holmes

13 Easter: Constructing Resurrection Narratives | 168
—Nigel Wright

14 Ascension: "Rich Wounds Yet Visible Above" | 181
—Anthony Clarke

15 Pentecost: The Rhythm of God on Monday | 194
—Paul S. Fiddes

16 Trinity: The Blessing of Almighty God . . . | 211
—Ruth Gouldbourne

17 Creation: Participation and Goal | 223
—Helen Paynter

18 All Saints': Remembering, Learning, and Attending | 237
—Andy Goodliff

Bibliography of the Writings of John E. Colwell | 249
General Bibliography | 253

Foreword

To be asked to write a foreword to a collection of papers honoring John Colwell is an honor. Of course honor is a description Baptists are rightly not sure they want to honor given the militaristic contexts in which the concept of honor is most determinatively exemplified. But that is why honor is so important for Christians to reclaim. If we are a people at war with war we will need a discipline every bit as demanding as those trained to be warriors. Over his distinguished theological career John Colwell has helped us see what such training must look like if we are to serve the Lord who is peace. His is a singular achievement.

But the work of theology is slow and frustrating. Many people, call them Christians if you will, who should demand that such work be done are often among those who ignore the work done by those like John Colwell. Given the subjects of the chapters in this book John has been quite busy. He has convinced students and friends that if we recover what we have been given the world will shout for joy. Moreover such a church will be a social witness making possible developments otherwise unthinkable.

If lives like his did not exist then this book could not help but seem like an advocacy for an illusion. John Colwell is rightly honored in this book as a friend, colleague, teacher, pastor, and theologian. But I am sure he finds the attention a bit overwhelming. I suspect he would pray that the focus not be on his life but rather that his life might be a witness to the One that has made his life possible. What the essays in this book suggest is that John has helped Baptists—of all people—to recover the Christian tradition, something as basic as the Christian year, so that the world might know that we are on God's time.

The manner these students and friends of Colwell approach their subjects is exemplary. I suspect they recognize that they could easily be accused of being Baptists who have gone Catholic. They avoid that far too easy put-down by showing what is at stake when we are shaped for example by the discipline of morning prayer. In the process they help us see Colwell's recovery of the great Catholic tradition is consistent with if not required if Baptists are to be faithful to their own tradition.

Colwell's project, a project also exemplified by my friend and colleague Curtis Freeman in his book *Contesting Catholicity: Theology for Other Baptists*, I believe to be the most important ecumenical development in recent times. We live theologically in a confusing and confused time to be a theologian. Christendom is surely coming to an end but what is to follow in its wake is not yet evident. I believe, as many of the essays in this book suggest, that Baptists particularly in England, under the influence of people like Colwell, have begun to discover ecclesial alternatives in ways unimaginable twenty-five years ago.

Finally I take this book to be a testimony to the importance of friendship for the work of theology. In almost every chapter there is a short story of how Colwell through his person and work changed a student or a friend's life. I suspect these testimonies may make John a bit nervous. When you are told that you made a decisive difference in someone's life you want to disavow you did so. We fear to take responsibility for what God has done through us. But this book is powerful witness to the significance of John Colwell. May his tribe increase.

Stanley Hauerwas

Contributors

Anthony Clarke is Tutor in Pastoral Studies, Regent's Park College, Oxford.

E. Anne Clements is Minister of West Kingsdown Baptist Church, Kent.

Geoff Colmer is Regional Minister Team Leader, Central Baptist Association.

Chris Ellis is former Principal of Bristol Baptist College.

Paul Fiddes is Professor of Systematic Theology, University of Oxford and Senior Research Fellow, Regent's Park College, Oxford.

Margaret Gibbs is Minister of Perry Rise Baptist Church, Forest Hill.

Andy Goodliff is Minister of Belle Vue Baptist Church, Southend-on-Sea.

Paul Goodliff is General Secretary, Churches Together in England.

Ruth Gouldbourne is Minister of Grove Lane Baptist Church, Cheadle.

Joe Haward is Minister of This Hope, Newton Abbott.

Stephen Holmes is Principal of St. Mary's College and Senior Lecturer, University of St. Andrews.

Richard Kidd is Honorary Research Fellow, Luther King House, Manchester.

Sally Nelson is Dean of Baptist Formation, St Hild College, Sheffield.

Helen Paynter is Research Fellow and Coordinator of Community Learning, Bristol Baptist College.

Ian Randall is former Tutor in Church History and Spirituality, Spurgeon's College, London.

Sean Winter is Director of Education and Formation for Leadership and Head of College at Pilgrim Theological College, Australia.

Nigel Wright is Principal Emeritus, Spurgeon's College, London.

Introduction

Andy Goodliff and Paul Goodliff

John Colwell is one of very few British Baptists who could sit in a room of the finest theological minds and, apparently, not be fazed (although Paul remembers one particular lecture in the early 1990s at King's College, London's Research Institute for Systematic Theology when, after a particularly dense lecture in philosophical theology he turned to John and expressed his dismay at understanding so little, only to be met by almost an equivalent degree of bemusement). John himself has contributed several important theological works. His doctoral thesis on Karl Barth's doctrine of election and eternity, *Actuality and Provisionality*, has continued to appear regularly in footnotes of subsequent theological engagements with Barth since it was first published in 1989.[1] His book on theological ethics, *Living the Christian Story*, saw Stanley Hauerwas write a long review article in response.[2] *Promise and Presence*, an argument for a theology of the seven sacraments of the Catholic Church, has found a wide readership, going beyond just the Baptist constituency.[3] This reflects the way in which John has always written for the church catholic rather than merely the church Baptist. His small book *The Rhythm of Doctrine*, a sketch of Christian faith, found an even wider audience following an appreciative review from the

1. It was reprinted in 2011 by Wipf & Stock. William Placher called it "the best discussion of the topic in English I know," *Narratives of a Vulnerable God*, 49.

2. Hauerwas and Sider, "Distinctiveness of Christian Ethics." The book is also called "insightful" by the Pauline scholar Michael Gorman, *Becoming the Gospel*, 1.

3. The Church of England's Bishop of Coventry Christopher Cocksworth gave it a warm review in *Ecclesiology* 5 (2009) 99–102, and it has also been a key text on a course on the sacraments taught by the Anglican theologian Joseph Mangina.

editor of *Christianity Today*.[4] In another review, Suzanne McDonald called it "beautifully conceived, theologically rich and engagingly written."[5] His most recent book, *Why Have You Forsaken Me?*, is his most personal as he explores theologically the experience of God-forsakenness and his own struggle with bipolar disorder.

Born in Brighton, and growing up in a deeply Christian home, John found his teenage home amongst the Baptists.[6] Attending the same school as one of the editors of this collection (Paul, with a school-career's interval between them), Varndean Grammar School for Boys did not bring out the best in John. Some of his teachers there would be amazed to hear of the successful academic career that was to blossom later. John Colwell went to Spurgeon's in 1970 where he trained for the ministry. He married Rosemary in the summer of 1973. His first church was Maldon Baptist Church, where he stayed until 1979 when he returned to Spurgeon's having begun his PhD at King's College, London, supervised by Colin Gunton.[7] Colin along with Stanley Hauerwas, who John began to read in the mid-1980s,[8] are the twin sources of much that has shaped John's theology, in addition to Barth and, via Stanley, the theology of Thomas Aquinas.[9] He returned to pastoral ministry in 1982, becoming minister at Catford Baptist Church, South London, where began deep engagement with one of the Restoration church movement's most enduring streams, New Frontiers (then known as Coastlands), associated with Terry Virgo. In 1994 he returned to Spurgeon's as tutor in applied theology. The following year he became tutor in systematic theology, and then in 1996 tutor in Christian doctrine and ethics, a position he held until 2009, when he returned to pastoral ministry once again, this time in Budleigh Salterton, Devon. Doctoral research by Paul Goodliff into the character of Baptist ministry and convictions about ordination suggests that John has done more than most to reshape Baptist ministry in a sacramental register amongst those who were formed at Spurgeon's during his tenure, as well as assisting in shaping a wider acceptance of Baptist ministry as sacra-

---

4. David Neff, review of *The Rhythm of Doctrine*, by John E. Colwell, *Neff Review*, August 25, 2007, http://neffreview.blogspot.co.uk/2007/08/baptist-theologizes-liturgical-year.html.

5. MacDonald, review of *The Rhythm of Doctrine*.

6. John tells some of his own story in Colwell, *Why Have You Forsaken Me?*, 11–23.

7. John says of Colin, "He was a loyal friend and confidant; virtually every academic thought I have had has, in some respects, been a response to him and to his theological perception," *Promise and Presence*, x.

8. John probably first encountered Stanley at a 1986 conference in Oxford marking the centenary of Karl Barth's birth, see Colwell, "Characterisation and Character," 1.

9. See Colwell, *Promise and Presence*, x, and *Rhythm of Doctrine*, ix, 1.

mental in character.[10] He retired from full-time ministry in 2014. Colwell's fifteen years at Spurgeon's College left an indelible mark upon several generations of students, who experienced his classes.[11] Many of us have been taught and nourished through reading his work, or in some cases, listening in as he and Paul Fiddes held court for many years, during Baptist Union Council, in the later evenings over cheese, wine, and the odd single malt.

John's impact has also been felt in the Order for Baptist Ministry, which he helped cofound in 2009. A group of his Spurgeon's students, in learning about the Order of Preachers (the Catholic Dominicans) had asked why no one from "The Preacher's College"[12] had anything similar to join. This began to spark the vision, which John subsequently shared with Paul Goodliff, who in turn took it to his fellow mutual support group of Geoff Colmer, Colin Norris, and Martin Taylor.[13] That group of five, and each with an invited companion (including for John's part one of those original students, now in pastoral ministry), and facilitated by Ruth Bottoms, spent thirty-six hours at Ivy Lodge, Warminster, from which emerged both the bones of the nature of the order, and its founding document, "The Dream" (which had come almost in that fashion to Ruth during the early hours of that time of vision-casting).[14] John continued as one of the core group members for a while after the founding of the order, and has been instrumental in the growth of membership in three small groups (cells) in the South West of England, where he continues to live.

A common feature of that original group of five was an early ministerial embrace of charismatic renewal (and, in John's case, at least, of a stream that was part of the movement called "Restorationism," although how far all that entailed was shared by John is debatable) and later, a desire to recognize the value of the wider Western and Catholic spiritual tradition.[15] This was neither a sign of any rejection of the reality of the charismatic, nor a muted flight to the Roman Catholic Church—all remain convinced Baptists, and therefore Protestants, and heirs to the Dissenters—but rather a recognition that where Baptists and charismatics were most deficient, the Western spiritual tradition offered treasure in a way that they found the Celtic, Northumbrian tradition did not.

10. Goodliff, *Ministry, Sacrament and Representation*, 151.

11. For example, Holmes, *God of Grace & God of Glory*, xi; and Southall, *Rediscovering Righteousness in Romans*, v.

12. As Spurgeon's College is known.

13. The group had met regularly ever since their time as students together at Spurgeon's College in the mid-eighties, incidentally, before John was resident.

14. http://www.orderforbaptistministry.co.uk/the-dream/.

15. For John's own account, see *Rhythm of Doctrine*, 5–6.

There was essentially a search for the unique charism of this fledgling order, and it was discerned to be a means by which Baptist ministry with a more sacramental character might find the resources to remain faithful to baptism, call, and ordination. This entailed devising a daily office of greater variety than that found elsewhere in English Protestantism (hence a diversity of offices for each day of the week, a project still in progress at the time of writing—that is closely linked to the liturgical year, reflecting John's own *The Rhythm of Doctrine*); commitment to a contemplative dimension to prayer; participation in a cell for mutual accountability and a gathering annually in convocation. Thus was born the only dispersed Baptist religious order at present in existence in the British Isles (the Northumbria Order, in which a number of Baptists participate, is ecumenical) owing something to the New Monasticism, as well as the renewal movement of half a century earlier. John's role in seeing this possibility, and ensuring it did not dissipate its unique charism cannot be overestimated. It is fitting, then, that this collection of papers should follow the structure of the Order for Baptist Ministry Daily Office, and the rhythm of the liturgical year by which John so imaginatively has shaped his own dogmatics.

Thus, this book is structured in two ways. The first part seeks to engage with the structured elements of the Daily Office of the Order for Baptist Ministry: becoming present to God, celebrating the presence of God, acknowledging our humanity, and so forth.[16] Some of those writing these chapters are members of the order.[17] Still in its infancy, we hope that by thinking more deeply about the Daily Office in this way, we can offer both something to those who are members of the order and those who might be interested to know more. The second part of the book seeks to offer further studies on the sketch that Colwell offers in *The Rhythm of Doctrine*, as well as engaging with the different days and seasons of the OBM Daily Office. During ordinary time the OBM Daily Office begins with Easter on Sunday, and then follows through Pentecost, Advent, Christmas, Epiphany, Lent & Passiontide, and Creation on the remaining days of the week, and some readers might like to follow that pattern.

---

16. We note here that there is one section of the Daily Office that we do not have a chapter on, which is called "Reflecting on Our Roots." This is a prayer based on the OBM's founding "Dream."

17. Paul Goodliff, Geoff Colmer, Margaret Gibbs, Richard Kidd are professed members, while others, such as Ruth Gouldbourne and Joe Hayward, have participated regularly in cells, and others, such as Paul Fiddes and Anthony Clarke, have encouraged the use of the Daily Office in the process of ministerial formation. Andy Goodliff uses the Daily Office with those in his church who gather for weekday morning prayer.

The contributors to the book were all invited to write their assigned chapter and then a good number of us gathered overnight at Regent's Park College, Oxford,[18] to discuss and comment on each other's work, seeking to model the Baptist practice of doing theology together. We hope this has led to a better book. Some of the contributors are working pastors, others practicing college tutors or lecturers in theology, and some have held posts of regional or national oversight, but all have great affection and respect for John. We are grateful to Stanley Hauerwas, a longtime provocateur for John's own life and thought, for agreeing to write the foreword. Final thanks go to the Whitley Committee for a kind gift that helped make the publication of this book possible.

The varied character of the contributions reflects the multifaceted nature of John's ministry as a Baptist minister, college tutor, and personal friend. Some contributors engage significantly with John's writings, especially *The Rhythm of Doctrine* and *Promise and Presence*, while others renew old controversies rehearsed in late-night conversations over congenial refreshment. Some attend closely to Scripture (which, as one who preached regularly throughout his ministerial life, is John's practice, too), while others engage more closely with the OBM Daily Office. John's appreciation of music is reflected in at least one chapter, and his engagement spiritually with the Western Catholic tradition finds its echoes in more than one place. As noted already, some contributors work mostly in the academy, others in local or regional pastoral oversight of Baptist churches, while others straddle both worlds with adept coherence. This is expressed in the variety of registers the chapters sound—some more pastoral, others more academic—and this is deliberate, for it expresses both the considerable achievement of John's theological endeavors, and his engagement with the quotidian life of the local church, and the way in which his theological writing always has an eye to the question "so what" for the discipleship and life of the people of God, and his preaching a vividly theological character.

John has been a teacher, a friend, a colleague, and for all of us a partner in the gospel. We hope this book both honors the impact he has made on our lives and at the same time, is the kind of theology, inspired by John, which will make an impact on many more lives, in proclamation of Christian faith and faithfulness.

---

18. We are grateful to Regent's for their hospitality.

PART ONE

PART ONE

1

Becoming Present to God

PAUL GOODLIFF

+ In the name of the Father, and of the Son and of the Holy Spirit.

JOHN WAS MY FIRST theological teacher. In 1982 I was called to a pastoral role at Streatham Baptist Church (Lewin Road), where I was already a member and elder and working as a schoolmaster at Tiffin School, just as its minister, Douglas McBain, moved on to a wider apostolic ministry.[1] Douglas suggested that some form of theological education might be beneficial (how right he was!) and arranged for me to see John Colwell, with the aim of teaching me Greek. Armed with a copy of Wenham, I duly arrived at John's manse, and sad to say, made not a great deal of progress with Greek—as we mainly discussed, as I recall, Barth. This continued until in 1984 I enrolled at Spurgeon's College. During those two years a friendship was born. We, at that time, shared a charismatic spirituality and a love of learning (John was completing his PhD) and that continued as the network of like-minded ministers across South London continued to meet monthly at "Lewin,"[2] for a while, John included.

1. Douglas McBain founded Manna Ministries to support this wider ministry, and subsequently became the Baptist Union's Metropolitan Superintendent (London Baptist Association).

2. The group, called "Norman's Boys" (yes, we were in those days, all men) was

We discovered we had been to the same Grammar School in Brighton, albeit five years apart, and recalled with fondness some of the masters who had taught us both—the roots of that friendship were deeper than we had imagined. After ordination, and a year teaching half-time at Spurgeon's, back-filling for the unplanned absence of a couple of tutors, I embarked upon postgraduate work at King's College, London, in systematic theology, and John and I would often sit together at conferences in the 1990s held there for the Research Institute in Systematic Theology. Colin Gunton taught me, and he had been John's doctoral supervisor—our paths continued to intertwine. They continued to do so in a variety of ways: membership of Baptist Union Council; John chaired a committee I was responsible for while head of ministry at the Baptist Union; and latterly, we played a founding role in the life of the Order for Baptist Ministry (a story told in the introduction) and which shapes the themes of this volume in tribute to him. John's friendship is counted amongst the longest and most important of my life, and it is a joy to contribute to this volume in two ways—as coeditor and contributor.

Each version of the Daily Office for the Order for Baptist Ministry (although, not its Midday Prayers, nor its Prayer at Day's Ending) begins with a section entitled "Becoming Present to God."[3] The daily office will often specifically suggest the rubric "through a sign of attentiveness like lighting a candle or + In the name of the Father and of the Son and of the Holy Spirit," and is always followed by a short word and response. For Sunday and Easter, for instance, that offers two alternatives:

> The Lord is risen!
> He is risen indeed! Alleluia!

or

> Risen Lord, In this place and at this time
> come and stand among us.[4]

Some of the offices use verses from a hymn: so, the Tuesday and Advent office offers a Taize chant[5] or a verse from "O come, O come Immanuel." That same season's Alternative Office offers the first verse from the Dodderidge hymn "Hark the Glad Sound," the Alternative Christmas Office two verses from "From Lands That See the Sun Arise," and an early

---

chaired by the Rev'd Norman Moss, Minister at Wimbledon Baptist Church, and was an effective mutual support group.

3. Midday prayer starts, nonetheless, with the + In the name of the Father . . .
4. The word and response also used in the Alternative Easter office.
5. "Wait for the Lord, his day is near."

version of an Alternative Advent Office had a verse from the carol "Lo! How a Rose, E'er Blooming"—in German! ("Es ist ein Reis entsprungen . . .") The wisdom of the core group for the order prevailed and such pretentiousness (mine) was removed (I had a mild obsession with that carol at the time, I remember).

This chapter seeks to explore what we might be doing when we seek to become present to God in the context of the Daily Office. In what ways are we present to God already? What does it mean by seeking to become present by the use of a sign? Is invoking the Trinity the sign, or the physical gesture suggested by the + that precedes it, and which invites the sign of the cross to be made across the torso of the one praying?

What John Colwell would emphasise is that encountering the presence of God is not dependent upon a felt-experience of some kind. This is not a search for spiritual goose bumps. John has suffered from bipolar depression for most of his adult life, and freely acknowledges this both in the book that focuses most upon this aspect of his life, *Why Have You Forsaken Me?*[6] and in this observation from the preface to *Promise and Presence*, "I write as one for whom felt-experience is frequently elusive; I write as one for whom spiritual and emotional darkness have become common companions; I write as one for whom promise and mediated presence have therefore become increasingly precious."[7] If all theology is in varying measure an outcome of personal experience, then John's has certainly been shaped by this. However, even those for whom this dark path is not familiar, becoming present to God dare not be merely a variety of emotional reassurance or inner peace. It may, in God's grace be both, but becoming present to God is never dependent upon them, but rather upon the promise of God, in the words of Jesus, "I am with you always, to the end of the age" (Matt 28:20b).

Also what such a move at the start of the Daily Office most assuredly is *not*, is a kind of wake-up call to remind God we are here, a knock at heaven's door to awaken God's attention, or a plea to turn his gaze upon us for a while. It is our attentiveness that is required, not God's, for his is constant and unwavering. Our attention is claimed by many objects—at present, my attention is upon these words being typed and the annoying habit of the two-fingered keyboard aficionado of misplacing letters, requiring retyping, and the fact that it is raining very hard outside my study window—but God does not suffer from limited attention. All things are present to him, and, indeed, sustained by that attention and power. Were God's attention to somehow be lost, then creation would lose its being, and all order return

6. Colwell, *Why Have You Forsaken Me?*
7. Colwell, *Promise and Presence*, x.

to primordial chaos. No, God requires no call to attentiveness, not even a gentle "ahem" represented by the lighting of a candle or gesture of the cross. It is always he who first welcomes us, not we who welcome him, as some contemporary worship songs would do well to understand. This "becoming present to God" is the drawing of *my* wayward attention to his eternal presence, a preparing of *my* soul to draw near to the One who is Father, Son, and Holy Spirit, and a settling of my spirit in preparation for God's disturbing presence.

This question of how God is present to us lies at the heart of a long and controversial discussion over many years between Colwell and Paul Fiddes. Where John claims that to make everything sacramental is to emasculate sacramentalism,[8] Paul responds that "signs signify in different ways and in different degrees."[9] That debate is reflected in John's contribution to a Festschrift in honour of Paul Fiddes, "On Language and Presence,"[10] and in Paul's contribution to this volume. As I understand it, at its heart lies the question of whether God's inner life is mediated by the Spirit, and how this predicates the mediated character of God's presence to creation. Both agree that the presence of God to creation is in some way a mediated presence, especially through the sacraments, but for John (unlike Paul) such a mediation requires that the love of the Father and the Son be mediated by the Spirit—everything in God is mediated. Paul insists that this is unnecessary, and there is a perichoretic flow of relationships that is eternal and unmediated in God, and so a more fluid way in which God is present to us.[11] Where Colwell speaks of mediation, Fiddes speaks of participation. So, God makes himself present to us through baptism and the bread and wine of the Eucharist, and both would agree upon this. For John, that presence is mediated through the Holy Spirit, and here his theology reflects the influence of Calvin. John, however, goes further. He attributes to the Spirit (never a depersonalized "thing" but always a personal being) the role of mediating the love of God between Father and Son:

> In every respect and in every instance the relatedness of the Father to the Son and the relatedness of the Son to the Father as narrated in the Gospel story is a mediated relatedness; it is never unmediated. And if that which is narrated in the gospel story is a reiteration of the form and manner of the love between Father and Son in eternity, if revelation is truly revelation, if God is in

8. Colwell, *Promise and Presence*, 55.
9. Fiddes, "Ex Opere Operato," 228.
10. Colwell, "In the Beginning Was the Word."
11 Fiddes, *Participating in God*, 281, 299.

eternity who he is in this narrative, then even in eternity the love between the Father and the Son is mediated and never unmediated . . . it is only because this absolute love and self-giving is mediated, rather than unmediated, that the persons of the Trinity remain distinct, that the Trinity does not collapse into an indistinct monad.[12]

It is this mediatory *necessity* of the Spirit between the Father and the Son that Fiddes disputes, and which has consequences for our becoming present to God through a sign. If even the love between Father and Son is mediated by the Spirit, then does this imply that we only encounter God when mediated by the person of the Spirit? While John, following Gunton, wishes to reinvigorate a role for the Spirit as person, a role which has often in the Western tradition been seen as attributed to a rather impersonal force, or something akin to a substance—grace, and this reinvigoration is to be welcomed, does this imply too distant a role for the Father and the Son in their presence to creation? To put it naively, when we pray, asking Christ to "stand amongst us in your risen power," is it the Spirit alone who is present, and when we pray, "Our Father in heaven . . . ," does he hear, or only the faint echo of that prayer as mediated by the Spirit? The vital doctrine that what one person in the Trinity does, all do (the unity of God's actions *ad extra*) would suggest that the Father, Son, and Spirit are equally present to us when our attention is drawn to their intimate presence in all things.

If, then, the Father, the Son, and the Spirit are present to us—the God who is three in one—as we attune our attention towards his presence to us, what means might we utilize to do so? Here both Fiddes and Colwell are helpful.

"A CANDLE MAY BE LIT . . ."

The rubric in the Daily Office that suggests lighting a candle might imply simply a nod towards the way in which many Catholic practices have become acceptable to those whose tradition suggests they should be entirely shunned. Growing up mid-century in a very "low church" Anglican Parish, in a rather anti-Catholic atmosphere, candles never appeared on the Lord's Table, and even at Christmas they were slightly suspect. It was a mark of how we differentiated ourselves from those Anglo-Catholics in the neighbouring Church of England parish as much as from the Catholics elsewhere in our parish. But evangelicals and Protestants seem now to be much more irenic when it comes to candles! The ecumenical movement, and the Second

---

12. Colwell, *Promise and Presence*, 39. Colwell attributes this insight to Tom Smail.

Vatican Council have helped, of course, but above all, it has been the discovery of Catholic spirituality, and its virtue, that has given many evangelicals, and not a few Baptists too, the freedom from reserve about such practices. So, is the suggestion, often followed, that becoming present to God through the lighting of a candle, merely a sentimental, or affective aid?

Fiddes's insistence that God is present to us through all he has made—that God is in all, and through all and for all—would suggest that there is a deeper significance. A flickering candle flame is a sign of God's presence. Colwell would no doubt say that this *may* be the case, but God has not promised *explicitly* so, and so we may not count upon it. With such caution in the background, let me proceed. A candle is living, responsive to the moving of air so that it flickers, and vulnerable. It gives light, such that even one small candle in an otherwise darkened room, illuminates. Above all, it speaks of the Son who is the light of the world—and not the Son only, although it is Jesus of Nazareth, the incarnate Son who speaks. The Father of Lights (Jas 1:17) and the Spirit, the Lord and Giver of Life speak as well. This draws our attention to the One who defines his glory not in totalitarian acts of absolute power, as any self-respecting despot might, but through the abject weakness of a newborn's cry and the wordless cry of a man dying on a cross.[13] God is living, responsive to the moving "breath" of our prayers, imparting light as we draw near. Through the Spirit, we might even venture a form of sacramentality about lighting a candle. It points by grace to what it signifies in itself. This is a sacramentality derived from the God who is present in all creation, while remaining utterly free from any demand and in his uncreated nature, distinct from it. The ability of creation to be truly and freely itself is not obviated by the sustaining Word that ensures its orderly existence and continuity. While this does not have the absolute quality of promise that accompanies the dominical sacraments, nor even the way in which God has promised to speak through the Scriptures, it has the quality of drawing our wayward attention towards the God who attends to our cry (Ps 145:18–19).

SILENCE AND STILLNESS

Second, while not explicit, the expectation in the opening section of the office is that there will be some silence and stillness, some pausing from the activity and speech that precedes it, in order to become attentive. This is not to propose that God cannot be met in the busyness of our daily work, nor met in the noisy conversation, and especially that he is not encountered

---

13. Cf. Gray, *Jesus in the Theology of Rowan Williams*, 105.

in the very vocal praise of communal Christian worship. For many, their primary means of "becoming present to God" is sung worship—and its absence from much of the life of the order is not to decry that dimension of worship, but rather to acknowledge that it takes its proper context from the life of the churches to which every member of the order belongs, and the order offers something else in addition.

Silence expresses the humility that acknowledges that my speech, my ideas, my power must become subject to God's, and so I keep silent to listen. Amongst the virtues of silence are the awareness of the sins of the tongue (contempt for others, domination, and malice), growth in the ability to listen deeply to others, as well as to our own inner world of the heart, an acknowledgment that at some point words fail in their adequacy (that is, the apophatic sense that words fail to do justice to the divine) and the ability to deepen concentration. In this context at the beginning of the daily office, as we become present to the God who hears our subsequent prayers, this enhancement of concentration and listening places the priority firmly with God. This is a quality most necessary in a world of noise—of traffic, of ubiquitous music (and "musak"), and of speech that skitters across the surface of things and those screens that mediate reality to us.

Stillness is associated with this, and the importance of bodily posture in preparation for prayer is well documented. Accompanied by a slowing of breathing, and a posture that is the opposite of frantic activity, this attention to our own body in stillness, as well as a deliberate avoidance of unnecessary noise, is more than a psychological trick. It is a *signum* of the God who precedes me, who is present before I am attentive, and before whom therefore, silence and stillness is appropriate worship.

Silence allows something more, though. It is possible to light the candle, say the *in nomine*, and even enter into silence, and still avoid an inner encounter, an interior sense of drawing near to God. While John is suspicious of *reliance* upon this for faith, I am not so sure that he denies its reality at times for himself and others, even if for him it is never predictable (apart from, say, its anticipated absence when in the depths of desolation). The *signum* are necessary steps, but do not exhaust the experience of an *inner* witness to the presence of God. This interior experience can be sought, even if it is never our property; it can be desired, even if in God's gracious wisdom it is never automatic, there being times when its absence is necessary to our growth in faith. There will be times, however, when we do find our heart crying, "Abba, Father!" and with Paul we recognize that "it is that very Spirit bearing witness with our spirit that we are children of God" (Rom 8:15b–16).

A way of actively seeking this inner response is to pay attention to Ignatius's Third Addition—to take a period of paying attention to God before anything else. Writing about this Ignatian discipline, Rob Marsh, SJ, writes, "When I look at the God who looks at me, it is not a matter simply of seeing the other as one object among many, but of looking, gazing, contemplating. We see each other. The look transforms—it is encounter."[14] More than an "introductory gambit in the game of prayer," more than just the first thing we do as we become present to God, this pause and attentiveness to God, enables all else that follows to be real encounter with the living God. "When prayer becomes an encounter with the living God, it becomes unpredictable. You thought you were doing something relatively safe—praying—and instead you find yourself face to face with someone real. Fierce or fond, bright or dark (who knows?), but it is someone other and someone real—not yourself."[15]

THE WORD MADE FLESH

Third, while silence and stillness is intrinsic to the process of becoming present to God, the last word in this becoming present to God is not *no*-word, but the Word. At the heart of every daily office is the reading of Scripture as organized by the Revised Common Lectionary and the Anglican pattern of daily readings. In his essay "In the Beginning Was the Word . . . ," John explores this at some length. While acknowledging that to say with John the Evangelist that the Word is God cannot be reversed to imply that God is simply speech, a language game, John claims that to say "the Word was with God and the Word was God" from the beginning, that is from eternity, then "God eternally is never without Word, speech, language. More radically still, if the Word *is* God, then Word, speech, language are inherent to God: it is not just that God is never without Word, it is also that God is only authentically God in this identification."[16] If Word is inherent to God, then he cannot solely be "one," but must be a plurality, not just in his communication with "another" (creation) but within himself.

Now, this might imply a *Logos asarkos*, an eternal Word and his relationship to the particular subject who is Jesus of Nazareth. Colwell notes how this has gained sharper expression in the dispute, sometimes acrimonious, that has divided Barth scholarship in recent times. Barth affirms Jesus

---

14. Marsh, "Looking at God Looking at You," 26.
15. Marsh, "Looking at God Looking at You," 27.
16. Colwell, "In the Beginning Was the Word," 48.

Christ as both electing God and elected man.[17] But the relationship of this two-sided election to God's eternal nature was left undeveloped by Barth, opening the way for a long-running dispute between Paul Molnar and Bruce McCormack.[18] John summarizes this dispute, with Barth's affirmation of the freedom of God's love, "that God is God in this way and not in some other way, that he elects us in Jesus Christ, that he creates and loves that which is other than himself . . . is wholly an outcome of God's freedom (so Paul Molnar and others)."[19] Barth, however, similarly everywhere affirms that this freedom is not caprice. Colwell continues,

> The positive freedom to be this electing, creating, reconciling, and redeeming God in Jesus Christ and not to be God in some other way, and in this respect, Barth's doctrine of election would appear to precede and to determine his doctrine of the Trinity—God elects himself as this God with the positive freedom to elect us for himself in Jesus Christ; eternal election specifies (if not determines) eternal nature and being . . . (so Bruce McCormack and others).[20]

Barth rejects the notion of *Logos asarkos*, an eternal Word of God other than this particular Word of God made flesh in Jesus Christ. This Word, "who was with God and was Himself God, participating in the divine being, before created time began, in the eternity of God"[21] is the incarnate One. Now, does the incarnation change God, or was he eternally never without this particular humanity now realized in human history in the man Jesus of Nazareth? This takes us the heart of the matter of God's changelessness, or otherwise:

> Here, surely, we encounter the most radical implication of God's changelessness. If, with Augustine and Thomas Aquinas, we reject the possibility of any potentiality in God, we are left with no choice but to affirm this Word's eternal humanness and, thereby, since the Word is not just with God but *is* God in the beginning, the eternal humanity of God. This is the radical step that Bruce McCormack ventures and that Paul Molnar and others resist . . .

17. Barth, *Church Dogmatics*, II/2, 94–194.

18. This dispute began in 2002 with Molnar's criticism of McCormack's chapter in *The Cambridge Companion to Karl Barth* (edited by John Webster) and is found in Molnar, *Divine Freedom*, 61–64, and has continued. A good starting point for this debate is Dempsey, *Trinity and Election in Contemporary Theology*.

19. Colwell, "In the Beginning Was the Word," 51.

20. Colwell, "In the Beginning Was the Word," 51.

21. Barth, *Church Dogmatics*, III/2, 484.

> If the Word who . . . *was* God in the beginning is this Word made flesh, Jesus Christ himself, then this flesh which is itself created flesh is eternally in and with God; then this flesh which is eternally in and with God is itself the eternal possibility of that which is other than God, the eternal possibility of creation.[22]

Colwell continues with a critique of biblical fundamentalism (the Word became text), since the words of Scripture remain human words, even when adopted and inspired by the Spirit. Even "divinely inspired human words are inherently vulnerable to imprecision, misapprehension and misapplication."[23] Claims to biblical authority can never be anything but thinly veiled totalitarian claims to authority, and when claims to inner illumination are married to dogmatic assertion, an authoritarian interpretation of Scripture is even more so a bid for power. Taking the argument in a direction that differs slightly from Colwell's, it is important that in our listening to the Word, and through it listening to the Word made flesh, as we become present to God, we keep silence, we refrain from that evangelical impetus to always comment, to always lay claim to understanding. We simply listen, and are silent. Perhaps many attempts to hear the Word, and then immediately to seek to interpret it, to apply it, to comment upon it, are subtle ways to avoid the Word made flesh who draws near.

Furthermore, as Colwell asserts, this word, this Scripture, is the church's Bible, and not simply an individual's. It is the gathering of the church—for us Baptists, the local congregation in fellowship with other gatherings of disciples—that has the corporate duty of discerning the mind of Christ through a communal interpretation of Scripture. Fiddes asserts the same principle, "[Baptists] have always seen 'private reading' in the context of congregational reading."[24] Steve Harmon suggests that this is the equivalent, for Baptists, of the Catholic *magisterium*.[25] While it is true that neither individuals saying the office, nor, equally, cells doing so in their habitual practice of saying the office together when meeting, are "congregations" or Baptist churches, and any attempt to apply such a status to the order is misguided, nonetheless, when there is a gathering of the whole ecclesial community, as at convocation, here is a context in which the understanding and application of Scripture might be communally discerned. Then, broader in scope, this is offered to both wider Baptist communities, and the catholic church,

---

22. Colwell, "In the Beginning Was the Word," 52.
23. Colwell, "In the Beginning Was the Word," 54.
24. Fiddes, "Spirituality as Attentiveness," 51.
25. Harmon, *Towards Baptist Catholicity*, 63–69.

but not arrogantly so, but with the grace of humility that is expressed in the silence and stillness that precedes any action or word.

+ IN THE NAME OF THE FATHER . . .

The second *signum* in the opening section of the daily office is a combination of word and action—a declaration that all that follows will be done in the name of the Holy Trinity, while signing with the cross. "+ In the name of the Father, and of the Son and of the Holy Spirit." It also is the final word spoken and action signed in every version of the office. As we noted with the lighting of a candle, this would have been an unthinkable gesture for an earlier generation of Baptists, and remains so for the great majority. Some members of the order use this sign, while others, while saying the words, do not sign.

Its biblical origins lie in the dominical command to go and baptize (Matt 28:19): "Go therefore and make disciples of all nations, baptizing them in the name of the Father and of the Son and of the Holy Spirit." Here, its use might reflect a commitment to living the baptized life: having been baptized into Christ in the name of the Father, Son, and Holy Spirit, this moment is the opportunity to reaffirm the faith and obedience that flows from that. The fact that it is a sign of the cross that is shaped is a daily reminder that the life of discipleship is a taking up of a cross in Christlike obedience. For Catholics it is a sacramental,[26] preparing an individual to receive grace and become disposed to cooperate with it, and as such it has its proper place at the start of the office.

There is no specific variety of signing that is encouraged. Differences between Catholic and Orthodox usage centre around the manner of shaping the fingers—the Eastern practice is to bring together the thumb and two forefingers, representing the Trinity, with the smaller two fingers pressed into the palm, representing Christ's two natures. A Western variant has an open hand, with the five fingers representing the five wounds of Christ. The practice is ancient, with Theodoret (393–457) being an early exponent describing in some detail its usage and meaning, and today is more widespread in its use than in its avoidance (Baptists again being in a minority, possibly for proper historical reasons that have long lost their significance). At its worst, I suppose, it degenerates into a form of folk religion, most visibly seen when some football teams enter the pitch (although those who do so may well have a sincere faith), but its misuse should not determine its prohibition.

---

26. Sacramentals, *Catechism of the Catholic Church*, 1670.

The fact that it is a visible action (alongside, say, a posture for prayer, such as kneeling, or an action in praise, such as the lifting up of the hands) places it in the realm of an enacted prayer, a *signum* of more than is immediately obvious. In this regard it has a gracious plenitude that is truer to the doctrines of the Trinity discussed above than those entirely cerebral and wordy practices that so often accompany the anxious and frantic activism of contemporary Baptist and evangelical Christians. It seems perverse to me to endorse the charismatic practice of raised hands, while frown upon the signing of the cross—both signs carry visible and wordless prayer that accompanies (or not) the spoken words used.

Its usage from the beginnings of the order reflects the conscious embrace of the Western Catholic tradition of spirituality that characterizes the origins of the Order for Baptist Ministry, but it does more than place it within a particular tradition. It gives depth to the way in which the office begins and ends with God the Holy Trinity (and so avoids a folky privileging of Jesus, so common in much contemporary spirituality and worship), and the cross-shaped way in which every day proceeds, not just Fridays and Lent and Passiontide.

Fiddes notes how attentiveness to others may not be matched by attentiveness to Christ, and indeed those who are not Christians may have become highly attuned to others, in the way Levinas has insisted is important, but lack entirely any attentiveness to Christ.[27] The obverse is also sadly common, with an attempt at attentiveness to God, but lacking any attentiveness to others, in whom, so claims Levinas, we see the face of the Other. The use of the "*in nomine*" at the close of each daily office is an invitation to go and look for the hidden face of God in the faces of others, and that little word "go" suggests a journey embarked upon. Fiddes also relates the stillness, of which we spoke earlier, to the metaphor of journey—one flowing into the other. From clamor we enter silence and stillness in the name of the Father and Son and Spirit, at the end we continue the journey, back into clamor and demand, in that same triune name, for God is not met just in the place that seems religious, but in those that are most determinedly secular and worldly. In other words, "the still point of the turning world,"[28] to quote T. S. Eliot, must be related to the continuing journey. In between we give our attention to the God who energizes that commitment to go in the way of the cross, signed upon us.

> The term "spirituality," understood as attentiveness, includes such aspects as a discipline of stillness and receptivity of the

---

27. Fiddes, "Spirituality as Attentiveness," 26.
28. Eliot, "Burnt Norton," IV, from *Four Quartets*, 183.

mind, an awareness of a mysterious reality of love and justice that transcends what can be empirically tested, and a journey of empathy that flows from such receptivity and attentiveness . . . For Christian believers, such a kind of spirituality will centre upon a journey into the fellowship of the triune God, through identification with the crucified and risen Jesus.[29]

In all of these practices, deeply embedded in the praying and liturgy of the church of Jesus Christ, we are rooted in a wider, corporate prayer, not only of those who pray this office with members of the order, but with the universal church at prayer. We read these Scriptures with the whole church. Colwell is very clear on this: "Prayer and worship are never individual activities: we pray and worship before the Father, in the Son, and by the Holy Spirit . . . When I pray my prayers, as participating in the praying of Christ by the Spirit, are simultaneously a participation in the Church . . . in every place and in every age."[30]

Becoming present to God, then, entails more complexity than simply "starting to say the office." It calls for theological insight, reflective practice, and, to move beyond mere repetition to deep engagement, the entering into those practices that open us up to the God who is always present to us—silence and stillness, bodily awareness, listening to the word through which we hear the Word who addresses us, and confirming time and again our desire to live in conformity to the crucified and risen Christ (or seeking to desire it, at least). In this regard, a fruitful conversation with two rather different theologians—John Colwell and Paul Fiddes—deepens our awareness of just what is entailed when we light a candle, become still, say the *in nomine*, and listen to the call of Christ once again.

---

29. Fiddes, "Spirituality as Attentiveness," 33.
30. Colwell, *Rhythm of Doctrine*, 6. Cf. Colwell, *Living the Christian Story*, 165.

2

Celebrating the Presence of God
Spirituality and the Arts

Geoff Colmer

> Triune God: community of creative and outpoured love,
> gatherer and shaper of dust, scatterer
> and weaver of beauty and meaning,
> we celebrate your gathering and scattering.[1]

A REMARKABLE MEETING TOOK place on October 19, 2009, when four friends[2]—Baptist ministers who had been meeting regularly for over fifteen years—gathered together in Oxford for a conversation with another friend, John Colwell. John had written a paper concerning a Baptist Order of Preachers, and on that occasion an exploration began as to the possibility of some kind of order which was distinctively Baptist. Over a meal at Brown's, the Oxford bistro, a glass of red wine was raised to what we felt to be an extraordinary venture, and the Order for Baptist Ministry was seeded. During the course of the next year, three foundations were established: first, a commitment to prayer, with a structured rhythm of daily office sustained

---

1. OBM Daily Office—Saturday and Creation.
2. Geoffrey Colmer, Paul Goodliff, Colin Norris, and Martin Taylor.

by spiritual direction and regular retreat—essentially a commitment with a strongly contemplative character; second, a commitment to gather in accountable relationships; third, a commitment to ministry.

What is strange, though maybe not so strange, is that when these five Catholic Baptists first met each other some twenty years previously they were all strongly committed and involved in what was then called "charismatic renewal." The "not so strange" part of this is the deep desire of both the charismatic and the contemplative to experience the presence of God through the action, or as John might put it, the mediation, of the Spirit of God.

"Celebrating the presence of God" is one of the movements of the Order for Baptist Ministry Daily Office, and in the course of this chapter I want to explore two of my particular interests in relation to this. These two interests do not feature specifically in John's writing but are nonetheless important aspects of his life and ministry, namely the arts and spirituality. My intention is to be even more specific and explore music and Ignatian Spirituality, each in relation to the experience of encounter with God.

In what seems like a previous life, before I became a Baptist minister, I was a professional musician playing the bassoon in the English Northern Philharmonia, the orchestra of Opera North. Music and the arts continue to be a passion. My interest in spirituality goes as far back as a book written in the eighties by Richard Foster, *Celebration of Discipline*, which opened up to me a world previously unknown and one that I have continuously sought to inhabit. More recently I have undertaken the Ignatian Spiritual Exercises and subsequently trained as an Ignatian spiritual director.

MUSIC IS RIFE WITH RUMORS OF GOD

It has been said that "spirituality defines our era."[3] The word "spirituality" has a wide usage in today's world and is applied to virtually anything. "Cooking, exercise, sex, and travel are just a few of the activities that popular publications characterize as spiritual."[4] Big businesses talk less about "five-year plans" and more about the spirituality of the organization. In education, spirituality is a significant consideration in the curriculum. So, has spirituality become an aerosol word that means anything you want it to mean? "'Spirituality' is a word suffering from runaway inflation," and "spirituality has become the mood-muzak of post-modernity."[5]

---

3. Sheldrake, *Spirituality*, 3.
4. Guthrie, *Creator Spirit*, xi.
5. Fabricius, *Propositions on Christian Theology*, 79.

The word spirituality is frequently applied to the arts. "For many, aesthetic experience has effectively substituted itself for religious faith as a perceived window onto 'spiritual' realities."[6] This would strike a chord with much of contemporary culture, which speaks of being "SBNR": "spiritual but not religious." People flock to art galleries to see exhibitions such as "Matisse: The Cut-Outs" at the Tate Modern, or the annual Summer Exhibition at the Royal Academy. A while back, prompted by exhibitions by David Hockney and Lucian Freud, the BBC published an online article by Jason Farago called "Why Museums Are the New Churches."

In the year 2000, George Barna found that 20 percent of Americans turned to media, arts, and culture "as their primary means of spiritual experience and expression." He expects that percentage to rise to 30 or 35 percent by 2025.[7] Spirituality and the arts, together, need to be taken seriously. But it prompts the question, what are we talking about when we link them? Is spirituality just a description of "what I really connect with" or "that which gives me goose bumps" when I hear a piece of music or experience some other form of art. A number of years ago, a program on BBC Radio 4 entitled "The Tingle Factor" explored people's experience of precisely this. So, is spirituality just a more sophisticated way of expressing an extraordinary feeling, or is it something much more? It is important to stress that this is not a new phenomenon. Throughout the ages, theologians, philosophers, and novelists have set the arts and the spiritual side by side: Augustine, Plato, Schleiermacher, Tillich, and Tolstoy, to name but a few.

For some time, as I have reflected more deeply on music and the arts from the perspective of Christian faith and spirituality, I have come to believe that the arts are not simply an add-on that we indulge in when we have the time and money, but are central to who we are as human beings. Art matters. Music matters. In *Simply Christian*, Tom Wright states, "The point is this. The arts are not the pretty but irrelevant bits around the border of reality. They are the highways into the centre of a reality that cannot be glimpsed, let alone grasped, any other way."[8]

From what we have already observed, contemporary spirituality would appear to be more assumed than defined. And defining it is in no way straightforward. As Jesus says in John's Gospel, speaking of the Spirit, "The wind blows where it chooses, and you hear the sound of it, but you don't not know where it comes from or where it goes."[9] This is my attempt

---

6. Hart, "Protestantism and Art," 270.
7. Detweiler, *Into the Dark*, 18.
8. Wright, *Simply Christian*, 201.
9. John 3:8.

at a definition, or perhaps a description, of spirituality: for me, as a follower of Jesus Christ, spirituality is the "living out" of my belief about God and my experience of God in all of life. It is about becoming the story I tell, or perhaps, becoming the song that I sing. Drawing on Don Saliers's exploration of this theme in his book *A Song to Sing, A Life to Live*, spirituality has to do with sounding life before God.

Upon reading Anthony Storr's illuminating book *Music and the Mind*, I was struck afresh by how very complex music is, and how it always seems to elude explanation. Reflecting on the nature of music can certainly help us to understand it, but ultimately music is to be experienced—it is to be played and listened to—and nothing else will do. What the dancer Isadora Duncan famously said about dance is true of all the arts: "If I could tell you what it meant, there would be no point in dancing it." Similarly, singer-songwriter Elvis Costello joked that "talking about music is like dancing about architecture." And Daniel Barenboim, the pianist and conductor: "I firmly believe that it is impossible to speak about music." The amusing thing is that this does not deter Barenboim, nor countless other people who agree with what he says—including myself!—from doing just that.

Although some people simply do not like music, music is universal. It can be expressed in numerous genres and styles, but it is a given of being human. I recall hearing Paul Tortellier, the celebrated cellist, declaim in his thick French accent "in the beginning was music." The desire for music is evident through its many forms—singing or playing instruments, alone or with others—and in a variety of contexts—secular, religious, formal, informal. The iPhone means that millions of people walk around "wired to sound" as they listen to their unique preferences. Celebrating important events in our lives is almost unimaginable without music that is significant to us. Favorite tunes have associations for us, and those connections are made in an instant. We have access to so much music in our world, from innumerable and diverse traditions, that we would need more than a lifetime to become familiar with even a small fraction of it. And then there is the music that comes to us indirectly, as the soundtracks to films and television programs. Music is used intentionally—manipulatively, even—to advertise, to create atmosphere in the shopping mall or the coffee shop, to calm us in tense situations, to rouse emotions, to stir patriotism, to express identity, to bring healing. Music does many things. But at its heart, it connects us with our innermost selves. It helps us to explore something of the vast expanse of our human experience, the agony and the ecstasy, without putting it into words. This is never more true than in times of grief, particularly national grief, when music has a power to hold us and express the inexpressible.

Wordlessly, music conveys beauty, truth, and goodness. It delights the senses, fires the imagination, shocks and provokes. It evokes memories and, I would suggest, instills hope, linking us with both past and future. It tells us who we truly are, and helps us to become more human.

I have often heard Jeremy Begbie, probably the most significant theologian writing on music and the arts, use the expression, "so much music seems rife with rumors of God." This resonates deeply with me. Experiencing some music can touch something in me in such a way that I seek the language of depth, and "God" is the word that comes to mind. My understanding is that though particular knowledge of God is mediated to us through the Scriptures by the Spirit, there seem to be many aspects of "ordinary" human life that point beyond themselves to the reality of God. I will now draw on a number of striking comments that people have written that I find particularly illuminating.

David Atkinson refers to "glimpses of God . . . those moments in our ordinary lives when the ordinariness points beyond itself to some deeper reality which is always there but not always seen, not always heard."[10] Peter Berger uses the phrase "signals of transcendence," while Paul Tillich speaks of God as the "depth" in things. He maintains that the experience of depth is the experience of God, for God is the depth-dimension in all reality.

Begbie observes that "there is some fundamental encounter with transcendence in the creation of art and its experiencing,"[11] and Hans Küng writes movingly of how the music of Mozart, more than any other, reveals how wafer-thin is the boundary between the human and the divine. Speaking of Mozart's Clarinet Concerto, he writes:

> To listen to the adagio of the Clarinet Concerto, for example, is to perceive something wholly other: the sound of an infinite which transcends us and for which "beauty" is no description . . . To describe such experience and revelation of transcendence, religious language still needs the word "God."[12]

Karl Barth would not have expressed this in quite the same way, but the music of Mozart was hugely significant for him. Begbie, commenting on this, speaks of "his extravagant devotion to Mozart, amounting almost to an obsession."[13] Barth himself recounts:

---

10. Atkinson, *God So Loved the World*, 24.
11. Begbie, *Voicing Creation's Praise*, xvii.
12. Küng, *Mozart*, 19.
13. Begbie, *Resounding Truth*, 153.

> My very first hearing of great music—I must have been about five or six years old—was of Mozart. I can still recall: my father struck a few measures of "The Magic Flute" on the piano ("Tamino mine, oh what happiness"). They thrilled me through and through.[14]

In Barth's adult life the music of Mozart found a place along with his daily prayers.

Nick Hornby, in *31 Songs*, makes a characteristically humorous contribution in his chapter on the song "One Man Guy" by Rufus Wainwright.

> I try not to believe in God, of course, but sometimes things happen in music . . . When things add up to more than the sum of their parts, when the effects achieved are inexplicable, then atheists like me start to get into difficult territory . . . When I say that you can hear God in [music], I do not mean to suggest that there is an old chap with a beard—a divine Willie Nelson, if you will—warbling along with them. Nor do I wish to imply that this surprise guest appearance . . . proves that Jesus died for our sins, or that rich men will have difficulty entering the Kingdom of Heaven. I just mean that at certain spine-shivering musical moments . . . it becomes difficult to remain a literalist. (I have no such difficulty when I hear religious music, by the way, no matter how beautiful. They're cheating, those composers: they're inviting Him in, egging Him on, and surely He wouldn't fall for that? I think He'd have enough self-respect to stay well away.)[15]

In *Resounding Truth*, Begbie engages with these "rumors of God" in music but makes as his starting point a Christian ecology in which he poses a number of questions. The first—and John Colwell would approve—is "What kind of Creator?" to which his response is christocentric and Trinitarian. He goes on to ask, "What kind of cosmos?" and reflects on a world crafted in freedom and love; a world that praises God, a world that is good but not God; a world made to flourish towards its end; a world of ordered openness; and a world of diverse unity. He then asks, "What kind of calling?" and writes, "In the midst of this breathtaking praise of creation, the speechless paean of the cosmos to its Creator, the Christian faith dares to affirm that a creature, *Homo sapiens*, is given a singular calling: not simply to acknowledge the cosmic symphony, but also to enable, articulate, and extend it in ever fresh ways . . . In the human being, creation finds a conscious answering voice, a mortal from the dust of the earth who can know

---

14. Barth, *Wolfgang Amadeus Mozart*, 15.
15. Hornby, *31 Songs*, 31–33.

and respond to God's love as a creature, love God in return, and as part of this response, 'voice creation's praise.'"[16] Note that at this point he has not specifically begun to explore music but as the title of his first book exploring a theology of the arts, *Voicing Creation's Praise* makes clear, music in God's calling becomes a natural and inevitable progression.

Tom Wright provides a structured theological framework to these "rumors" when he says, "Though I am not so confident [as Sayers] that one can argue a kind of natural theology by starting with artistic integrity and going right the way up to the Christian doctrine of God, I am certainly prepared to think in terms of the revelation of God in Jesus and the Spirit moving towards us and meeting artistic integrity coming the other way. Without the first, the artist is in danger of producing form without substance, a classic problem of both modernity and post-modernity. But without the second, the theologian and preacher, struggling to hear what the Spirit is saying to the churches, might easily fail to speak the full truth."[17]

Albeit a slight digression, it is worth acknowledging that while there are specific pieces of music that seem to draw a similar response from many people, there are many pieces which are particular to the individual. Music is intensely personal, as is our experience of God. What moves me, musically, may well not move you. My experience of God will be different to yours. Music has a sticky quality. It attaches itself to events in life and creates powerful associations. Psychologists call this the "Darling, they're playing our tune!" theory. For me, many pieces of music have powerful associations that take me to different places and people in an instant. This can be a total delight or, sometimes, an unwelcome intrusion as the association overrides the music.

In reflecting on this dimension of the music experience, one concept that I find especially illuminating and instructive is allusiveness. One of the things that makes art "art" is the quality of allusion. It alludes beyond itself, refers indirectly. Another word for allusiveness is suggestion. Art suggests or hints at, it beckons and points beyond itself. Begbie speaks of how a work of art does not normally make a direct or literal statement, and if it is reduced to such its power is destroyed. Art communicates symbolically, allusively. Begbie writes: "The most enriching art is suggestion-rich, multiply evocative. Art can generate multiple meanings, disclose more and more of something, evoke more and more as we are drawn into it, a 'more and more' that is potentially inexhaustible . . . Art reminds us that in fact the world

---

16. Begbie, *Resounding Truth*, 201.
17. Wright, "Resurrection: From Theology to Music and Back Again," 202.

always exceeds our grasp and perception . . . All of this makes music's meaning irreducible. Who can sum up a piece of music in words?"[18]

One of Emily Dickinson's poems begins: "Tell all the Truth but tell it slant—Success in Circuit lies." Here she captures the notion that we tend only to catch glimpses of truth. We see it in our peripheral vision, out of the corner of one eye. Later, in the same poem, she calls such insights "Truth's superb surprise."[19] Poetry uses words in a way that allows us to remain alert to that which we cannot quite see, and not be fixated on what is clear and lies straight ahead. The result is that music, and indeed all art forms, does not merely exist, but draws us in, draws us out of ourselves, and enables us to participate in it. To be experienced as art it must be received and, as it were, reconstructed in the perception of the listener or viewer. Allusiveness—suggestiveness—it could be argued, is why Christians can sometimes produce bad art. Christian artists can try too hard to present a message or be too obvious in a portrayal. The quality of allusiveness, of being understood in a number of possible ways, and possibly misunderstood, leaves too much to chance for some Christian artists.

Steven Guthrie, reflecting on "art and ineffability," recognizes a coherence between aesthetic experience and spiritual experience. He notes that, in both cases, the experience communicates and reveals, but in a manner which is often subtle. Allusiveness has an elusiveness about it and maybe music's particular "elusive allusivity"[20] is on account of its being aural, not visual—not being held within a frame as with a painting, or positioned on a page as with a poem, but dependent on sound which emerges out of silence and ultimately disappears into silence.

Proceeding from this, the encounter, as we have already observed in music, cannot be reduced to words, but within our part of the Christian tradition at least, this is precisely what we seem to be eager to do. I am struck by Edwin Muir's observation that, in the case of the incarnation, we reduce the mystery to words and in so doing lose the mystery: "The word made flesh is made word again." Both aesthetic experience and spiritual experience originate in love and invite us to participate as we open ourselves and give ourselves to the experience. Guthrie concludes, "The role of mystery, however—again in both art and the life of the Spirit—is not that we would remain in a constant state of 'not knowing.' Rather, we are given a taste—but only a taste—that we might accept the invitation to come to the fountain."[21]

18. Begbie, *Resounding Truth*, 51.
19. Dickinson, *Everyman's Poetry*, 82.
20. Brand and Chaplin, *Art & Soul*.
21. Guthrie, *Creator Spirit*, 19.

FINDING GOD IN ALL THINGS

For a change of perspective, I draw on the Spiritual Exercises of Ignatius of Loyola, the founder of the Jesuits. Ignatius lived from 1491–1556 and was a Basque nobleman from Loyola, Spain. He underwent a spiritual conversion and formed a movement based upon his writings known as the Spiritual Exercises. Although these are commonly considered one of the most influential spiritual texts of all times, one would not think so at first reading them, because they are essentially a series of practical notes for the retreat-guide as they accompany the person taking the retreat. The intention of the Exercises is to help a person to grow in spiritual freedom that they might respond to the call of Christ. Put another way, they enable an individual to experience personal encounter with God and make a response. "Finding God in all things" is a phrase that is central to Ignatian spirituality. Unlike some Christian approaches that tend towards a divide between the sacred and the secular, Ignatius refuses this. His method is deeply incarnational, embodied, earthed. It recognizes in the words of the poet Gerard Manley Hopkins, a Jesuit, that "the world is charged with the grandeur of God,"[22] that God is present in all things, and cannot not be present. The "finding" is the experience and recognition of this together with response.

Ignatius's expectation is that we are, in the words of William A. Barry, "beings on the lookout for God,"[23] and as a person examines their life so they will encounter God in all of life. This requires contemplation, or to put it more simply, being aware, paying attention, noticing life in all its dimensions.

This being aware, paying attention, noticing, contemplating, seems to me to be the sort of thing that is required of us if we are to engage with any form of art, and especially music. In December 2013, I attended a performance of Wagner's Parsifal at the Royal Opera House. I reflected in my journal afterwards, "The experience was contemplative in that on account of its length (about five hours) you are not in control and simply have to place yourself attentively before the music and allow it to do its work." James MacMillan, the Scottish contemporary music composer, who writes with a keen awareness of Christian theology, makes a similar point when he says, "What's required of us when we go to a concert or put on some music that is not simply background music is giving up something of ourselves in order to contemplate this other that is bigger than ourselves."[24] If God is to be

---

22. Hopkins, "God's Grandeur," 128.
23. Barry and Connolly, *Practice of Spiritual Direction*, 21.
24. Langley, "Music, Modern Art and Mystery," 9.

found in all things, surely music, and the arts, on account of their capacity to engage with our innermost selves across the broad range of our human experience, and touch us at a deep place in our lives, are a privileged place of encounter.

My interest has been piqued by suggestions as to how a contemplative approach to experiencing music and the arts might be more intentionally nurtured. I am grateful to Rob Marsh, a Jesuit and personal friend, for a resource that I have adapted here. When preparing to engage with a work of art, whatever form it takes:

1. Come with a passive expectancy and an active openness. Be ready to be moved, for there to be some kind of response from within, when you listen or view. And be ready to wonder if God might not be waiting to be found in what moves you.

2. When your attention has been caught—gently or forcefully—by a work of art, a film or a piece of music, be prepared to linger, to repeat, to give the moment time to develop. As we have already observed, this is more challenging with music, which is aural and takes place in time, here and then gone, than, for example, a painting, which is visual and contained within a frame. It is more challenging still if the piece of music is lengthy, and you may need to go back to just one section unless it is a song that can be played again!

Do you get the same reaction or something else when you listen again? What is it doing to you? What are you are feeling? Maybe you know and maybe you don't. Can you stay with the movement for a while contemplatively, i.e., just noticing it and not trying to work anything out or get a result? Even without hearing it again, go back to what the music did to you.

3. Who is the God who seems to be present as you stay with the music or scene? How is this God looking at you, present to you, speaking to you? Is God watching/listening with you or is God somehow "in" the scene/music that has moved you?

4. Notice what you find yourself desiring in all this. Let yourself feel the desire. If it feels right let yourself express the desire to God. But notice also what God seems to be desiring. Let yourself take that desire to heart. What is God inviting you to be or do?

5. Stay with the thing that moves you until it loses its flavor. Keep coming back to it as long as you feel drawn back. Rob Marsh says, "I am embarrassed to say how many times I have seen the film *Shakespeare*

in Love because of a scene near the close where the heroine says to young Will 'write me well.'"[25]

6. The first rule of any kind of prayer is to go where God is and do what helps God be present and communicative. Go where you are drawn; follow the scent; trust your graced instincts to lead you were God is to be found.

Our friend, John Colwell, in common with Karl Barth, is a great lover of music and particularly Mozart. So, I conclude with an extract from a book, *Unapologetic,* by Francis Spufford, which describes a profound experience of music which is rife with rumors of God and in which God is found, and so celebrates something of the presence of God. The year is 1997 and the author has spent the whole night having a row with his wife that has gone round and round. He is exhausted and despairing, sitting in a cafe over a cappuccino, when someone puts on a cassette of the Adagio from Mozart's Clarinet Concerto:

> It is a very patient piece of music. It too goes round and round, in its way, essentially playing the same tune again and again, on the clarinet alone and then with the orchestra, clarinet and then orchestra, lifting up the same unhurried lilt of solitary sound, and then backing it with a kind of message-less tenderness in deep waves, when the strings join in. It does not sound as if Mozart is doing something he can only just manage, and it does not sound as if the music is struggling to lift a weight it can only just manage. Yet at the same time, it is not music that denies anything. It offers a strong, absolutely calm rejoicing, but it does not pretend there is no sorrow. On the contrary, it sounds as if it comes from a world where sorrow is perfectly ordinary, but still there is more to be said. I had heard it lots of times, but this time it felt to me like news. It said: everything you fear is true. And yet. And yet. Everything you have done wrong, you have really done wrong. And yet. And yet. The world is wider than you fear it is, wider than the repeating rigmaroles in your mind, and it has *this* in it, as truly as it contains your unhappiness. Shut up and listen, and let yourself count, just a little bit, on a calm that you do not have to be able to make for yourself, because here it is, freely offered. You are still deceiving yourself, said the music, if you don't allow for the possibility of *this*. There is more going on here than what you deserve, or don't deserve. There is *this*,

---

25. Marsh, "Praying through Film, Story, Song, Art."

as well. And it played the tune again, with all the cares in the world.[26]

Francis Spufford continues,

> The novelist Richard Powers has written that the Clarinet Concerto sounds the way mercy would sound, and that's exactly how I experienced it in 1997 . . . I think that I was not being targeted with a timely rendition of the Clarinet Concerto by a deity who micromanages the cosmos and causes all the events in it to happen. I think that Mozart, two centuries earlier, had succeeded in creating a beautiful and accurate report of an aspect of reality . . . I think that the reason reality is that way, is in some ultimate sense merciful as well as being a set of physical processes all running along on their own without hope of appeal . . . is that the universe is sustained by a continual and infinitely patient act of love.[27]

---

26. Spufford, *Unapologetic*, 15.
27. Spufford, *Unapologetic*, 15.

3

Acknowledging Our Humanity
Confessing Our Sins Together

Christopher J. Ellis

*God of grace, we acknowledge before you that
we are not the people you want us to be, nor the people we want to be.*[1]

WHATEVER THE DAY, WHATEVER the season, the Daily Office of the Order for Baptist Ministry follows a regular pattern of prayer. Each day, the sequence begins with *Becoming Present to God* through a sign or word of attentiveness and continues with *Celebrating the Presence of God* through prayers of praise and thanksgiving. God is rightly the focus as this daily discipline of devotion begins, but the mood then shifts as the worshipper is invited to share in *Acknowledging Our Humanity*. This is an opportunity to confess our sins and our persistent sinfulness, and it is the notion of general confession in Christian worship I would like to explore.

My primary intent here is theological and pastoral. Theological, in that I want to explore what it means to confess our sins and seek forgiveness in worship, and pastoral, in that I wish to bear in mind what this might mean for worship leadership and pastoral care. These two questions are, of course, both distinct and interrelated.

1. OBM Daily Office—Tuesday and Advent—Coming Lord.

It will be noted that I have widened my brief to encompass corporate Sunday worship as well as the personal devotions of those who use the Daily Office for their daily prayers,[2] and perhaps this wider remit needs some justification. This is a good place to reaffirm the conviction that there is no real distinction between personal and corporate prayer. As a matter of semantics, I always try to avoid referring to *individual* prayer or *individual* spirituality, usually preferring the language of *personal* prayer or spirituality. It has often been said that there is no such thing as "individual prayer" because whenever we pray we pray as part of the body of Christ and the communion of saints. This is clearly the case for anyone who uses the Daily Office for, in part at least, there is an intentional joining with others who are using the same words on the same day.[3]

Pastorally, there are clear connections between the focus of this study and what in some parts of the church would be called "the sacrament of Penance or Reconciliation." While we may note that most of the Reformers rejected the practice of individual auricular confession,[4] a wider study might usefully explore the links between corporate prayers of confession and other pastoral practices which might encourage self-examination, penitence, or continuing conversion in the following of Jesus Christ. The approach which I will take here, however, in addressing the current pastoral and theological questions, will be informed by the perspectives of liturgical theology. This is a form of systematic theology which explores the convictions of the Christian community through a study of what is expressed, enacted, and implied in its worship. Its foundation is the belief that in worship the church is most clear in its articulation of what it believes—that the evocative and proclamatory nature of its language is at least as deserving of our theological attention as carefully nuanced, and sometimes hotly contested, dogmatic statements.

Approaching its doctrinal work through an exposition of what may be called the "primary" theology of, for example, hymns, prayers, and symbolic actions,[5] liturgical theology offers a form of theology which has similarities

---

2. For historical studies of the Daily Office, see Bradshaw, *Daily Prayer in the Early Church*, and Guiver, *Company of Voices*.

3. It was Cyprian who made this comment on the opening phrase of the Lord's Prayer, *Our* Father: "Our prayer is public and common; and when we pray, we pray not for one, but for the whole people, because we the whole people are one." Cyprian, *De Oratione Dominica*, 8.

4. The exception is the Lutheran tradition, which has maintained the practice of auricular confession. For Bonhoeffer's communal interpretation of this, see Bonhoeffer, *Life Together*, 86–96.

5. Sallie McFague, for example, in her examination of the use of models in theology, equates primary and secondary language with "metaphorical language" and

with spiritual or mystical theology. Although, in its present form, it is a relatively modern form of enquiry,[6] it can trace its roots to the mystagogical addresses of the early Christian centuries in which the fundamentals of the Christian faith were presented to those preparing for baptism by means of an exposition of worship and its meaning.[7] Despite its expository nature, there is a cycle of reflection, critique, and adjustment available to the liturgical theologian which can ensure that the worship event is not approached in a "fundamentalist" way which might assume that "anything goes" in worship. Indeed, I believe that it is important to critique the worship event by testing its own implicit theology against other credal formulations of the church.[8] For example, anecdotal evidence of the apparent absence of prayers of confession in some Christian worship might well be critiqued by a wider theological reflection and the practice of worship planning adjusted accordingly.

GENERAL CONFESSION

I remember as a young teenager my early experiences of liturgical worship in a local Baptist church in Cardiff. The green hymnbook, *The Baptist Hymn Book*, was published in early 1962 and I was presented with a music copy at my baptism that Easter. Inside the hymnbook covers, there were printed a number of traditional prayer texts from *The Book of Common Prayer* of 1662, including "A General Confession" which had been included in the order for Morning Prayer since Cranmer's second prayer book of 1552.[9]

"conceptual language," respectively, and argues for their interdependence, McFague, *Metaphorical Theology*, 118.

6. See esp. Schmemann, *Introduction to Liturgical Theology*, and Kavanagh, *On Liturgical Theology*. For Free Church perspective and method, see Ellis, *Gathering*, esp. 15–24.

7. See the homilies of Cyril of Jerusalem, Ambrose, John Chrysostom, and others. For a contemporary approach to mystagogy, see Regan, *Experience the Mystery*.

8. For a critique of Schmemann at this point and a Protestant adjustment proposed, see Ellis, *Gathering*, 23–24.

9. The inclusion of the General Confession in 1552 may well have been part of the attempt to increase the devotional introduction to morning worship. The first prayer book of 1549 had envisaged Holy Communion as the main Sunday service, but many churches reported low attendance at this first revision of the Roman Mass. Consequently, the "light" 1549 Morning Prayer (probably envisaged as a discipline for clergy and a few others) was strengthened with more penitential material with a view to providing an adequate Service of the Word for most Sunday worship. Indeed, Matins became the main Anglican Sunday service until the liturgical renewals of the twentieth century. See MacCulloch, *Thomas Cranmer*, 504–13.

The inside covers also contained the Lord's Prayer, a General Thanksgiving, the Sursum Corda, and a number of Benedictions. Conveniently printed for occasional use, these prayers offered a liturgically minded minister a means of enabling the congregation to participate actively in a handful of specific prayers. The two previous denominational hymnbooks[10] which had been published since the union of Particular and General Baptists in 1891 had also used their endpapers for additional material. They had both included the Lord's Prayer and some scriptural benedictions, along with the words and music of the Genevan Doxology (Praise God from whom all blessings flow) and the Trinitarian ascription "Glory to the Father and to the Son" with the curious (for Baptists) Latin title *Gloria Patri*.

The printing of the *Book of Common Prayer* (*BCP*) General Thanksgiving and General Confession in 1962 is indicative of a number of reforming trends in the worship of some Baptist churches of the time.[11] The Liturgical Movement of the mid- and late twentieth century had a range of emphases and points of impact in liturgical renewal across various denominations.[12] Two are relevant here. First, a concern for greater congregational participation because, to quote an oft-used phrase, "Liturgy is the work of the people." James White has made a very helpful distinction between "active" and "passive" participation in worship: "'Passive (or receptive) participation' means people hearing or seeing someone else do something . . . 'Active participation' means people doing things themselves: praying, singing, shouting, dancing."[13] Enabling a congregation to utter the words of a prayer, rather than just being led in prayer by a representative voice from the front, may not only be seen as a move towards corporate utterance, and therefore action, on the part of the congregation but also an opportunity for individual worshippers to engage with that prayer at a deeper level by their own active participation.

Second, a concern for the shape or pattern of worship, as well as a modern aversion to verbosity, led to a move away from the Long Prayer.

---

10. *The Baptist Church Hymnal* and *The Baptist Church Hymnal (Revised)*.

11. However, their usefulness, even in those (few?) churches which took advantage of this resource, was to be severely time-limited as the revolution in the language of public prayer was soon to gain momentum. Cranmer's English, the "Thees and Thous" of Payne and Winward, and the archaicisms of much extempore public prayer were to be challenged by the surge of new translations of the Bible "in modern English" and a desire for accessible language. For the present writer, the turning point was the publication, a year before beginning ministerial formation, of an influential book of prayer produced by a group of young Congregationalist ministers, including Caryl Micklem and Brian Wren, in Micklem, *Contemporary Prayers for Public Worship*.

12. See Fenwick and Spinks, *Worship in Transition*.

13. White, *Protestant Worship*, 17.

This extempore prayer was traditionally a collection of concerns addressed to God and would include all the modes of Christian prayer in the one item of worship. Praise and confession would be interspersed with petitions, pastoral concerns, and any other matters which the minister thought should be addressed to the Almighty. Spurgeon advised his students that twenty-five minutes was too long for this prayer and that his friend Dr. Charles Brown of Edinburgh believed the limit should be ten minutes.[14] The move away from a single catch-all Long Prayer, to shorter, more focused prayers, was a trend which would, amongst other things, encourage more specific acts of corporate confession in Free Church worship.

Payne and Winward's *Orders and Prayers for Church Worship*, first published two years before the green hymnbook, was the first Baptist service book to include collections of prayers under a variety of thematic headings, such as adoration, thanksgiving, intercession, and, most relevant here, "Prayers of Confession and Assurance of Pardon."[15] Despite the section title, all the prayers are either prayers of confession and/or prayers requesting pardon. There are no announcements assuring forgiveness and we shall return to this in a moment when we consider the question of absolution and what we think is happening when we collectively confess our sins.

THE NEED TO CONFESS

When the crowd asked Peter how they should respond to his Pentecost sermon proclaiming Jesus as God's Messiah, he replied, "Repent, and be baptized every one of you in the name of Jesus Christ so that your sins may be forgiven; and you will receive the gift of the Holy Spirit" (Acts 2:38). Of course, there are distinctions which need to be made. Many preachers have insisted that repentance (*metanoia*) is more than confession of sins, or a statement of regret, as it includes the intention to change direction and

---

14. Spurgeon lists some of the things which do not need to be included in the prayer, including extensive scriptural quotations, and concludes, "It *is* necessary in prayer to draw near unto God, but it is not required of you to prolong your speech till everyone is longing to hear the word '*Amen*.'" Spurgeon, *Lectures to My Students*, 62.

15. Its predecessor, first published in 1927 and edited by M. E. Aubrey, only included orders of service for marriages, funerals, the Lord's Supper, etc. No additional prayers were included and the number of prayers available in the services was quite limited, with a large dependence on passages of Scripture. Indeed, the order for "The Communion of the Lord's Supper" includes no written prayers and only provides a prompt for "a prayer of thanksgiving and consecration" which would normally have been extempore, Aubrey, *Minister's Manual*, 39.

live differently in the future.[16] This was to be made explicit in the questions which developed with pre-baptismal anointing and the renunciation of Satan found in various baptismal rites from at least the third century.[17] By the mid-second century, Justin Martyr was describing baptismal preparation in Rome:

> Those who are persuaded and believe that the things we teach and say are true, and promise that they can live accordingly, are instructed to pray and beseech God with fasting for the remission of their past sins while we pray and fast along with them. Then they are brought by us where there is water, and are reborn.[18]

But the decision to be a disciple of Christ, to "turn to Christ" as many of the early (and now recent) liturgies have put it, and to follow in his way is only possible when once we have received the forgiveness of our sins through his saving death and resurrection. Repentance includes confession as well as intention to change and is logically positioned at the beginning the life of faith, even when we see discipleship as a life of continuing repentance.

Whether we call that beginning "conversion" or not, it is signified in baptism and is a key aspect of proclaiming the gospel and living as a Christian. But it is this "living as a Christian" which is at the heart of the present discussion. How is post baptismal sin to be dealt with? How might we follow Jesus more closely? What spiritual practices do we need in order to deal with failure in the pursuit of holy living? Is it necessary to confess our sins continually and, if so, how is it to be done?

The medieval church developed a practice of auricular confession and penance and, while this is beyond the scope of this study, the pastoral context is clearly linked to any general confession in worship. Indeed, current Roman Catholic teaching does not recognize general confession in worship, and the words of absolution which follow it, as sufficient for normal Christian practice.[19] Using traditional language, we could observe that baptism

---

16. Commenting on the definition of repentance in *The Westminster Shorter Catechism* (question 87), H. R. Mackintosh observes, "This emphasis on the volitional aspect of repentance is of special value. Stress is laid, not on storms of feeling but on the act of turning from sin," Mackintosh, *Christian Experience of Forgiveness*, 236.

17. But we need to heed Paul Bradshaw's cautions about the range and variety of initiation practices in different parts of the ancient world. See Bradshaw, *Search for the Origins of Christian Worship*, 161–84.

18. Martyr, *First Apology*, 61. Cited in White, *Documents of Christian Worship*, 147.

19. After commenting that "Christ is at work in each of the sacraments, and that he personally addresses every sinner: 'My son, your sins are forgiven,'" the *Catechism of the Catholic Church* concludes that "personal confession is thus the form most expressive of

expresses the forgiveness of sins which is made possible through God's justification of the sinner, with the human response of thanksgiving and the intent to live in the future a life "worthy of the Lord." The pastoral question remains as to how the process of sanctification might require and include the need for continuing self-examination and the confession of our sins.[20]

Part of the Protestant critique of the medieval sacramental system was to see confession and absolution by a priest as an instrument of ecclesiastical control over the laity. However, a rejection of medieval penance was not the same thing as a rejection of the practice of confession *per se*. The Reformers were close readers of Scripture, especially such passages as Matt 18:15–20, and the role of the church in challenging sinfulness could not be ignored and pastoral practices were developed to take account of this. The "fencing of the table," or exclusion from the church, were not seen as cosmic power games over the lives of poor sinners but challenges, which it was hoped would lead to repentance and a return to Christ and his ways.

It might seem self-evident that continuing self-examination and confession should be an integral part of the Christian life. However, with a view to our focus on worship we need to explore what the dynamics are in this, both for the believer who is also a sinner and the church which provides pastoral opportunities for the life of faith and corporate opportunities to express repentance and faith.

LITURGICAL MEANINGS: A PROPOSED INTERPRETIVE LENS

As we reflect on the meaning of what takes place in worship, I believe we can organize at least some of the questions a liturgical theologian might ask into a cluster of themes which might provide a tool for continuing reflection on, and assessment of worship. This interpretive tool might be seen as a lens which distinguishes three areas of meaning:

1. *Performative* words and actions, in which we believe that we are doing or achieving something which results in an outcome different from what was the case beforehand. Someone may be married or ordained, someone may commit their life for Christian service or be welcomed into church membership. God may be thanked, offerings may be given, or prayers of intercession offered.

---

reconciliation with God and with the Church," *Catechism of the Catholic Church*, 334.

20. The place of spiritual direction and pastoral care is also relevant here.

2. *Proclamatory* words and actions in which explicitly or implicitly some truth is announced. Scripture is read, sermons are preached, and the promises of God are received. The gospel of Jesus Christ is announced, not only in the sermon, but in the body language of the welcomers, in the sharing of the peace, in the breaking of bread, and the sharing of wine, and in the singing of songs. Much of what we do and say in worship will say more than one thing, which is why worship can be so dangerous. "Bad" theology can be expressed as well as good—which brings us to

3. *Formational* words and actions which influence and shape the development of the congregation in Christian living and faithfulness. The words we sing, the language we use about God and about people, the things we claim and celebrate—all these shape and influence the aspirations and attitudes, the self-image and beliefs of the members of the congregation.

Often, all three of these areas of meaning will intersect in a single liturgical action. For example, prayers of thanksgiving do not only do the business of offering thanks (a transaction within a relationship), but they proclaim something about the goodness and faithfulness of God and, over time, they shape worshipers in the habits of gratitude and trust.[21]

Such an interpretive matrix offers both theological and pastoral benefit when applied to the design, leading, and review of specific worship events. Are the beliefs embodied and expressed in this particular worship event going to build up the body of Christ or erode its convictions? Is the presentation of the character of God offered in these songs worthy of God and the gospel of Jesus Christ, or are they merely reflective of human emotion and sentiment? Here are three questions which a responsible worship leader should be continually asking:

- What is happening here?
- What are we proclaiming here?
- How are people being shaped for discipleship here?

But let us now apply this interpretive tool to the practice of the general confession of sins in Christian worship.

---

21. For an extended exposition of liturgical "thanksgiving," see Saliers, *Worship as Theology*, 85–105.

GENERAL CONFESSION: WHAT IS HAPPENING HERE?

In a prayer of general confession there are a number of distinct actions. While not all the elements will be present each time, there is a logical sequence to them such that it might be claimed that when not always explicitly and verbally present, one or more elements may be present by implication.

1. *We say "Sorry."* This might sound like a very obvious thing to do—something intrinsic to all well-functioning relationships. We begin with the internal acknowledgment that something is wrong and that at least some ownership of responsibility is taken for it. We might see this as the first step in a process of repentance. There is truth-telling to be done and the beginning of any true worship will need to start from, or at least build on, a place of honesty about ourselves. John Colwell points out that while the practice of individual confession is likely to focus on sins of commission, actions we have undertaken which we regret and attitudes of which we repent, a larger, underlying concern is the matter of our sins of omission. He suggests that the comprehensive nature of general confession in worship has the potential to draw these also within the attention of the worshippers.[22] Beneath our sinning, there are dispositions which need redeeming and worship provides the true focus for this redemption. Colwell links his observation to Jesus's summary of the Law (Matt 22:37–40) and it is significant that in the first order for Communion in *Common Worship* this summary of the law is used as the introduction to the prayers of penitence.[23]

2. *We ask for forgiveness.* Saying "Sorry" is an interpersonal action in which we seek to achieve reconciliation with someone we have injured in some way. It has a momentum which moves towards reconciliation through a request to the other for their forgiveness. This reconciliation is beyond our power to achieve but requires our doing what we can to make it possible. Between human beings, forgiveness is about the restoration of a relationship, but in our dealings with God it also includes a request that we be cleansed, or healed, as well as forgiven.

3. *We ask for a new beginning.* This, again, is interpersonal, because it encompasses the desire for reconciliation and a new phase of healed

---

22. Colwell, *Promise and Presence*, 188.

23. *Common Worship*, 168. Alternatives are offered in the rubric, but the summary is what is printed in the main text. The second order for Communion follows the *BCP* and begins with the Ten Commandments, followed by the Kyrie (including a general confession at the approach to the Table; see 230 and 250).

relations.[24] But it also implies the need for our being "fixed" in some way—hearts cleansed, release from guilt, and a spring in our step.

4. *We ask for help in the future.* We know our own frailty, our own wilfulness and waywardness, and we ask for divine assistance to lead a godly life from here on.

To see these steps as "performative" or "transactional" is to see them as actions we take in order to see a change in our relationship with God and a change in our state as human beings. The implication of these actions is that something should be different in the cosmos afterwards from what it was before. This might well be seen as the heart and purpose of the act of confession, even before we explore the proclamatory and formational dimensions.

Following Mackintosh, Paul Fiddes writes of "the journey of forgiveness,"[25] and we can see that forgiveness is indeed an interpersonal process leading to reconciliation. Accordingly, we should view confession and forgiveness within the framework of relationships rather than the forensic absolutes of the law court. This will influence the language we use in worship, as well as our interpretation of what we "do." Words of "assurance" will be more prominent than pronouncements of "absolution." This is not because of a suspicion of absolution as such, so much as a belief that the relevant discourse is personal rather than juridical. What we "do" in confession is to continue our journey with God.

THE ASSURANCE OF FORGIVENESS

Pastoral need, as well as scriptural warrant and theological exposition, lead us to want to make some announcement about the triumph of grace in the face of genuine repentance. For many churches this will be expressed in congregational song as the wonders of grace are celebrated. But is this enough, or should our worship practice include some words of assurance at the point where we express our penitence and seek God's forgiveness? Indeed, it is "Words of Assurance" which tend to be the order of the day in recent Free Church service books. For example, the first British Baptist service book to include specific prayers of confession was Payne and Winward's *Orders and Prayers for Church Worship*, published in 1960.[26] Although the section is

---

24. On the eternal love of the Triune God as the basis for forgiveness, see Jones, *Embodying Forgiveness*, 113–19.

25. Fiddes, *Past Event*, 173–75.

26. Payne and Winward, *Order and Prayers*, see 64–67, and also prayers of confession in the "Order for the Lord's Supper," 10, and the orders for "Morning or Evening

headed "Prayers of Confession and Assurance of Pardon," it contains no announcements on the part of the minister and the title is clearly a contraction of "Prayers of Confession and Prayers Asking for the Assurance of Pardon," a concern well known to our Puritan antecedents.[27] This shying away from announcing absolution is particularly clear in Payne and Winward's Order for the Lord's Supper, where the words of absolution in 1662 *Book of Common Prayer* have been transposed into a prayer by the minister on behalf of the congregation.[28] The confession section of *Praise God* in 1980 did not include any assurances of pardon although, arguably, the extensive selection of Scripture verses offered by way of introduction to the general confession might be interpreted as providing such assurance in advance as boldly we approach the throne of grace![29]

By 1991, *Patterns and Prayers for Christian Worship* included a section entitled "Assurance of Forgiveness" which included a mix of Scripture verses with some pastoral expansion.[30] This approach was extended in the larger *Gathering for Worship* which now includes, after a series of scriptural phrases emphasizing the atoning work of Christ, these bold words:

> Receive his pardon and peace
> to stand before him in his strength alone,
> this day and evermore.

More circumspect are the conditional words on the following page. Sandwiched between 1 Timothy 1:15 and 1:17, we read:

> To all who confess their sins
> and resolve to lead a new life,
> he says:
> Your sins are forgiven,
> and he also says:
> Follow me.

Service," 32, 38, 42.

27. See, e.g., Gillett, *Trust and Obey*, 42–43.

28. Payne and Winward, *Order and Prayers*, 10. This transposition from pronouncement of absolution to petitionary prayer also includes the additional phrase that the promised forgiveness is "to all those who forgive their brethren," as well as to all those who "with hearty repentance and true faith turn unto Thee." Perhaps this is a reference not only to the Lord's Prayer but to the Baptist ecclesial view of the church as the "fellowship of believers."

29. Gilmore et al., *Praise God*, 59–65.

30. Baptist Union, *Patterns and Prayers for Christian Worship*, 27–28.

This conditionality is significant and seems to be found even when the language of absolution is used. In Cranmer's second prayer book of 1552 the words announce that

> Almighty God . . . hath geuen power and commaundment to hys ministers, to declare and pronounce to his people, beinge penitent, the absolution and remission of their synnes

and continue with a declaration which is conditional: "he pardoneth and absolveth all them which truly repent, and enfeynedly believe his holy Gospel." This conditionality is so significant that the minister continues with an exhortation: "Wherefore we besehe him to graunt us true repentaunce and his holy Spirite."[31] This wording was to be continued in 1662 and is reprinted in the BCP text in *Common Worship*.[32]

There is still a modicum of conditionality in the absolution announced in the orders for Holy Communion in *Common Worship*:

> Almighty God,
>   who forgives all who truly repent,
> have mercy upon you,
>   pardon and deliver you from all your sins,
>   confirm and strengthen you in all goodness,
>   and keep you in life eternal;
>   through Jesus Christ our Lord.[33]

While these words do seem to have a performative dimension to them ("have mercy upon you"), the efficacy is still dependant on an assumed true repentance.[34] It leaves this Free Church author wondering why such words need to be reserved for a priest and what the difference is between such general statements of theological truth (that God forgives those who truly repent) and Free Church assurances of forgiveness, especially when Anglican discipline reserves "you" forms of absolution for those ordained priest.[35]

What, then, is the performative nature of confession in worship? It is more than simply a statement of general truth. In the journey of worship

---

31. Edward VI, *First and Second Prayer Books of Edward VI*, 148.

32. *Common Worship*, 64.

33. Order One, *Common Worship*, 170. See also Order Two which speaks of promising forgiveness "to all those who with heartfelt repentance and true faith turn to him," 258. In the thirteen approved additional absolutions printed in pp. 135–37, nine begin with "May" and two others imply it either by use of the prayer formula "for the sake of Jesus Christ, our Saviour," or through the use of the word "us" rather than "you."

34. For a discussion of general confession in Cranmer and *Common Worship*, see Atherstone, *Confessing Our Sins*.

35. See *Common Worship*, 122.

nothing is taken for granted, the personal and gratuitous nature of grace remains and the need for faith and repentance continue to be vital. We confess our sins because, if our relationship with God is to be transparent and our gathering for worship have integrity, we *need* to confess, and our relationship with God is healed and deepened as a consequence of our confessing and God continuing to forgive.

GENERAL CONFESSION: WHAT ARE WE PROCLAIMING HERE?

Quite apart from the personal appropriation of the prayer by individual worshippers, so that repentance is heartfelt and confession truthful, the congregation is also making a statement about the nature of God, the promises of the gospel, and the nature of the church.

When the members of the congregation are invited to confess their sins, there is an underlying assumption that God is a God who forgives. This needs to be said clearly and repeatedly. Pastorally, such an announcement is the beginning of the way to truthfulness about our lives and condition. That God is a forgiving God sets us free from self-justification or diplomatic blindness, or even worse, the mire of self-criticism. Doctrinally, it speaks the truth about God in the face of misrepresentation and misunderstanding. Baptists do not normally recite a creed in worship, but in confessing our sins we are saying with the wider church that we believe in the forgiveness of sins—but more than that, we believe that at the heart of the cosmos and the center of our worship there is a merciful and gracious God whose nature "is always to have mercy."[36] This is made clear in the prefaces or words of Scripture which may often introduce a prayer of general confession or in the text of the prayer itself.[37]

Why do we need to proclaim this through the confession of our sins, rather than just credally in sermon or song? I want to propose that there is some added value through the worshippers' relationship to this truth and its articulation. Participation in worship is a continuous exchange between the one and the many—between what is generally true and what is true for me, between what we are taught and what we know to be true as a matter of personal testimony and appropriation. That God forgives is an important tenet of *the* Christian faith; that God forgives *me* is a different kind of knowing which provides the basis for my living a grace-filled life.

---

36. See the Prayer of Humble Access in *BCP*.
37. See, e.g., Ellis and Blyth, *Gathering for Worship*, 308.

There are two further corporate aspects to this proclamation. First, prayers of general confession will often acknowledge our sharing in the wider structural sins which contribute to the sin of the world. This dimension is an important aspect of our identity as human beings, and therefore social beings, as well as a vital element in our understanding of what it means to be a disciple of Jesus.

Second, the corporate nature of general confession is not only to be found in its content but in those who do the proclaiming. The community of faith which gathers for worship is a community of forgiven sinners. Pastoring a congregation which included the families and descendants of members of Cromwell's Parliamentary Army, Isaac Watts penned this glorious Eucharistic hymn:

> Jesus invites his saints
>   to meat around his board;
>   here pardoned rebels sit and hold
>   communion with their Lord.[38]

The gathering for worship can be both portrayed and designed as a journey—the active gathering of a community, which gathers before God and around God's Word and the Lord's table, and which eventually continues back into the everyday world.[39] That journey may begin with praise but needs to pass through the crisis of confession and continue in the knowledge of being forgiven and accepted. There is a gospel dynamic to this process in which shared confession plays a crucial (and I use the word deliberately) part. The Daily Office also follows a journey and the OBM's daily inclusion of penitential material offers a daily opportunity to proclaim, with others, the gracious mercies of God.

GENERAL CONFESSION: HOW ARE DISCIPLES BEING FORMED HERE?

In worship we not only speak the truth but learn the truth as well: we learn about God and what it means to trust God. In worship Christians have an opportunity to become more Christian and the church has an opportunity to become more truly itself. In speaking the truth we give ourselves the

---

38. Watts, *Hymns and Spiritual Songs*, III.II, reprinted in *Baptist Praise and Worship*, 438.

39. For more on worship as journey, see Ellis and Blyth, *Gathering for Worship*, 4–11, and Ellis, *Approaching God*, 47–61.

possibility of growing into that truth, whether it is the truth of forgiveness, or hope, or whatever.[40]

But Christian truth is not only doctrinal—there is orthopraxis as well as orthodoxy. Repeated acts of thanksgiving in worship can sharpen our observational skills to see the generosity of God each day, and also shape and nourish us as generous, as well as thankful, people. Similarly, repeated acts of confession can shape and nourish us as forgiven sinners, with eyes open to our own failings as well as to the grace and mercy of God. In addition, it can lead us to see others as people who can be released by our forgiving, not objects of our judgment but companions on the road to redeemed wholeness. The dependant linkage of forgiving and being forgiven in the Lord's Prayer is a testimony to the gospel simplicity and human complexity of this reality.

I have suggested elsewhere that there are at least two ways in which we can see worship having a formational character.[41] On the one hand, its repetitions have a *patterning* effect on the community and the individual worshippers. We are shaped by the gospel of grace. On the other hand, we *rehearse* for faithful living through what we do, say, and experience in worship. We practice, in a safe environment, virtues which will be tested more rigorously elsewhere. We examine ourselves before the cross, we give thanks, we share peace and much else.

In recent years there has been considerable interest in so-called "Christian Practices" in which intentional and repeated actions are undertaken in order to shape the community and its members in the way of Christ.[42] The notion of "practices" is similar to the more traditional understanding of "spiritual disciplines." The discipline or practice is not seen as a means to improve the person concerned but to provide the space within which the Holy Spirit might work formationally. It is an opening of oneself to God in an intentional and consistent way through means which have been either divinely ordained, such as prayer, worship, and the Lord's Supper, or have been received from the wider church as proven means of blessing. Clearly daily prayer comes within this compass and the Daily Office, as a received and corporately owned practice, is a means which God can use to shape disciples—and minsters—in gospel ways. Not all forms of the Office include penitential prayers, so the OBM Daily Office is clearly in a good place here.[43]

40. Irvine, *Art of God*.
41. Ellis, *Approaching God*, 158–61.
42. See esp. Bass, *Practicing Our Faith*, and other books in the series.
43. Psalmody and inclusion of the Kyrie have meant that there has been some penitential material in the Daily Office, but often there have not been prayers of general confession. *Common Worship*, however, following Cranmer, requires their inclusion

IN CONCLUSION

Worship is a dangerous business, leading the American essayist Annie Dillard to suggest that we really needed to wear crash helmets for it.[44] Poor songs can feed bad theology and dysfunctional views of God and of ourselves. Whatever we might mean by the "quality" of worship, we surely must mean something about its potential effect on the worshippers. Worship events which don't include intercessions are likely to encourage a self-absorption which is dangerous and, arguably, heretical. Worship events which do not include an opportunity to confess our sin are also dangerous and can lead to a sanitized form of discipleship in which we ignore aspects of our own lives and dispositions. It is vital we acknowledge our humanity in its sinfulness, as well as in its created beauty and its redeemed glory.

---

when Morning Prayer is the principal Sunday service. See *Common Worship*, 26.

44. Dillard, *Teaching a Stone to Talk*, 52.

4

Listening for the Word of God
Divine Speech, Scripture, and the Task of Interpretation

Sean F. Winter

>Listening Lord, whose word brings new life;
>when we do not heed your voice and live as though you are still dead;
>Shake us awake and whisper your ways and will within our soul.[1]

>It has seemed to me sometimes as though the Lord breathes on this poor gray ember of Creation and it turns to radiance—for a moment or a year or the span of a life. And then it sinks back into itself again, and to look at it no one would know it had anything to do with fire, or light . . . Wherever you turn your eyes the world can shine like transfiguration. You don't have to bring a thing to it except a little willingness to see. Only, who could have the courage to see it?[2]

---

1. OBM Alternative Daily Office—Sunday and Easter.
2. Robinson, *Gilead*, 279–80.

If this is true of our seeing it must also be true of our hearing and reading; what is true of perception must also, by inclusion rather than extension, be true of communication.[3]

Marilynne Robinson's Bonhoefferian novel *Gilead* is suffused with the language of sight and perception.[4] Narrative and narrator make it clear that sustained, rigorous, and joyful attention to this world makes possible a glimpse of glory, a partial but real sighting of the "eternal breaking in on the temporal."[5] Despite his vocation as a preacher, and his role as the narrator of his own story in the novel, Rev. John Ames is suspicious of the capacity of language to capture and so communicate the realities of human existence or the truth of God's love for the world. These truths are perceived instead: in the instant of an encounter with creation, or the face of a child, or the joy of human laughter. Ames catches a glimpse of a young couple getting soaked by rainwater from a tree. "It was a beautiful thing to see," he writes, "like something from a myth . . . it is easy to believe in those moments that water was made primarily for blessing, and only secondarily for growing vegetables or doing the wash." Ames wants his young son to learn to see material, mundane reality for what it is: the location of mystery and presence. "This is an interesting planet," he concludes, "it deserves all the attention you can give it."[6]

Those of us who belong to Christian traditions that place significant weight on the importance of language, words, and (certain) texts in relation to divine revelation do well to note the challenge here. Any account of the ways that God *speaks* through *texts* must emerge from a broader theological consideration of the ways in which God is *present* in *creation*. Of all the things I have learned from John Colwell, this is the most significant: it is only the "truly gratuitous and mediated manner of God's relatedness to creation" that makes possible our knowledge of God through "the truly gratuitous and mediated nature of God's presence and action through sacramental

---

3. Colwell, *Rhythm of Doctrine*, 49.

4. Much has been made of the apparent "Barthian" tone of *Gilead* (see Willimon, *Conversations*, 149), but my own reading leads me to suspect that the theology undergirding the work is derived from Robinson's reading of Bonhoeffer. See Robinson, "Dietrich Bonhoeffer."

5. Robinson, *Gilead*, 272. The tone of the whole novel is set by Ames's early reminiscence of accompanying his father to search for his grandfather's grave at sunset. The young Ames notices the "most wonderful light" cast on them by the setting sun and rising moon, "palpable currents of light passing back and forth . . . taut skeins of light suspended between them," leading Ames to confess that "I hadn't given much thought to the nature of the horizon" (16–17). For a discussion of this theme in the novel, see Holberg, "Courage to See It," 283–300.

6. Robinson, *Gilead*, 31–32.

signs within creation."[7] God's "perception" makes our perception of God possible, and this is as true for Scripture as for any other form of "mediated immediacy."

But this connection opens up the possibility that by paying attention to the dynamics of this broader sacramental view, we gain some critical purchase on the whole question of what we think we are doing when we engage with Scripture. John's own articulation of an answer to that question deeply affected me the first time I read it, not least because of its sensitivity to some of the hermeneutical concerns that, as a biblical scholar, I am invited to confront head on. In this essay I intend to do little more than sharpen the focus and perhaps build on John's discussion of the "Sacramentality of the Word" by considering how we might consider the ubiquitous commitment made in the Daily Office of the Order for Baptist Ministry to "listen for the Word of God." In so far as that liturgical phrase encapsulates the conviction that in the hearing of the words of Scripture God will speak to those who listen, we are invited to go deeper and ask what is happening in the act of listening, and how can such listening be the means of revelation.

I have also learned from John that theological work is generally most interesting when it takes the form of constructive proposal rather than, say, even-handed description or ruminative reflection. So, by way of making things as clear as I can from the outset, I am insisting in what follows that *listening for the Word of God consists in the fundamentally human act of interpretation, oriented towards the fully human words of the biblical text.* Of course, within any theological understanding both words and interpretation are taken up by the Spirit in fulfillment of the divine promise and become the means by which God speaks, something that without God's promise and work would be impossible. But just as there is no bypassing the human words of Scripture, so too there is no possibility of bypassing human interpretative activity in pursuing the circumstances within which, in God's own freedom, God's voice might be heard. In moving beyond a fundamentalism that claims a special and spiritual status for the biblical texts, insured against every possible implication of their historical locatedness and human authorship, we should not and need not seek equivalent protection for our reading. The argument of what follows constitutes a case for recognizing *both* elements as crucial for understanding the possibility of God speaking to us through Scripture. When a Baptist minister, or any other person, ordained or lay, reads Scripture as a central part of a daily office, or when a Baptist assembly (ambiguity intended) or any other ecclesial community hears Scripture read and proclaimed in the context of public worship, they

---

7. Colwell, *Promise and Presence*, 60.

do not bypass the ordinary opportunities and constraints pertaining to reading and understanding. It is precisely within the concrete, embodied, subjective, and messy realities of these ancient texts and their interpretation that God deigns to speak.

In what follows I unpack this proposal with reference to a famous and enigmatic debate between Barth and Bonhoeffer (though "debate" would be overstating the circumstances in which a clear point of theological difference emerged). I proceed to identify the ways that Colwell's own writing on Scripture supports the proposal, and I conclude by provoking some thoughts about the difference the proposal might make to our ongoing liturgical engagement with Scripture.

As is well known, Karl Barth had no problem in providing an unqualified affirmation of the humanity of the biblical text within his broader articulation of the theology of revelation. "In the Bible we meet with human words, written in human speech, and in these words, and therefore by means of them, we hear of the lordship of the triune God."[8] A number of interpreters have noted, however, that this assertion is not matched by an equivalent concern for or affirmation of the hermeneutical task undertaken by the interpreter of Scripture.[9] This may be unfair to Barth, who was able to assert that a "pure," "clear in itself" (Colwell's term would be "unmediated") Word of God "would not have come to us and we could have nothing to do with it." He concludes:

> For that reason *it has come to need interpretation* in so far as it has assumed the mode of our intellectual world and is thus exposed to the risk of being understood, or rather not understood, by us according to the habits of our mentality, in the relationship of reciprocal activity by which we are normally accustomed to understand human words.[10]

Barth's overall emphasis on the humanity of Scripture as witness is consistent with his overall account of revelation, the one-sided emphasis of which comes into focus in Bonhoeffer's famously enigmatic criticism of Barth's "positivism of revelation."[11] While Bonhoeffer never abandoned his

---

8. Barth, *Church Dogmatics*, I/2, 463, cf. the excursus on 466–68. See Hunsinger, "Postcritical Scriptural Interpretation," 29–48.

9. See, e.g., Jeanrond, "Karl Barth's Hermeneutics," 96, Colwell, "Word of His Grace," 192. The fullest exposition of Barth's understanding of the task of interpretation is Wood, *Barth's Theology*.

10. Barth, *Church Dogmatics*, I/2, 717. Trevor Hart has noted that it would be unfair to expect Barth to address the issues raised by the "turn to the reader" in the hermeneutical discussion that postdates his discussion. See Hart, *Regarding Karl Barth*, 117.

11. What follows draws on my discussion of Bonhoeffer's value for thinking

Barthian formation as a theologian of the Word of God, he came to see that Barth's critique of religion by means of his doctrine of revelation was only partially successful in so far as he "did not pursue these thoughts all the way, did not think them through."[12] Attention has rightly focussed on what Bonhoeffer might then have meant by his call for "non-religious" or "worldly" forms of (biblical) interpretation. But in another sense the issue is that in Barth's "like it or lump it" portrayal of revelation there is insufficient room for interpretation *per se*. Bonhoeffer's growing sense of a "world come of age" raised for him the key question of how in such a world Scripture or "biblical concepts" might be "received." In a long letter of June 8, 1944, the issue comes to a head. Despite the value of his ethics, Barth offers "no concrete guidance" for nonreligious interpretation. The story of the Confessing Church is testimony to the fact that a "positivist" theology of revelation can lapse back into a form of "conservative restoration" that communicates genuine theological concepts which nevertheless "remain undeveloped, remote, because they lack interpretation."[13] Rather than stripping away the mythology of the New Testament texts, "these concepts must now be interpreted in a way that does not make religion the condition for faith."[14] It is not enough to affirm that God speaks. There is a strong christological rationale for equally affirming that God's word is only heard in the fullness of human hearing, in interpretation. As is well known, Barth expressed no small degree of bemusement when he came to learn of this critique.[15]

It is now clear that the difference between Barth and Bonhoeffer at this point relates not merely to alternative assessments of the significance of a "world come of age." If that were the case, we might be rightly suspicious of Bonhoeffer's proposals in so far as they would be the product of what now (not least in the light of the "hermeneutical turn" in philosophy) turns out to be an unnuanced diagnosis of the state of human understanding. Michael DeJonge argues that the difference is the product of an early point of clear

---

through issues of biblical interpretation in Winter, "Word and World."

12. Bonhoeffer, *Letters and Papers*, 364, letter of April 30, 1944. The centrality of the theology of the Word for Bonhoeffer is to be explored in Philip Ziegler's forthcoming *Dietrich Bonhoeffer: Theologian of the Word of God* (London: Routledge, 2018).

13. Bonhoeffer, *Letters and Papers*, 429–30.

14. Bonhoeffer, *Letters and Papers*, 430. Bonhoeffer has Bultmann in his sights here although, like many others since, has not grasped that the Marburger's demytheologization project is exactly the kind of hermeneutical program for which Bonhoeffer was calling.

15. Barth, *Christian Life*, 200.

theological divergence relating to the identity of God as person, in contrast to Barth's understanding of God as pure act.[16] As DeJonge later summarizes:

> Barth understands God as a subject whose being remains outside history, while Bonhoeffer understands God as a person whose being is in history... Bonhoeffer's understanding of God as person means that he sees the reconciliation of God and the world as an accomplished fact in the historical person of Christ. Such an understanding of reconciliation requires not dialectical but hermeneutical thinking.[17]

DeJonge's either/or account of the difference between Barth and Bonhoeffer on the relationship between God and history is probably overstated. Both are concerned to affirm divine freedom, even as both recognize that, in so far as this freedom is *for* us, it is known and experienced *within* creation, *by* creatures.[18] It is also fair to say that neither Barth or Bonhoeffer drew the lines of their respective accounts of revelation all the way through to the point of considering in detail what it means to say that the human act of interpretation, properly understood, constitutes the means of encountering God's word. But the debate illuminates two alternative ways of construing what it might mean to "listen for the word of God." On the one hand, we might be satisfied simply to affirm that God speaks and we listen. On the other, we can insist that attention be given to the nature of that listening as an act of interpretative labour that takes place fully in the world: human, creaturely work, essential to our encounter with God in Scripture. It is to Colwell's credit that he sees the necessity of the latter perspective.

As noted above, Colwell's own reflection on the nature of Scripture and the relationship of the believing community to it is refreshingly attentive to questions of interpretation. He reminds us at one point that the term hermeneutics is conspicuously rare in the *Church Dogmatics*.[19] The same cannot be said of the chapters and essays that discuss the Bible in John's

---

16. DeJonge, *Bonhoeffer's Theological Formation*. In his foreword to the book Clifford Green rightly notes that DeJonge's analysis "fundamentally illuminates Bonhoeffer's late epithet about Barth's 'Offenbarungspositivismus,' showing that the term had serious theological substance and was not simply an infamous piece of polemic," xii.

17. DeJonge, "Bonhoeffer from the Perspective of Intellectual History," 204. DeJonge's understanding of what "hermeneutical" means at this point is different from that under discussion in this essay but, by extension, easily incorporates the relationship between divine speaking and human interpretation that might otherwise be treated in dialectical terms.

18. I am indebted to Paul Fiddes for clarification of this point.

19. Colwell, "Word of His Grace," 193.

own theological *oeuvre*.[20] In addition to his explicit recognition, and indeed affirmation, of the importance of hermeneutical theory, Colwell, like Bonhoeffer, engages in critical dialogue with Barth. The result is an account of Scripture and hermeneutics that, in my view, gives correct attention to the humanity of both text and interpreter/interpretation.

Colwell's insistence that Scripture is to be understood as a sacramental entity establishes the theological framework for his statements about interpretation. Scripture is sacramental in so far as it is "established by a promise of God to mediate [God's] presence and action through the agency of the Spirit."[21] The argument of chapter 4 of *Promise and Presence* is carefully drawn with consideration given to, among other things, the failure of historical-critical hermeneutics and fundamentalism alike to do justice to the mediatory role of the text in relation to divine revelation, and the inadequacy of appeals to speech-act theory as a way of shoring up against the challenge of interpretative relativism. At its heart, though, lies the claim that the material human words of the biblical text are taken up through the Spirit's agency to become the means of divine address and encounter.

> To affirm Scripture as Scripture, then, is to affirm that, through the means of this human word . . . we are encountered by God's mediated speaking; this human word is the instrumental means of the divine word. But Scripture is the instrumental means of this mediated divine word without ceasing to be a truly human word . . . though, even in its human origins, a word that is a mediation of God's mediated speaking.[22]

In addition, however, Colwell hints at a more historical argument that requires us to incorporate the act of reading and interpretation into this sacramental reality. It is the particularly (post)modern account of interpretation that lends itself to theological appropriation.[23] In a later essay, he takes Barth's famous assessment that "general hermeneutics" is "mortally sick" as a starting point and offers a more hopeful prognosis to the effect that: "general hermeneutics may not yet be in truly perfect health but I doubt whether

---

20. In addition to the essay in the previous note, see Colwell, "Perspectives on Judas," and *Promise and Presence*, 88–105.

21. Colwell, *Promise and Presence*, 61. Scripture is a sacramental entity in so far as it confers "context, definition, and validity on all other ecclesial sacramental action and event" and is therefore not a sacrament *per se*. See *Promise and Presence*, 3.

22. Colwell, *Promise and Presence*, 101. Cf. 103: "Within the Church, Scripture is a means of grace; through this human text God promises to mediate his speaking, acting, and presence by the Spirit."

23. Colwell, *Promise and Presence*, 90–92, tipping a hat to Saussure and Derrida.

Barth would *still* consider it to be 'mortally sick.'"[24] Exposure to the critique and claims of early post-structuralism gave Colwell "permission to engage with the text itself without the constant academic constraint of (often futilely) attempting to peer behind it" and afforded "a recognition and welcoming of the event of reading and at least the intention of letting the text be itself in that event."[25] This emphasis builds on the sacramental affirmation about the mediating role of the human text, by insisting that such a role can only ever be operative when complemented by the instrumental role of the human interpreter. Once the core insight of more contemporary hermeneutical theory is granted, namely that texts don't "contain" meaning but that meaning emerges out of the encounter between a text and its reader(s), we are able to affirm rather than explain away the work of interpretation and the identity of the interpreter as basic to a theological account of revelation as event. Appeals to the divine authorship of Scripture are otherwise likely to collapse into fundamentalism. As is so often the way, Colwell makes the point with delicious sharpness:

> Believing that Scripture has a divine author, beyond its human authors, does not help me one wit in knowing how to interpret the speeches of Elihu in Job, or the moral turpitude in Judges . . . More basically, this focus on the divine author entirely ignores this all too human reader—precisely the hermeneutical question—and thereby betrays its irredeemably Foundationalist rootedness, its uncritical and deluded assumption of unsullied access to pure objective truth.[26]

In short, those of us who listen for the Word of God in the time after Heidegger, Saussure, and Derrida should be aware that we are never just "listening," and should "admit the dynamic and inevitably interpretative nature of knowledge, *of reading, of hearing*."[27] Said differently, "there can be no event of reading of hearing without personal interpretation."[28] This enables Colwell to be refreshingly conscious of the implications of such a view of interpretation: a suspicion of all claims to objectivity; an awareness of the problem of interpretative pluralism; the inevitability of interpretations being shaped by history, culture, identity, and experience. It also provides the context within which he can affirm a nuanced understanding of the

---

24. Colwell, "Word of His Grace," 195 (emphasis mine).
25. Colwell, "Word of His Grace," 195–96.
26. Colwell, "Word of His Grace," 197.
27. Colwell, "Word of His Grace," 197.
28. Colwell, "Word of His Grace," 198.

church's catholicity as that community which inhabits a living "tradition of signification."[29]

All of this is to suggest that there can be no "listening for the Word of God" without the human work of interpretation. When we read Scripture, or hear Scripture being read and proclaimed, we are not passive auditors of divine speech but mediators of it in and through the interpretative work that we undertake. This means that, in the end, we cannot be satisfied with an account of the hermeneutical task that insists on the notion of "reading" or "hearing" as a way of downplaying attention to the constituent features of interpretative effort.[30] That work is sometimes on the surface of our engagement with a text, as we ask questions of ourselves or others about meaning, translation, coherence, or relevance. On many occasions it is instinctive; our interpretations shaped by presuppositions of which we are barely aware and that in some, more likely many, cases require significant challenge. In each and every case, however, when it comes to the Bible, interpretation goes all the way down.

The implications of this admission for understanding the commitment to reading or listening to Scripture as part of a daily liturgical discipline can now be briefly considered. Clearly at one level, engagement with the Scripture in the few minutes devoted to reading or hearing the texts appointed for the day lacks explicit layers of interpretation. There is no exegesis, no exposition, no commentary. But this is not to say that interpretation is absent. Our first observation is to insist that what happens when we read or hear Scripture in the context of the Daily Office is connected to other modes of scriptural engagement where interpretative work is more obviously visible and explicit. We must challenge any notion that one form of biblical interpretation is, by virtue of its mode or context, capable of mediating divine speech than another. Traditions of private, devotional reading of the Bible are often assumed to be somehow distinct from, say, the act of preaching or listening to preaching. Again, devotional and liturgical reading can very often be understood as being qualitatively different from, say, academic or intellectual approaches to the Bible. The former can, in some accounts, come to be regarded as somehow more "spiritual" than the latter, which is to say that claims can be made that imply that levels of human mediation of divine speech, presence, action are somehow lowered or, at worst, removed entirely. On this view, God's voice is more clearly available in the quiet contemplation of *lectio divina* than through the pages of a Hermeneia

29. Here summarizing the comments in Colwell, *Promise and Presence*, 90–93.
30. I have in mind here in particular the otherwise important account in Webster, *Holy Scripture*.

commentary. Yet, the work of a scholar exegeting a text in a commentary and the work of a Christian believer or disciple listening to a text read in the Daily Office and asking about its meaning *is the same kind of work and as such equally capable of mediating divine speech*. This means that the work of scholarship is indeed capable of offering spiritual guidance, but also that the act of reflecting on Scripture being read is shot through with the human work of interpretation. In all of these instances—the silent reflection in the moments after a daily lection is read, the imaginative entering into a gospel scene through an Ignatian exercise, the wrestling to translate a text into another language, the struggle to speak God's word to a congregation on the basis of a set text—the work of interpretation is the instrumental means of divine speech.

None of these different forms of encounter with Scripture are unhelpful, however, nor should we try and collapse them into one another. In relation to the practice of reading the Bible within the framework of a Daily Office, we might affirm the importance of hearing or reading Scripture without the encumbrance of explicit questions about what the text meant or means for us today. Nevertheless, these texts are read and heard with a view to hearing God speak and that demands interpretative effort on our part. The use of a lectionary to determine the selection of Scripture to be heard on a particular day reminds us not only of the importance of liturgical seasons but of the ways in which the breadth and diversity of the biblical witness demands the attention and effort of the reader or listener. We are invited to consider the relationship between selected texts for the day, the points of connection and difference between readings from Old and New Testament, Gospel and Epistle. Lectionary use also invites us to consider how God might choose to speak through texts that are unfamiliar, challenging, or problematic. We cannot just "listen" to warnings of eschatological judgment, threats of divinely sanctioned violence, or narratives steeped in a patriarchal "point of view"; we must seek to make sense of them in the light of history, experience, culture, theology, and moral conviction. The same goes for a parable or a dense part of epistolary argumentation: God speaks to us in the process of our seeking understanding of what we read or hear.

The use of Canticles in the Office also invites a particular form of interpretation as we take enough time with the texts to consider implications of selection (in relation to liturgical time), translation (where a less than familiar version is chosen), meaning (where words or phrase are unclear), and versification (where texts are laid out to be spoken by different voices). The familiarity with Scripture facilitated by repeated reading and hearing (of the Psalms for example, or of Canticles) should lead us more deeply into the complexities of language, imagery, structure, and thought that they contain. It is in our attention to these things that God's voice can so often be heard.

Finally, these observations would suggest that there is a liturgical necessity to holding a space within the Office for this kind of reflective interpretation to take place, prior to "Reflecting on our Roots" and "Bringing our Concerns." Perhaps the liturgical provision for "Listening for the Word of God" could include not just instructions about what text is read, or spoken but should also invite those saying the Office to ask the question, "What might God be saying through what these texts say?," allow space for that question to be considered, and provide an opportunity to ask God to continue to speak, as we continue to interpret, through the day.[31] We listen for the Word of God not just in the act of reading, saying, or hearing the words of Scripture alone, but as those words meet our intellect, imagination, and identity, and so take on meaning. In this way "the word of God is living and energizing and sharper than double-edged sword" (Heb 4:12).[32] We are invited to have the willingness, and the courage, to interpret, and so to hear.

---

31. The simplest way of achieving this would be through specifying a time for silent reflection following the readings, concluding with a response such as "May your Word live in us . . . and bear much fruit to your glory," or the like.

32. If I can be allowed a moment of exegetical indulgence, it is worth noting that the "word of God" here refers to God's direct address in promise and warning to the implied audience of Hebrews (cf. 13:7). However, the very possibility of that address is predicated on the interpretative work undertaken in relation to Ps 95:7–11 in the whole argument from Heb 3:1–4:11.

5

Bringing Our Concerns

Richard Kidd

*God who is gathering all things together in Christ,
hear us as we bring before you . . .*[1]

I can think of no better heading for the intercessory section in the Daily Office of our Order for Baptist Ministry than "Bringing Our Concerns." We are invited simply to bring our concerns, sincerely believing that these are already God's concerns too, and that naming them will in some way strengthen the living relationship we enjoy as creatures of a loving Creator. As a model of intercession it is, of course, a million miles from the demeaning caricatures of making demands or twisting God's arm. "Bringing our concerns" has, I suggest, precisely the right measure of tentativeness and humility, appropriate to this prayerful moment in the daily liturgy.

Tentativeness and humility, however, do not necessarily preclude genuine confidence in our act of "bringing." The foundations of our confidence are not built on any particular merit or skill as "bringers"; our confidence is rooted entirely in the consistent, faithful, and enduring grace of a loving God. Our confidence grows out of a deep conviction, honed over many years as would-be disciples, that "our concerns" are also the concerns of

---

1. OBM Daily Office—Saturday and Creation—Creating God.

God. As I reflect on where I have seen evidence of this confluence of humility and confidence in companion disciples, prominent amongst them is my colleague and good friend, John Colwell. I am reminded of his manner as a person, the tone of his writing, and his strong and consistent testimony to the boundless grace and love of God.

The simple formula, "Bringing Our Concerns," leaves us in no doubt about what we might expect concerning the tenor of the prayers that follow. Scriptures, hymns, and spiritual headlines come to mind: "While we were still sinners,"[2] "Nothing in my hand I bring,"[3] "*Grace Abounding*."[4] I can imagine John Colwell telling us that this tenor of prayer makes good theological sense because of its consistency with whom it is we understand God to be; our approach to intercession must be theological in the true sense of that word, John would say, flowing out of everything we have come to know about God, through our immersion in the narratives of Scripture.[5] This, then, is whom I have discovered God to be, for me: never entirely unveiled from the hiddenness that is intrinsic to God's god-ness, drawing us into the dynamics of grace, and building in us the confidence we need to trust that it really does make good sense, deep spiritual sense, to bring our concerns.

It would be foolish, of course, to think that bringing our concerns is something that we will be able to do confidently on every occasion, without further reflection on what we think we are doing or how indeed we might begin to do it. There will undoubtedly be times when our experience of living in a broken world means that our confidence is badly shaken; even if, at rock bottom, God still holds the foundations secure. The New Testament is no stranger to the idea that disciples must walk an indeterminate path, along which certainties and uncertainties will often be encountered in parallel formation. On the one side we are encouraged boldly to bring our requests to God,[6] but on the other we get the impression that it is unlikely that we will even know how to ask.[7] Disciples at prayer, it seems, will forever

---

2. Rom 5:8.

3. So begins the third verse of the much-loved hymn, *Rock of Ages*, written by Augustus Montague Toplady in 1763.

4. Words from the title of the book by John Bunyan, *Grace Abounding to the Chief of Sinners*, published in 1666.

5. In this chapter, I will often have in my mind the way that John Colwell sets about the exploration of a theological theme, as in his book *Promise and Presence*. There, as elsewhere, John always begins with God, as he has come to know him in Scripture and then builds on the foundation he has laid.

6. John 14:14.

7. Rom 8:26.

be torn between getting on with the job of praying and agonizing with God over what it is they should pray. I can easily identify with that dilemma.

As I write, I am aware that, as soon as we begin to spell out in more detail our personal interpretations of what it is we think we might be doing when we come to prayer, each of us will need to tell it with our own unique signature and with nuances that have taken shape along our particular disciple journeys. This means that what I suggest in the following pages is unlikely to rest easy with readers of every persuasion and, indeed, if I am true to my own disciple journeying, it will not even rest entirely at ease with some of the things I read in John's extensive writings. I offer, however, these windows onto my own understanding as someone who has talked long and often with John, and I offer them in the full spirit of our continuing friendship.

Over the years, I have developed a number of key words around which my thoughts naturally gather. I would like to think that they will awaken at least some resonances for others who tread similar, although not identical, paths. Some of my key words are these: mystery, grace, participation, connectedness, confidence, strangeness, hopefulness, and amazement. Let me try and gather some of these key words into a single statement that I can briefly expand by way of explanation:

> Despite the darkness that sometimes accompanies my experience of the mystery that is God, I sense that there is, deep down, a profound movement of grace that is never fully extinguished, and continually draws me back as a willing participant in the vast connectedness of this universe, the fruit of God's creative love; despite the myriad doubts and uncertainties that repeatedly needle away at my confidence, I continue to experience an elusive but inspiring strangeness in the way that God's grace is at work in the world: grace that builds and sustains hopeful confidence that God actually shares my concerns, and would have me bring them, laying them bare between us; and despite everything that might appear to the contrary, I never cease to be amazed that, so far at least, there always seems to be grace enough to sustain my disciple journey, and to keep alive the hope that was born in me when first I came alive to the gospel story.

In the spirit of our daily office, perhaps, this statement would better be expressed in the form of a prayer:

> *Loving God, the mystery of your grace*
> *never ceases to amaze us; from the womb,*

> *creative love births and re-births us,*
> *connecting us, ever-reluctant participants,*
> *into one vast inter-connected web*
> *that is your abundant life in the world.*
> *As each fresh wave of doubt threatens*
> *to break over these, our fragile lives,*
> *hold us secure in the courage of faith,*
> *confident in your love, and alive in your hope*
> *for the earth, and for all its people. Amen.*

In what follows, I break down these confessions into three sections, offering additional theological reflection on my experience as a would-be "bringer."

PARTICIPATION IN THE MYSTERY OF GOD

Once again, I can hear John telling us to begin with God. So, in my case, that means I will explore the phrase "God of Mystery." For starters, I am struck by the creative ambiguities sequestered in that little word "of." The power of an ambiguous "of" first came to my attention in Jürgen Moltmann's *Theology of Hope*.[8] We soon discover a hidden force buried in the double meaning, not just in the title but everywhere in his use of the phrase "God of hope." For Moltmann, the "God of hope" is both: the God who is and enables our hope, God who is hope's origin and continuing vitality; but also the God who Godself hopes on a godly scale, hoping with and for the world as it falters along its somewhat perilous way.

I would say that something similar is at play in the phrase "God of Mystery." Mystery is an essential part of God's repertoire, something to which we become acutely alert, for example, when we experience God as hidden; but God is also mystery to the very core of Godself, at the deepest level of God's being. This kind of mystery is, of course, nothing at all to do with puzzles to be solved, or codes to be cracked. When we say we experience mystery as God's "hiddenness," we mean God's real mystery, God's real hiddenness, and we have no choice other than to work with it for what it is, even if that reality is hard. It can lead to great frustration and anxiety. When we listen to the anguish of the psalmist, "Do not hide your face from me,"[9] or of Isaiah, "Truly, you are a God who hides himself,"[10] we hear them raising real questions born of bitter experience. These are questions, however, that I never expect to find answered; rather, I must learn to receive them as

---

8. Moltmann, *Theology of Hope*.
9. Ps 27:9.
10. Isa 45:15.

some of life's givens, part and parcel of God's way of relating to our world, and I must endeavour to learn from them, as well as contest them.

It is useful to think about mystery alongside the Bible's consistent testimony to important distinctions that are made between creatures and God, their Creator. When it comes to origins, for example, the relationship between God and humans is by no means symmetrical. The bottom line is this: we are only here because of God, and not vice versa. We thank God, however, that very real disparities between Creator and creatures are not the only things worthy of notice; what appears to be a very real gulf between God and God's creatures is not without significant bridges. Christians have long worked with variations on a theme that was eventually gathered under the Latin label, *analogia entis*, the analogy of being. When we affirm that there is an analogy of being, we are saying that although God's being (I find it useful to call it "Being") cannot simply be identical with ours (I call that "being"),[11] else the distinction between Creator and creature would simply disappear without trace; nonetheless, there is such a profound kinship between Being and beings, a real *analogia entis*, which makes it possible for us to do God-talk using analogies and metaphors that enable us to get some verbal leverage on God—even if its extent is seriously limited. We could put it another way and say that the kinship between Being and beings, God and God's creatures, is not entirely broken by creation's exercise of freedom, God's most significant gift. When, for example, we make an analogy between our ways of communicating with each other and God's ways of communicating with humanity, we are bold to say that God speaks to us. If there were no analogy of being, this would simply be a nonsense; but the truth is there is sufficient kinship for us to make sense of God's speaking, even if there remains a permanent residue of hiddenness that we will never manage to bypass.

In reading some of John's writings and recalling many of our late night conversations, I have never yet been convinced by, what seems to me to be, John's over-hasty rejection of "process theologies" and so-called "panentheism" as credible foundations for theological discourse.[12] "Panentheism" is a technical term, most often, but not exclusively, associated with "process"

---

11. Experimental uses of Being with a capital "B" and terms like "Being-itself" were common in the systematic writing of so-called existentialist theologians in the early and mid twentieth century. I first met it in Paul Tillich's *Systematic Theology*, and later in Macquarrie's *Twentieth-Century Religious Thought*.

12. See Colwell, *Promise and Presence*, 23–24, where "process" in general and the theology of Charles Hartshorne in particular are quickly dismissed as incompatible with a fully Christian understanding of God.

models of theology.[13] Meaning literally "all-things-in-God-ism," panentheism offers a way of holding two difficult ideas in a single dynamic relationship: that God is in some sense "in all things"; and that, also in some sense, "all things are in God." It is, then, a model that seeks to express a strong mutual participation between God and God's world, without losing the distinctiveness either of God's god-ness or of humanity's humanity. When John and I talk about these things, I am not arguing for the inerrancy of one particular panentheistic schema; I do think, however, that ever since the innovative work of Alfred North Whitehead, it is no longer possible entirely to dismiss the questions that his writings have raised. After much reflection, I simply cannot agree with what seems to me to be too easy criticisms of process-type theologies. I am not convinced by the claim that panentheistic models necessarily undermine anything essential concerning God's god-ness; neither am I convinced by the claim that, as creatures, we lose anything of our proper creaturely independence. On the contrary, I cannot credibly imagine what it might mean for a Creator-God ever to "Be" without an inter-penetrating participatory relationship with "beings" broadly along the lines that process writers suggest; after all, what is a Creator but one who is in relationship with creatures?

If my readers are beginning to wonder how all this will connect with intercessory prayer, I can only ask for patience. We will be there soon, but I need to explore a little more widely first. For me, there is genuine pleasure and fulfilment to be found in testing out the strengths and weaknesses of different models, analogies, and metaphors for the relationship between God and God's world. I am not committed simply to one or other form of words that somehow became fixed at a particular point in Christian history, and I rarely find the process of exploration threatening to the foundations of a personal faith. Most of the formulations we inherit were already second or third order reflections of our inheritance through Scripture. The modern world has, in fact, presented us with a fascinating and highly fruitful array of images from which to choose. Analogies with a "web," both spidery and worldwide, can be helpful, for example, in exploring the deep interconnectedness of beings and Being; and I find the language of "participation," to which I have already made reference, models extremely well how a "web of beings" might be thought to be held in dependence on Being: its ground, its depth and its ultimate home—metaphors and analogies abounding. I

---

13. The roots of process theology are associated with A. N. Whitehead's seminal work *Process and Reality*. Since that time, the term *panentheism* has surfaced in a wide range of theological traditions: existentialist and liberation theologies, as well as later promoted by committed process thinkers such as Norman Pittenger and David Pailin, whose book *God and the Process of Reality* provides a thorough overview.

sometimes wonder if terms like these might have surfaced in some early statements of the church's famous ecumenical councils—had they been gathering, not in the fourth and fifth, but in the early twenty-first century.[14]

Many of the terms most readily available at the time of these great councils had a Greek philosophical ring to them, now quite alien in the modern world, so that today we struggle to feel for their intended meanings. Many of the earliest attempts to reflect theologically on what it means to speak about Jesus of Nazareth as the incarnation of God's Messiah were constructed by navigating a winding pathway through some difficult concepts, then familiar from Greek philosophy: in particular, *homoousios* (same-being) and *homoiousios* (similar-being). Put simply, the question was, is the being of Jesus identical with the Being of God; or is it enough simply to say they are similar in being? After much thought, I find myself at ease with what has become known as a Christology "of degree";[15] rather, that is, than a Christology "of kind." Starting from the *ousios* (Being) of God, I am in no doubt that all we humans are *homoiousios* with God; we have much that is similar in our being with God's Being. We beings were, after all, made in the image and likeness of Being;[16] there is a fundamental kinship between ourselves and God. To talk like this is not, I hasten to add, a sign of inappropriate *hubris* on our part; it is simply testimony to a gift of God. Because this kinship is so strong, I do not find it hard to imagine some kind of spectrum such that, as similarity is progressively strengthened and nears the asymptote of identity, it is entirely possible that there should be a person for whom the distinction between Being and being blurs into relative insignificance. Whilst I do not doubt that there have been those, other than Jesus, who have been much further along the being-Being spectrum than I ever expect to attain myself, I find myself a committed follower of Jesus because he is the one in whom I have glimpsed Being more fully than in any other being. In my understanding none of this would make sense at all, were it not for a profound and universal kinship between Being and beings.

But what, you say, has all this to do with "bringing our concerns"—a great deal I answer. My conviction that our concerns are God's concerns is rooted in the intimacy of this very relationship between God and God's world. Our confidence that our "bringing," even if it is to one who remains in part hidden and concerning whom we are so easily prone to doubt, is

14. Most famous amongst the seven major ecumenical councils, and always demanding careful attention, are the Council of Nicaea (AD 325) and the Council of Chalcedon (AD 451), both major turning points in the lengthy struggle to formulate coherent statements about the person of Jesus Christ and the doctrine of God as Trinity.

15. A well-respected mid-twentieth-century version is Baillie, *God Was in Christ*.

16. Gen 1:26.

because we sense a surprising movement from beyond ourselves, from Being to beings, which we can never manage to contrive or manipulate—the movement we call grace. We are concerned to bring not just our own concerns but the concerns of the entire world, because we are all of us so webbed into the fabric of Being and beings. Twentieth-century writers, concerned about processes of empowerment and freedom, have been quick to say that our suffering and the suffering of others cannot ultimately be separated, as if I could be fully healed while a sister or brother remains in pain. Some have gone as far as to say that either we receive salvation together, a universal gift of God's grace, or we do not credibly receive it at all—and I warm to that.[17] It is the whole creation, in its entirety and not merely its parts, that groans with longing for the God of Mystery, God in God's hiddenness.[18]

Here we could explore a whole suite of analogies that have taken shape, especially through detailed study of deep-laid patterns in the universe we inhabit. Cosmologists and particle physicists often work with images that greatly help us describe, even if it is still within the limits of metaphor, our weblike interconnectedness and our inseparable participation in a greater whole. We do not need to understand much about quantum entanglement, the strange ability of particles at remote edges of the universe to show signs of intimate connection with each other, to feel grateful for the image it provides of just how interconnected we and all things are. We do not need to be able to quantify and analyze the data from ecological studies to get a feel for the interconnectedness of life on planet earth; it makes such obvious sense that when one part is manipulated, another will be altered too, and we rightly recognize our growing responsibility, weighing upon us as primary agents of change. Never have I heard this better expressed than on the lips of one of the real life characters in an inspiring film called *Waste Land*, shot on location on one of the world's largest landfills, Jardim Gremacho, near Rio de Janeiro.[19] In this real life drama, Valter dos Santos, a natural leader with no formal education at primary or secondary level, and twenty-six years amongst the "pickers" who scrape a living from the tip, speaks with extraordinary wisdom about the value of the contribution we make to the planet

---

17. Typically views of this kind are expressed by those who experience firsthand the impact of injustice and oppression, often committing themselves to a lifetime in solidarity with the poor. Such a view of the relationship between salvation and liberation can certainly be found in the work of Gustavo Guttierez, whose book, *A Theology of Liberation*, pioneered a new way of thinking for a whole generation of theologians around the world.

18. Rom 8:22.

19. *Waste Land*, available on DVD, was directed by Lucy Walker and was winner of an Amnesty International Award in 2010.

with each item we recycle. Asked why recycling every single abandoned aluminium can is significant, his answer is the one-liner that stays in memory long after the film is over. "One single can is of great importance," he says, "because 99 is not 100, and that single one will make the difference." This man clearly understands interconnectedness, and his "picking" is a model of transformative prayer in action. As we learn from the credits at the end of the film, Valter sadly succumbed to illness and an early death soon after filming was complete.

Not even Valter's massive gesture of solidarity with the world and its people makes any sense unless, as he appears to do, we also grasp the true importance of the interconnectedness of all beings. This is the interconnectedness that also drives us to bring each other, with all the weight of our many concerns, and name them in our daily prayers. What begins in a prayer can also spill over into the whole of life as we become living testimonies to the mystery of God's grace in the world, expressing God's concern not only with our words but, like Valter, in solidarity of action for justice, expressed in educating, campaigning, and restorative work. Only in this way do we do justice to the truth that our Creator shares the concerns of creation.

And so we pray. The Offices, originating out of our Order for Baptist Ministry, rehearse on a daily basis the shared concerns of Creator and creation. Each time, they rightly begin with God, then progress, echoing many of the themes to which I have already referred. The section "Bringing Our Concerns" in the Office for "Sunday and Easter" expresses this with clarity and force. Each new stanza begins with an affirmation of God's initiative, God's coming to us; only then are we invited to bring our concerns for those known and unknown. We bring those who are overwhelmed by grief, those who are fearful and without hope, even those who have denied God. Later in the week, in "Tuesday and Advent," we "celebrate your coming as a human being and the gift of your presence"; and then we pray in solidarity without boundaries, bringing our concerns for all the world. By the end of the week we have prayed for all God's creation; especially for: the broken ones, the sorrowful, the anxious, the suffering, the persecuted, the abandoned, and the lost; and we bring with them and for them: healers, peacemakers, activists, educators, scientists, artists, and musicians, all who have potential to become instruments of transformation in a broken world.

CONFIDENCE AMID THE STRANGENESS OF THE WORLD

Again, I can hear John calling me back to God, and his prompting demands that I say more about what I have been calling God's hiddenness. God's hiddenness certainly keeps us humble, and sometimes it becomes so acute that we are left wondering if hiddenness is just a polite term for absence or even nonexistence. I have no experience of what it might be like to live a life of faith that is free from doubt. I do, of course, occasionally meet companions who claim to live all well nigh doubt-free lives; but I am usually left wondering if in truth there lurks a measure of self-deception, a bit like the emperor exhibiting new clothes. I know that I cannot count myself amongst them.

There is, it seems to me, an ultimate rightness about doubt that demands it be recognized as the inevitable shadow-side of faith. Its rightness is all of a piece with the way that our Creator effects a living relationship with all creation, enabling us to become aware of God's presence. In part, the fullness of God's grace is inevitably hidden because it is always mediated through materiality, the fabric of the universe. John is strong on this. It is never, as many theologians have agreed, "unmediated-immediacy."[20] If it were other, and God did touch our lives, unmediated, Being on being, then there could be no space for doubt at all. If we found that God bypassed all mediating forms to speak or touch or heal, then what more would there be to say than "I believe"; whereas many of us are glad to complete the famous biblical saying with its additional words, "help my unbelief."[21] Aquinas had another technical phrase to identify this process by which God is only mediated through the materiality of the world; he called it "conversion to the phantasm." What he had in mind is this: whenever we are alerted to the possibility of God's presence in a parable or a healing, this only becomes possible because God has converted that presence into something we can hear or touch in the actual material of creation. That is a major reason why the arts—literature, poetry, music, and so on—are so very powerful in communicating what we might hear as a result of God speaking. The arts make imaginative use of material forms—sounds, shapes, colours, and so on—to effect Aquinas's "conversion" into media with which we can engage with our

---

20. This is most clearly stated in what we think of as the Aristotelian strand in Western theological thought, relaunched in the writings of Thomas Aquinas at the turn of the first millennium, and fundamental to the theology of leading Roman Catholic theologians in the twentieth century, notably Karl Rahner. It contrasts with a more Platonic approach to Christian theology which, amongst its many dualisms, can easily find itself so dividing Creator from creatures, that it becomes necessary to resort to "unmediated immediacy" as a mechanism for revelation.

21. Mark 9:24.

everyday senses. In matters of healing, the "conversion" is most often effected through the skill of doctors and the love of carers. It would not, in my own understanding, make any sense for such healing to bypass the chemical and physiological structures that constitute our creaturely bodies; if it were so, neither faith nor doubt could find a place in the picture at all; God would simply be self-evident as given.

The truth is that God is always mediated into the world of creatures like ourselves. The downside, I have admitted, is that this leaves people like me sometimes doubting whether there is a God at all; but God's hiddenness is not always and entirely to our disadvantage. I am reminded of the saying in the Letter to the Hebrews, "It is a fearful thing to fall into the hands of the living God."[22] We would most surely be badly burned; but God relates with us in much more gentle and protective ways. When I try to articulate God's gentle ways of relating with us, I am drawn to the old-fashioned word "intimation," or perhaps even better the more modern word "glimpse." My own testimony, in common with many companions, is that there are just enough occasions in my own life when an intimation or a glimpse of God's grace is enough to rebuild confidence and keep me on the disciple way. This is not, of course, a testimony that readily yields itself to empirical examination; that could only happen if immediacy were to be unmediated and God could be measured as an indisputable cause in a sequence of cause and effect. In reality it is only by steady growth in confidence rather than by proofs that disciples gather a strong and potentially lasting conviction that almost everything precious in life is down to God's deep and loving concern.

I suspect that not everyone will be able to identify with me if I say that what I often find myself calling the "strangeness of God's world" is very important to me in building the faith that I live by. There can be genuine delight in our experiences of strangeness, often things that deep down we will never manage to explain—why should we want to? Becoming aware of the strangeness of God's world can encourage growing confidence in God, but only in the God who always remains strangely hidden. Limited understanding does not prevent some scientific insights into the deep working of the universe from bringing great pleasure and strengthening my experience of faith. I am not amongst those who expect science to crack the theory of everything: to have, as it were, the boxed-set of proofs. Gödel's incompleteness theorems[23] prove good companions to my theological conviction that,

22. Heb 10:31.

23. Roughly speaking, these theorems from the discipline of mathematical logic suggest that in any system of thought there will always be some things that remain beyond proof within the terms of the system. A useful analogy might be the difficulty of picking oneself up by the handles of a basket in which we are already standing.

at the very deepest level of reality, by which I mean God, hiddenness cannot finally be exposed. There is, I suggest, an irreducible strangeness that continually creeps in and disturbs our best attempts to harness a theory of everything; it is as though, Babel-style, God forbids it.[24] This is as true in the developments in physics as, more importantly, it is true in almost everything else that matters most to us in our humanity: the strangeness of love, of providence, of coincidence, of salvation, of human freedom—the list is never-ending.

This is reason enough for me to "bring my concerns," because in the midst of all this strangeness there are just enough intimations that there is another who shares my concerns, but measured on a different scale. This reminds me of a much-quoted statement in which Desmond Tutu summarizes his core conviction about God, "there's no question about the reality of evil, of injustice, of suffering, but at the centre of this existence is a heart beating with love."[25] That same conviction energizes us as we are "bringing our concerns" as part of our daily office; and the fact that we bring our concerns with humility need not in any way diminish the confidence with which we bring them.

It is probably worth noting at this point that sometimes, when we faithfully bring our concerns, we can be shocked by the events that rapidly follow. It is not at all unknown to bring our concern for someone who has a severe illness and for that person to die very soon after; I can bring my concern for someone who has been taken hostage, and they are murdered; I can bring my concern for someone who has sunk into the darkness of depression, and they bring an abrupt end to their life. Strangely, however—here comes the strangeness word again—none of these is enough to stop me continuing to bring my concerns to God. On the contrary, the lure of God's love continues to draw me; and, at just such times, some simple framework of daily prayers is often all that it takes to keep me on track when things are especially dire.

AMAZEMENT BEFORE THE GOD OF GRACE

But I can still hear John saying I should keep returning to God, and I will do that one more time under a heading that includes the words "God of Grace." We are back to the ubiquitous "of," another example of an ambiguous genitive. On one hand, we find God who is, Godself, grace through and through;

24. Gen 11:1–9.
25. Tutu, interview with Krista Tippett, *On Being*, March 20, 2014, https://onbeing.org/programs/desmond-tutu-a-god-of-surprises/.

on the other, we find God energizing the dynamic of grace in the world: unbidden, free from manipulation, the fullest expression of unconditional love. How amazing is that!

In the sections of the Daily Office entitled "Bringing Our Concerns," we are invited through simple prayers to rest our troubled souls on the boundless grace of God, and to bring the whole of creation with us. One striking feature of our Christian Gospels is their frequent repetition of the observation that the disciples and the crowds were amazed.[26] Many Christians would, I think, rest more effectively in God's grace, if only they could discover the joy in amazement, resisting the temptation to go on striving after explanations and proofs.

For many years, people the world over brought their concerns for the people of South Africa during the bitter days of apartheid, as now in 2018 we bring our concerns for Afghanistan, Sudan, Israel/Palestine, Myanmar, Syria, Yemen, and so on. We bring these concerns with a heavy heart, usually struggling to imagine what meaningful transformation would look like and, even harder, what could enable transformation to happen. Sometimes, however, even against enormous odds, transformation does happen, and it is tempting to ask if this is an "answer" to our prayers? I am more comfortable just to receive the news of transformation with amazement, and to be thankful that another manifestation of human wickedness has been erased from the world. It is not that I am questioning God's involvement; these nations and their peoples are God's concern even more than they will ever be mine, and it is right to be thankful. Whether there is anything to be gained from an autopsy into the mystery of grace and its relationship to our prayers, that I doubt.

Is it not enough that, when a Nelson Mandela or a Desmond Tutu emerges on the world stage and becomes a catalyst for transformation, we simply acknowledge our amazement and express our thanks to God? If we bring our concern for a friend with advanced symptoms of cancer to God, and there comes about a surprising remission that doctors would not normally expect, is it not enough that I am amazed and hugely thankful? To reach too far beyond our amazement is to enter dangerous water, in which the possibility of serious disillusionment is not far below the surface. South Africa might still descend into fresh violence; my friend might have a recurrence of the invasive cancer. If I have put too much emphasis on explanation and proof concerning the detail of God's involvement, there is now the possibility that counter-evidence and counter-proof will expose my amazement

---

26. There are no less that twenty-nine occurrences spread across the synoptic gospels.

and gratitude as premature and misplaced. But that is not a necessary scenario. Instead I can choose to stay with my amazement and learn from it, and when hard times return (even Lazarus had to die again, one day) I will keep on "bringing my concerns" and trusting the God of Grace.

BY WAY OF CONCLUSION

I do not doubt that John Colwell will keep telling us to go back to God, and I for one am grateful for his reminders. John, from what I have written in this paper, it is clear that my mind has not yet found a theological home in the same place as yours. I keep finding so much that excites me, heart and mind, in those models of thinking that we associate with "process theologies" and the concept of "panentheism." At the end of the day, however, I would like to think that in most of the things that matter deeply, our spirits will not be found far one from the other; were it not so, I doubt we could find such pleasure in our conversations, nor would we delight when there is opportunity to pray together at the Order for Baptist Ministry's annual convocation. Your arguments carry much weight and continue to challenge me. Gladly it has not been too hard to find bees that appear in both our bonnets: I fully share all your disclaimers about immediacy, and your warnings about the danger in any claim to manipulate grace; and I affirm wholeheartedly your emphasis on the priority of God in all matters of faith and all the workings of grace.[27] Let us, then, continue together with humility and confidence to bring our concerns to God.

---

27. These are the summary themes that struck me so forcibly in John's book *Promise and Presence*, to which I refer in the opening section of this chapter.

6

Going to Love and Serve
As the Father Sends Me . . .

Margaret Gibbs

Enlarge our dreams and enthuse our minds,
Inspire our faith and empower our resolve[1]

"Weep if you must
Parting is hell
But life goes on
So . . . sing as well"[2]

There is a 1960 painting by Graham Sutherland called *Noli me tangere* which hangs in the Mary Magdalene Chapel at Chichester Cathedral,[3] and which depicts the moment in the garden when the risen Christ tells Mary to overcome her natural instincts on meeting him so unexpectedly, and to let him go.[4] Christ is shown purposefully ascending a staircase, yet his gaze and gesture are directed towards Mary. The ambiguous positioning of his

---

1. OBM Daily Office—Monday and Pentecost—Living Spirit.
2. Grenfell, "If I Should Go."
3. A copy of the painting can be found here: https://www.chichestercathedral.org.uk/about-us/delve-deeper-1/graham-sutherland-painting/.
4. John 20:14–17.

hand may indicate either affection or restraint. Mary kneels in humility below the stair, but her eyes are lifted up to him and her hand reaches through the balustrade. One with the Father and Holy Spirit, the Christ figure is enclosed within the triangular structure he climbs. He strides away from a keyhole perhaps signifying all that has been permanently locked or unlocked through his unique death and resurrection. Following Rembrandt, Christ wears a gardener's hat, though his shadow does not. He is no longer earth-bound.

Noli me Tangere is a Latin expression which has become associated with this story and which means "do not touch me" or more strongly "do not interfere with me."[5] Rendered in Greek, Μή μου ἅπτου, it can bring out a direction to stop clinging to or holding on to Christ.[6] It captures a significant moment of transition in a devoted relationship which, in demanding a sacrifice would grow through that sacrifice.[7] For us the painting could represent another hinge moment which comes towards the end of every experience of corporate worship. Eventually the participants each need to let go of the gathering, square their shoulders and face whatever is waiting beyond, as they go out to love and serve Christ in the world to which he sends them.

LEAVING WELL

Significant transitions of any kind can be delicate and unpredictable. After some years spent managing cross-cultural mission workers and their families, through their calling, sending, service, and finally through the often painful process of withdrawal and relocation, I can testify to this. Sometimes a fruitful and effective ministry built over long years can falter when the time comes, often earlier than anticipated, to begin to let go, hand responsibility over to others and leave. A clean break in these circumstances is very rarely made. Motivated by love for a situation which has become a precious part of personal identity, the tendency is to stay in close touch, to visit, to continue to exert influence and "to help."

Concluding anything of importance successfully can be even more challenging, sometimes calling for sacrifices beyond those of the ministry

---

5. *Collins English Dictionary* online, s.v. "noli-me-tangere," https://www.collinsdictionary.com/dictionary/english/noli-me-tangere.

6. Perschbacher, *New Analytical Greek Lexicon*, 50.

7. Wright, *John for Everyone*, 147.

itself. At worst, ending poorly can allow sin or even evil to gain a foothold, disrupt fruitfulness and destabilize relationships.[8]

When in gathered worship participants have enjoyed a sense of God's presence, affirmation of identity and belonging, and the comfort of familiar words and actions, it can be equally hard to let go. Mary Magdalene stood in this kind of dilemma in the garden. She loved Jesus dearly and was thrilled and overcome at meeting him once more in the flesh. Perhaps she assumed things could now revert to how they had been before, or she simply wanted to remain in her attitude of adoration, but both he and she were called to move forward rather urgently from their all too brief reunion. Jesus would soon ascend to his Father in order that the Holy Spirit might be sent to his followers. Mary would be commissioned to communicate this first meeting with the risen Lord to the other disciples. The joy of being together was great, but the temptation to linger could have become a stumbling block.

It is important to note here how natural it is for followers of Jesus to long to come permanently into the unhindered presence of God. Humanity was originally created for this purpose and destination. As the psalmist expressed it in his poetry:

> One thing I ask of the Lord,
> that I will seek after:
> to live in the house of the Lord
> all the days of my life,
> to behold the beauty of the Lord
> and to inquire in his temple.[9]

The Apostle Paul couched it in practical terms in his letter to the Philippian church.

> For to me, to living is Christ and dying is gain. If I am to live in the flesh, that means fruitful labour for me; and I do not know which I prefer. I am hardpressed between the two: my desire is to depart and be with Christ, for that is far better.[10]

Nonetheless Paul had accepted that the Father sets the appointed time for each one, even the risen Christ, to come to him. In the meantime believers must be sent onward from gathered worship, continually and purposefully, in loving service to the world.

---

8. Hale, *On Being a Missionary*, 258.
9. Ps 27:4.
10. Phil 1:21–23.

SENT OUT TO BE POURED OUT

Paul followed in the tradition of Jesus who was himself sent as a pattern for his subsequent followers. Jesus's *modus operandi*, bequeathed to his disciples, is recorded by John the Evangelist:

> Very truly, I tell you, the Son can do nothing on his own, but only what he sees the Father doing; for whatever the Father does, the Son does likewise. The Father loves the Son and shows him all he himself is doing.[11]

Just before Jesus died he prayed to the Father:

> As you have sent me into the world, so I have sent them into the world.[12]

After his resurrection he reiterated:

> "Peace be with you! As the Father has sent me, so I send you." When he had said this, he breathed on them and said to them, "Receive the Holy Spirit."[13]

John Colwell talks of the dynamics of sending within the Trinity: "Within the relatedness of the Trinity there is a sending and being sent, though, as with all the works of God with respect to creation (with respect to that which is other than God) these actions are distinctly appropriate to the persons of the Trinity."[14] Having first been sent himself, and having fulfilled his sending, Jesus understood from the inside how to go about sending others. As we reflect on sending, and in particular on how to send out from worship, we see that Jesus apparently intended his disciples to be sent in the same way that the Father sent him. With the help of the Holy Spirit Christians are to look at what Christ did and do the same in his name. Following this pattern Mary was indeed sent out from the garden in the manner of Jesus. She was sent as his first resurrection messenger, and therefore with his authority, with this message for his followers:

> Say to them, "I am ascending to my Father and your Father, to my God and your God."[15]

---

11. John 5:19–20.
12. John 17:18.
13. John 20:21–22.
14. Colwell, "Mission as Ontology," 8.
15. John 20:17.

It was hard for her to depart, but she delivered the message immediately and obediently.[16] Following a scriptural trajectory down through the ages, the dynamics of sending out from worship should reflect this same transaction. Worshippers are sent out just as the Father sent Christ, sacrificially, in his authority and with his good news to share.

A key Scripture which fills out in more detail the manner of Christ's transition from heaven to earth is the christological hymn in Phil 2:5–11, which is given expressly as an example for us to follow.

Jesus's sending meant willingly letting go of equality with God, including unhindered communion within the Trinity and the culture and community of heaven, in order to become human; to be emptied, become nothing and serve. The fullness of what Jesus had to give up in order to be emptied remains a mystery to us. As human creatures we can only approach an understanding of what he took on from our familiar condition instead. Such a Christlike *kenosis*, with the purpose of inhabiting a new context and ministry authentically, becomes a blueprint for all disciples of Jesus as we serve him in our own small ways. The manner of our sending should facilitate this kind of voluntary emptying in order that, sacrificially, we can assume aspects of our particular contexts to communicate the gospel more effectively wherever God has placed us.

SENT OUT INCARNATIONALLY

In 2004, having returned from serving with BMS World Mission in various settings overseas, I had the opportunity to prepare for Baptist ministry at Spurgeon's College. I remain grateful for the chance to process aspects of what I had experienced of God through other cultures and Christian traditions in John's theology and ethics classes. Inclining towards activism I found this an especially helpful way to come to theology. It was around that time that John was preparing his book *The Rhythm of Doctrine*, which includes an examination of the implications of the incarnation. In a chapter entitled "The One Who Takes Our Humanity," John explores how taking flesh was a transition which required Jesus to assume particular aspects of the human condition and experience. He emphasizes the uniqueness of Christ's coming among local cultures some of which expected lesser gods to take temporary material form, but which would never have imagined the ultimate reality would do so as fully divine and fully human, and in such an earth-changing way.

---

16. John 20:18.

> The very idea of the Word becoming flesh, of God becoming human, of the Creator becoming a creature, of the divine becoming matter, was deeply incongruous if not offensive to those amongst whom the Christian gospel was first preached and it remains incongruous and offensive still.[17]

The shocking and unexpected event of the incarnation, envisaged before creation but brought about in a particular moment of time, manifests eternal qualities in God's character.[18] God comes in Christ, mysteriously, freely, particularly, "grounded in a promise and sought in prayer."[19] Since God acted in this way, it is also fundamental for the way humanity should reflect his image.[20] The narrative of the incarnation is inherently material[21] says John, and so are our own narratives. "He makes the flesh his own and thereby affirms it and fulfils it."[22]

> It is not only that the true God is truly identified in Christ; it is also that true humanity is truly identified in his real and risen humanity; and, in this real and risen humanity the goal and fulfilment of all creation is disclosed and effected.[23]

His nature, his coming, his service, and his destination become definitive for us, and should be reflected through our worship, love and service today.

> That there is a material creation is because this, the true God, invites and destines us together with all creation to participate in his glory in and through Christ and by the Spirit.[24]

Incarnation by emptying is thus definitive of the Trinity, and Jesus's incarnation could not have come about without the Holy Spirit's mediation. Streaming outwards from this, the marks of the Spirit's particular inspiration and involvement are evident throughout the scriptural record, through hovering over the waters of creation,[25] to the heartfelt cry, raised together with the bride, of "Come!"[26]

---

17. Colwell, *Rhythm of Doctrine*, 31.
18. Colwell, *Rhythm of Doctrine*, 32.
19. Colwell, *Rhythm of Doctrine*, 30.
20. Colwell, *Rhythm of Doctrine*, 34.
21. Colwell, *Rhythm of Doctrine*, 35.
22. Colwell, *Rhythm of Doctrine*, 35.
23. Colwell, *Rhythm of Doctrine*, 36.
24. Colwell, *Rhythm of Doctrine*, 37.
25. Gen 1:2.
26. Rev 22:17.

And here as everywhere else and always the Spirit is the agent of this mediated presence and purposefulness.[27]

Since the Spirit was integral to Christ's incarnation, how much more so for us sent with his authority and message, and hoping to connect effectively into our own contexts?

In his teaching Jesus emphasized: "As the Father has sent me, so I send you."[28] He, emptied, was sent to a certain place, time, culture, and society. Rather than springing as it were fully formed from the head of Zeus, he chose to invest the time needed to grow up and acquire everyday skills in an ordinary human family just as we all do. (In mentioning this I am reminded of times in lectures at Spurgeon's College when John playfully suggested to students, that the baby Jesus probably behaved exactly like any other baby boy!)[29] Jesus had to learn to eat, to walk, to listen, and to speak; to relate as a person within his community. Of these the acquisition of human languages provides us with a fascinating practical aspect of how Jesus was emptied in order to assume humanity.

SENT OUT TO CONNECT IN A CONTEXT

Inheriting a "mother tongue" is an important example of cultural and social particularity coming to each person born on the planet. A person's first language is formative for their initial worldview; that is their foundational beliefs and values. Each subsequent language learnt forms new connections in the brain, making it easier to acquire more. This in turn leads to enriched overall insight, breadth of understanding and communication possibilities. Individual languages are the chief repositories of their particular culture's content[30] and each one is unique. When a monolinguist understands for the first time that translations given in bilingual dictionaries are not exact equivalents, it is a genuine *eureka* moment. It becomes difficult for that person to persist in believing that there could only be one way of understanding or expressing anything.

In taking flesh, Jesus became no different to any other "third culture kid"[31] in respect of communication. Emptied as it were of the speech of

27. Colwell, *Rhythm of Doctrine*, 37.
28. John 20:21.
29. http://www.paolo-veronese.org/Holy-Family-With-St-Barbara-And-The-Infant-St-John.html.
30. Everett, "From Threatened Languages to Threatened Lives."
31. Pollock and Van Reken, *Third Culture Kids*, 13.

heaven, he had to start with the ABCs of human and therefore unique but limited languages. Through them he would announce the coming of the kingdom of God.

Like so many in today's world Jesus grew up in a multilingual society. The gospel accounts imply that Jesus could speak and understand several languages; Aramaic day to day, Hebrew for the synagogue, probably Greek in the wider public sphere, perhaps Latin and regional dialects. Analyzing his speech and teaching we see Jesus intentionally matching the manner and content of his speech to different situations. He spoke of everyday rural scenes and artefacts in his parables to the multitude, quoted the torah to teachers, and spoke in intimate language to his family and close friends. The gospels, written down in Greek for more efficient communication across the first-century world, bring many of Jesus's sayings to us in translation. From this we infer that, unlike with the Koran, it is permissible, even beneficial to translate Christian Scripture and use other languages in order to spread the gospel, making it sound less culturally foreign to each hearer.

In contrast, a first experience of entering a church in the UK today can feel like stepping into a foreign land. Language, symbols, and actions based on traditions which "initiates" find familiar and comforting can be impenetrable to newcomers. If Christianity is to continue as a prophetic and not become a reactionary movement, regular revision of our worship vocabulary and study and practice in communicating effectively in increasingly varied contexts are urgently needed. A society where most had attended Sunday School or church, or had learned bible stories in school, is long departed. Christians cannot depend on common terms, let alone concepts and narratives as starting points for outreach any more. Annual debates about what to include or omit from leading dictionaries prove that "last year's words belong to last year's language."[32]

Communication challenges for sharing the gospel in contemporary Britain include immense and growing ethnic diversity, the social media boom, often hidden communication differences across generation gaps, and all amid a rhetoric of increasing political and social divisions and differences. In some ways, UK society is becoming more like the one Jesus addressed and to which he sent his first disciples. Prophetic insights are needed to help us bridge the widening gap between our forms of gathered worship and the world we hope to serve.

Such a prophetic insight was demonstrated at Pentecost when the Holy Spirit enabled a group of Jewish disciples to speak spontaneously in diverse languages. As a result, a very diverse crowd found that they could each

---

32. Eliot, "Little Gidding," II, from *Four Quartets*, 204.

miraculously understand and therefore respond to the gospel.[33] Despite the evident impact of this event in multicultural Jerusalem, the disciples still struggled to follow in the wake of the Spirit's direction. They did not get to grips with practical contextualization of the gospel until persecution forced them out of their comfort zone. In contrast, the cosmopolitan city of Antioch did spawn a church fellowship that was willing to send workers voluntarily further afield: and yet even for them the task proved far from straightforward.[34]

To understand practically how hard it was for the fledgling church and its trainee missionaries to communicate the gospel in a diverse world, we need look no further than Paul's experiences in Lystra.[35] Sent out from a multiethnic church, by the time he arrived in Lystra Paul had accrued a range of mission experiences and had met with some success in planting new fellowships. His approach to evangelism thus far, and which we see repeated in Iconium[36] immediately before arriving in Lystra, had been to find a local population of Jews and start with them. Paul could count on some familiar cultural assumptions, perhaps some hospitality, and above all common languages and knowledge of the torah which provided an easy transition for him into preaching the gospel of Christ, starting from the prophets.

In Lystra for the first time Paul had none of these helps available, and he soon found out that his previously successful approach was all wrong for this new context. Bystanders could not understand his preaching, nor, disastrously, could he understand what they said in response. He had not anticipated the serious misapprehensions that could arise from an impressive visual miracle divorced from a spoken explanation. Nor did he apparently remember the Phrygian myth that the gods would be returning as humans to that locality one day.[37] (The people of Lystra had been found wanting on the first occasion, and so kept the appropriate sacrifices in constant readiness so as not to be caught out a second time.)

Paul came to Lystra with the authority and message of Christ, but found, as many cross-cultural workers do, that even these would not automatically lead to a connection. He had apparently not taken any time to study the new culture in order to develop a more effective way in. Perhaps he could have capitalized on their belief that God would indeed come to

33. Acts 2:4–11.
34. Patterson, *Antioch Factor*, 28.
35. Acts 14:8–20.
36. Acts 14:1.
37. Ovid, "Philemon and Baucis," in *Metamorphoses*, book 8.

them in human form, though not in the way they expected. Perhaps he could have introduced them to Jesus through an interpreter who could frame his message in a culturally appropriate way. Perhaps some kind of high street survey,[38] however clumsy might, while not in itself constituting mission, might have revealed locally held beliefs and aspirations in such a way as to enable Paul to find a touching point for the gospel later on. Instead Paul jumped into a situation unprepared, using the wrong language and an outmoded approach, and ended up being drummed out of town. (The continuing narrative in Acts shows that, by God's grace and the work of the Holy Spirit, Paul's first visit to Lystra did yield some fruit. At least one person there did understand the Greek language and the Hebrew Scriptures through his parentage.[39] Ironically, it was probably Timothy's uniquely appropriate cultural heritage that enabled him to respond to Paul's tried and tested approach, and later become his coworker.)[40]

Paul's rather inglorious beginning in Lystra, faithfully recorded by Luke, could be seen to preempt much of the continuing history of evangelism as the gospel continued to be carried across immense boundaries of culture, worldview and communication. Paul, sent from Antioch in Jesus's name, was knowledgeable, gifted, and moreover willing to undergo immense suffering for the sake of his Lord, but he was not yet sufficiently emptied of aspects of his own cultural heritage and assumptions to be able to communicate effectively everywhere. The painful experience of Lystra however, seems to have started him on a personal "Pentecost" journey, in which he learned to be continually reordered as he travelled in order to assume more localised approaches, so that others would be able to hear and understand more easily. It apparently set him on the path to reflection and, whilst the content of his message remained unchanged, he gradually developed much more flexible styles of ministry to suit subsequent varying contexts. His attempts to connect culturally with the people of Athens perhaps represent a halfway house on this journey of adaption,[41] which he continued to the end of his ministry.

Disciples today, just like Paul in the first century, are still born into and absorb specific cultures, languages, social conventions, and so on. Influenced by these we gather to worship, and we are sent back into them to love and serve. For those committed to sharing the good news, worship is never to become an exercise in pure escapism. Each gathering for worship

---

38. Colwell, "Mission as Ontology," 7.
39. 2 Tim 3:15.
40. Acts 16:1.
41. Acts 17:23.

should involve some kind of emptying of what needs to be laid aside for realignment to the identity and perspective of God's kingdom. Then we are refilled with what is needed for effective and relevant ministry back in the world. The totality of the worship experience should take this process into account, and the hinge moment of sending out should help to make the transition back to the world sustainable. We are sent as Christ was sent, not only in his name and with his authority, but in his tradition of self-emptying in order to assume whatever is needed to engage with the cultural and social context effectively. As John says, corresponding to the sending of the Spirit, and in response to the sending of the Son, "The existence of the Church as that which is sent into the world in the power of the Spirit is itself a sign and sacrament of the sending of the Son into the world: it is the means and promise of his presence and action through the Spirit."[42]

SENT OUT EFFECTIVELY

The Order for Baptist Ministry, which originated in part to help Baptist Ministers as disciples of Jesus remain true to their ministry vows, has developed a range of daily liturgies to provide frameworks for regular gathering and personal reflection. Following a common structure, each liturgy ends by sending participants out to love and serve Christ in the world. The liturgies may include actions, symbols, silence, and gesture but are chiefly made up of words. That means that they are particular to the English language, and are written for a broadly British cultural setting. Members of the Order are Baptists, and so the liturgies also reflect Baptist heritage but with a wider appreciation for a catholic spirituality.

Do the OBM liturgies fulfil the pattern of sending participants out as Christ was sent; in his name and authority, providing helpful transitions back into the communities they seek to love and serve? Some excerpts from the original set of daily liturgies may help to answer the question.

An implication of the Pentecost communication miracle in Acts 2 is that the gospel bearers themselves must first change and grow, before their hearers can. This is reflected in the sending words in the liturgy for Monday and Pentecost. Together with those endeavouring to speak new languages we pray:

> Enlarge our dreams and enthuse our minds,
> inspire our faith and empower our resolve,
> that growing in the likeness of Christ,

---

42. Colwell, "Mission as Ontology," 9.

> we may be unafraid to live this day
> to your praise and glory.[43]

Tuesday and Advent's form reminds us that all are sent just as Christ was sent:

> Engaging in the mission of Christ this day, open our eyes to see
> his coming,
> and guide our feet to follow in his way.[44]

Wednesday and Christmas makes the same message personal.

> As the Father sent Jesus into the world so he sends me.
> Yes and Amen![45]

Thursday and Epiphany acknowledges the transforming role of the Spirit enabling us to become more like Christ through ministry.

> By your Spirit
> help us to grow more
> into the likeness of Christ,
> bearing his light
> as we seek to serve you
> in the church and in the world.[46]

Friday and Lent with Passiontide's words are a reminder that whether we go out into joy or sorrow, it is Christ who calls us and wherever we go we remain within the breadth of his love.

> Holy God, may we live this day
> with Christ's call to discipleship ringing in our ears.[47]

His love, fundamentally sacrificial, is restated in the liturgy for Saturday and Creation.

> We are created from love, of love, for love.[48]

Returning in the weekly cycle to Sunday and Easter, the liturgy of the risen Lord leads, just as it did for Mary Magdalene in the garden, straight back into being poured out in loving service to the world.

---

43. OBM Daily Office—Monday Morning and Pentecost—Living Spirit.
44. OBM Daily Office—Tuesday Morning and Advent—Coming Lord.
45. OBM Daily Office—Wednesday Morning and Christmas—Incarnate Lord.
46. OBM Daily Office—Thursday Morning and Epiphany—Revealing Lord.
47. OBM Daily Office—Friday Morning and Lent with Passiontide—Suffering God.
48. OBM Daily Office—Saturday Morning and Creation—Creating God.

> By your Spirit
> enable us this day
> to participate in his dying and rising
> and so share the life of Christ
> with all whom we meet. Amen.[49]

So far so good, but although liturgies rightly provide communities with stability, structure and continuity, yet the liturgies themselves should not be entirely static. Whilst maintaining the rhythms of structure and truth, elements can be refined or augmented with words and forms that reflect the changing and varied world we come from, as well as helping to bridge the gap back into it. John warns, "I know that language is a living dynamic, that words are slippery, that words change their significance, that words only signify within a community of communication, that a community's use of words change over a period of time."[50] Remembering that the OBM is currently rather homogenous, could not the vocabulary and use of images in its liturgies be regularly revisited to reflect the increased ethnic and social diversity already present in the UK, prophetically anticipating and encouraging the day when the OBM and our churches' membership does likewise?

Yet there is a helpful conciseness in these liturgies. We gather, acknowledge our faults, hear and respond to the word, and pray. We know where we have come from and why we are going forward. The words for sending are intentional and purposeful, and having pronounced them it should become awkward to stay. All may be sent as Christ was, to reflect the image of God mysteriously, materially, and at times scandalously in the world. We leave eager to participate in God's mission as he brings all things by the Spirit to eventual completion in Christ.

In contrast with this impetus a tendency to linger in gathered worship and cling on to the experience has featured in some Baptist gatherings recently. Charismatic renewal for example has helped enrich and refresh much Baptist worship. It has affirmed personal experiences of God's presence and encouraged a greater flexibility appropriate to "Spirit-led worship." But as a consequence the "ministry time" and the use of spiritual gifts in meetings can sometimes become lengthy, with the result that there is no distinct ending to an event. People drift away individually instead of being sent out corporately. This represents a lost opportunity foundational to the whole purpose of gathering for corporate worship in the first place and should be addressed. As John argues, "The church's mission is constituted by its being sent out into the world. It is a matter of identity before it is a matter

---

49. OBM Daily Office—Sunday Morning and Easter—Risen Lord.
50. Colwell, "Mission as Ontology," 7.

of function. It is a matter of 'being' in the world rather than 'doing' within churches. We are a missionary people."[51] We gather specifically in order to be sent out.

A practical clue to this tendency to cling is the appearance of worship songs which have no written endings. Technically speaking they have no final cadences, but can be repeated indefinitely without being resolved musically.[52] (This is nothing new for musicians, and even some of the greatest composers found it hard to conclude pieces of music gracefully at times. The greatly extended final cadences of the last movement of Ludwig van Beethoven's otherwise "perfect" Fifth Symphony is an oft-cited example.) Good endings do not generally come about by chance. Some skill or art combined with intent are needed to end well. At its best a good ending fulfils the purpose of gathered worship by providing a springboard into reengagement back in the world.[53]

Human creatures necessarily experience time chronologically. However hard we try to guess at or preempt the future, leaving gathered worship must still be a walk into the unknown. Through the Spirit however God gives prophetic gifts which enable disciples to be people of hope. They can value and learn from the past, but fundamentally must focus ahead and work towards alignment with God's continuing good will for his creation and its eventual complete realization. The ongoing rhythm of gathering for worship and dispersal back into the world should enable a necessary and regular realignment to this perspective. It is helped by having, under the Spirit's guidance, a clear and corporate end point for each worship event in mind, rather than an unforeseen or an individualistic drifting away.

Like Mary meeting the risen Lord in the garden, we need to be sent out intentionally with authority and a message. Our worship should equip us to deliver this message effectively in whatever context we inhabit: "Where every word is at home, / Taking its place to support the others."[54] An effective ending to corporate worship makes it possible to go out with confidence and peace into service, hardship, the known and the unknown:

> committed to the way of Christ,
> faithful to the call of Christ,
> discerning the mind of Christ,
> offering the welcome of Christ,
> growing in the likeness of Christ,

---

51. Colwell, "Mission as Ontology," 11.
52. Howlett, "Ending a Song on a IV Chord."
53. Hargreaves, *Whole Life Worship*, 145.
54. Eliot, "Little Gidding," V, from *Four Quartets*, 208.

engaging in the mission of Christ,
in the world that belongs to Christ.[55]

---

55. OBM Daily Office-Risen Lord-Sunday Morning and Easter.

PART TWO

PART TWO

7

Advent
The Light Who Dawns

Joseph Haward

> Just when we thought the story had been told;
> rumours surface and disturb the world.[1]

Rust: "There was a moment . . . when I was under in the dark, that something, whatever I'd been reduced to, not even consciousness, just a vague awareness in the dark . . . I could feel man, I knew, I knew my daughter waited for me, there. So clear. I could feel her . . . And all I had to do was let go, man. And I did. I said, 'Darkness, yeah' and I disappeared. But I could still feel her love there. Even more than before. Nothing. Nothing but that love. And then I woke up."

Marty: "Didn't you tell me . . . you used to make up stories about the stars?"

Rust: "Yeah, that was in Alaska, under the night skies."

Marty: "And look up at the stars and make up stories. Like what?"

Rust: ". . . it's just one story. The oldest."

---

1. OBM Supplementary Advent Office—Coming Lord.

Marty: "What's that?"

Rust: "Light versus dark."

Marty: "Well, I know we ain't in Alaska, but it appears to me that the dark has a lot more territory."

Rust: "You're looking at it wrong..."

Marty: "How's that?"

Rust: "Well, once there was only dark. You ask me, the light's winning."

True Detective

In him was life, and the life was the light of all people. The light shines in the darkness, and the darkness did not overcome it.[2]

ADVENT AS A TIME of waiting, a recognition of the in-between time in which we live, is aware that God has come to us in the vulnerability of the Christ child in order to bring the "corruptible to incorruption," and in doing so also reveals to us our own vulnerability and therefore how we wait for this One who is now seated on the throne who will gather all things together and make everything new; that which *will be* is still *not yet*. John Colwell's own personal account of depression highlights for us all that it is clear how our lives are not always marked out by joy, nor a sense of the enduring presence of God. In our opening lines of the TV drama *True Detective* the character Rust Cohle speaks of a "vague awareness in the dark," an echo of his life consumed by depression, and the pain of the death of his daughter, this character Rust is symbolic of many today, beaten by the pain of despair. This is why an Advent theology of hope matters, one that is enacted through the breaking of bread. Here in this meal God meets with us by the Spirit of the resurrected Jesus, the gospel story becoming our own story, and the God of the gospel story present with us through this human-divine act of Eucharist.[3] As the cry of the newborn Jesus reveals, there are times when we, as it were, feel cold, hungry, and alone, where the promises of God are beyond our realm of understanding or consciousness, and all that we have is the rawness of our current state of being. Yet in the God who comes to us in Jesus we do not have a God who is beyond us but with us; Immanuel. God, then, is not hidden behind the walls of empires, within the rooms of palaces, protected by the swords of guards, but is exposed to us, naked and present, here with us in the complexities and profundity of life,

2. John 1:4.

3. See Colwell, *Why Have You Forsaken Me?*, 40–41 for an example of the importance of Eucharist within John's own life, spirituality, and theology.

> And the Word become flesh, and lived among us. (John 1:14)

And as the writer of the Letter to the Hebrews puts it,

> Long ago God spoke to our ancestors in many and various ways by the prophets, but in these last days he has spoken to us by a Son, whom he appointed heir of all things, through whom who also created the worlds. (Heb 1:1–2)

This is what God is like; the God who Israel waited for is the same God who came to his creation in Christ, is the same God whom the church anticipates returning. And so we come to Colwell's deeply insightful suggestion that there are only two theological questions, "What kind of God?" and "So what?"

> Cosmic God, beyond time and space,
> yet within history and our world
> We look for signs of your coming.[4]

The Advent daily offices for the Order for Baptist Ministry reminds us of the mystery of God, of how all our "God-ideas" are disrupted by the reality of the God who comes to us in Christ, and how it is so often in the strangeness that we encounter the Lord of history; it is in this "strangeness" that we look for signs of the Cosmic God's coming, this One who, within our history and world, has been presented to us in the person of Jesus of Nazareth. If, then, God really is like Jesus, a God found in the strangeness and absurdity of the incarnation, that in the incarnation we encounter a God who is revealed in the "shit and stench of the stables,"[5] and the cries and darkness of the cross, then it is this "kind of God" who is truly with us. Certainly, to say that here we encounter a God who is utterly and totally with us is not in the first instance a pursuit of triumphalistic models of theological thought, where one assumes that because God is with us, by default, God is not with others. Nor is it to say that if God is with us then we will be "blessed" and "capable" in truly remarkable ways, rather, it is to say that this God who has been revealed through the incarnation, this God who is made known through Jesus of Nazareth, is wonderfully and truly and wholly God. As Irenaeus puts it,

> The Word of God, our Lord Jesus Christ, who did, through His transcendent love, become what we are, that He might bring us to be even what He is Himself.[6]

4. OBM Supplementary Advent Office.
5. Pound, *Theology, Psychoanalysis and Trauma*, xiii.
6. Irenaeus, *Against Heresies*, 5.preface

Dietrich Bonhoeffer sought to reorientate the church to a theology and vision of God that was determined and grounded within the Crucified Jesus. In his remarkable *Letters and Papers from Prison* he writes,

> God let's himself be pushed out of the world on to the cross. He is weak and powerless in the world, and that is precisely the way, the only way, in which he helps us. Matt. 8.17 makes it quite clear that Christ helps us, not by virtue of his omnipotence, but by virtue of his weakness and suffering. Here is the decisive difference between Christianity and all religions. Man's religiosity makes him look in his distress to the power of God in the world: God is the *deus ex machina*. The Bible directs man to God's powerlessness and suffering; only the suffering God can help . . . the God of the Bible . . . wins power and space in the world by his weakness.[7]

God is not known through his glory but through the cross. Of course Bonhoeffer, as a Lutheran pastor, followed Luther's significant insight of a *theologia crucis*. In the Heidelberg Disputation that took place on April 26, 1518, Luther was invited by the Augustinian Order, of which he belonged, to expand upon and defend his views. In thesis 20 from the Heidelberg Disputation, Luther states,

> He deserves to be called a theologian, however, who comprehends the visible and manifest things of God seen through suffering and the cross . . . The manifest and visible things of God are placed in opposition to the invisible, namely, his human nature, weakness, foolishness . . . and it does him no good to recognize God in his glory and majesty, unless he recognizes him in the humility and shame of the cross . . . For this reason true theology and recognition of God are in the crucified Christ.[8]

The cross is the supreme revelation of God, and Luther calls us to this revelation and knowledge. Irenaeus fourteen hundred years earlier puts it thus,

> But in every respect, too, He is man, the formation of God; and thus He took up man into Himself, the invisible becoming visible, the incomprehensible being made comprehensible, the impassible becoming capable of suffering, and the Word being made man, thus summing up all things in Himself.[9]

---

7. Bonhoeffer, *Letters and Papers*, 196–97.

8. Luther, Heidelberg Disputation, thesis 20, http://bookofconcord.org/heidelberg.php#20.

9. Irenaeus, *Against Heresies*, 3.16.6, in *Ante-Nicene Fathers*, 1:315–567.

The Crucified Christ is the full revelation of God, and in the visible suffering of the Son we encounter the fullness of who God *is*, of who God has come to us *as*,

> He comes to us as the one he eternally is, or rather, he eternally is as he is in his coming to us.[10]

To live in a theology of Advent is to live as people of hope, defined by the hope of the One who came and is coming again. From his birth, through his life, to his death, and then his resurrection, Jesus reveals a God who has eternally been who he is; One who in triune simplicity is Love, a love expressed in the freedom of who God is, indeed, of who God has always been. God cannot be anything other than who God is, a God whose "is-ness" we are invited to witness and participate in through the Spirit. As the New Testament affirms,

> His divine power has given us everything needed for life and godliness, through the knowledge of him who called us by his own glory and goodness. Thus he has given us, through these things, his precious and very great promises, so that through them you may escape from the corruption that is in the world because of lust, and may become participants of the divine nature.[11]

The early church fathers attested to this participation in God through Jesus as we have already seen with Irenaeus. Athanasius even more boldly suggested, "For he was made man that we might be made God."[12] Of course such language can appear almost blasphemous without qualification, yet what the church fathers were seeking to declare was that God in Christ has come to us in order that we might be called children of God,[13] that we would share in and proclaim the universal hope consistently spoken of throughout the New Testament witness and through the testimony of the early church. As Colwell rightly points out, "such universal hope ought not to be confused with cheap universalism,"[14] but understood entirely christologically. This is a proper theology of Advent, a recognition that the God who comes is the God of inclusive love, an unconditionality that echoes out into eternity beyond the human cries of retribution, vengeance, and violence. We are a people of hopeful anticipation, who look towards the One who came and in

---

10. Colwell, *Rhythm of Doctrine*, 21.
11. 2 Pet 1:3–4.
12. Athanasius, *On the Incarnation*, 54, 107.
13. 1 John 3:1.
14. Colwell, *Rhythm of Doctrine*, 27.

faith trust that this same One will come as he went,[15] and, on his return, be who he has always been,

> the one who will come is not other than the one who came. This is not some strange Jesus. Worldly images of majesty, power, and violence are consistently and systematically deconstructed. He comes to judge, but he comes to judge justly. He comes to conquer, but he conquers as the Lamb who was slain. At the end of this age Christ does not resort to the worldly violence and power he once rejected—to fail to recognise this is to fail to recognise the rhetoric of this vision—at the end of this age Christ comes as the slaughtered Lamb and conquers by his word. He comes as the one he ever is and ever was.[16]

Such a hope, such an Advent hope, must be shaped though the cross. As the Revelation of John testifies, this One in eternity is the Lamb who has "been slaughtered" (Rev 5:6) and is therefore the One who is known and revealed through the crucifixion:

> Look! He is coming with the clouds; every eye will see him, even those who pierced him; and on his account all the tribes of the earth will wail. So it has to be. Amen.[17]

Humanity as a whole are those "who pierced him" and so together, in observing the darkness of the cross, cry out in lamentation as we come face to face with the Alpha and the Omega, aware that it is us who sought to extinguish the Light of the Cosmos, being, as we are, "children of wrath"[18] pouring out our wrath upon the One who is Love in all eternity. Yet this One speaks eternal forgiveness to us as those who do not know what we are doing, such is our disorientation because of sin, a disorientation that has corrupted the whole cosmos, a corruption that damages and distorts our true humanity in often painful and dehumanizing ways. So whilst Advent brings expectant hope, we live also in the reality of our painful cries into the sometimes long and desolate night.

In *Why Have You Forsaken Me?* Colwell speaks plainly about the reality of his depression, a felt darkness that has been present in his life for decades. Yet it is not his depression that ultimately determines his theology (whilst of course being part of it), rather it is the Crucified One who determines for him who God is into all eternity, this One who before all things

---

15. Acts 1:11.
16. Colwell, *Rhythm of Doctrine*, 22.
17. Rev 1:7.
18. Eph 2:3.

has always been Trinity. It is this God whom Colwell has implored us to remember as the One who mediates his presence to us through that which he has created, enabling us to know that God is true to his promise that he will never abandon us, that Jesus's cry of forsakenness is the cry of John, of us, and of all humanity as we live in the now of a cosmos corrupted and disorientated by sin,

> The cry of abandonment that Jesus cries is nothing less than our cry of abandonment: his cry is the cry of the child murdered by Herod's soldiers; his cry is the cry of the abused slave; his cry is the cry of the woman being raped; his cry is the cry of terror from the gas chamber; his cry is the cry of despair from the one contemplating suicide; his cry is the cry of lament from the psalmist; his is the desolation of every man and woman. Every human cry of despair is unique and particular—the particularity of individual suffering is not abolished at the Cross—but every human cry of despair is echoed in his cry; he enters fully into our desolation, our sin, our pain, our abuse, our dying, our death; he becomes what we are that we, through his entering into this desolation, might become what he is, the true humanity that is our destiny and calling.[19]

And it is because this Crucified God enters into the fullness of humanity's desolation that we can live in hope:

> A theology of Advent will not subscribe to false optimisms . . . a theology of Advent confronts the truth of creation's present bondage to decay with the truth of its prospective liberation, its participation in the glorious freedom of the children of God; a theology of Advent expresses itself in hope.[20]

Colwell calls the church to prophetically live "full of hope," a hopefulness and prophetic witness enacted and lived in and through baptism and the Lord's Supper. This God who promises his presence to us through these sacred events meets with us in his graciousness, his Spirit with us as we break through the waters, and break into bread. A theology of Advent is a theology of hope, a hope witnessed and revealed through the God of all hope,[21] Father, Son, and Spirit. Advent reminds us that God has not given up on us, has not abandoned us like orphans,[22] but will draw us, once and for all,

---

19. Colwell, *Why Have You Forsaken Me?*, 99.
20. Colwell, *Rhythm of Doctrine*, 25.
21. Rom 15:13.
22. John 14:18.

into the fullness of the Trinitarian love, and this is why, as Rust Cohle puts it, we are "looking at it wrong" when we believe that the darkness is gaining more territory; God mediates his presence to us, by the Son, through the Spirit, with creation an instrument through which "the Son and the Spirit are truly agents of God's presence and action."[23] This presence and action of God has an eschatological goal and orientation, the *telos*, "to reconcile to himself all things."[24] As a result, Advent calls us to be a people of expectant worship, a community whose lives are shaped by the Spirit's creativity, who, albeit provisionally, "live and speak prophetically within a world otherwise devoid of hope."[25] This hope is in "the one who can perfect his strength even in my weakness and, with the benefit of hindsight, this has been the case over and again; Good Friday and Holy Saturday are torturous, long, and dark, but they are not unending and Easter morning dawns."[26] The Spirit invites us, through the liturgy and worship of the church, to be a people of Advent hope, invited into and shaped by the life of the One who cries out in a manger and on the cross, a people of prophetic hope who can, with expectancy, declare that the light is indeed winning:

> The light shines in the darkness, and the darkness did not overcome it.[27]

Disturbing Rumors

The 2006 dystopian film *Children of Men* imagines a world where humanity is on the brink of collapse and extinction due to an unknown cause of global human infertility. The story follows a young pregnant woman called Kee, and a man called Theo who has promised to look after her and get her to a safe place. We, the viewer, are invited to be part of this perilous journey of getting Kee to safety, with the camera often reverting to first-person perspective, as well as shaking and jerking as though we are in the story. The most remarkable scene within the whole film happens after Kee has had her baby and, with Theo, are attempting to find the boat they are due to board that will guarantee safe passage where the baby and Kee will be looked after. Emerging from a building, Kee, Theo, and the baby are confronted by a scene of soldiers and refugees engaged in extreme fighting, bullets flying

---

23. Colwell, *Promise and Presence*, 60.
24. Col 1:20a.
25. Colwell, *Rhythm of Doctrine*, 27.
26. Colwell, *Why Have You Forsaken Me?*, 137.
27. John 1:4.

everywhere and bombs dropping with constant regularity. At the sound of such violence the baby begins to cry, screaming out from the top of her lungs. This is a world without children, a world that has not heard the cry of a baby for eighteen long years; at the sound of the crying child the soldiers stop fighting, and look in awe and wonder at the baby being carried in her mothers arms. It is a moment of pure transcendence as humanity remembers the sound of a child, and the lost power of the child's cry, a cry that reminds us of hope. The cry, for that one moment, brings the fighting to a halt as people watch this baby being carried through the war-torn streets. Earlier in the film one of the characters, Miriam, remarks,

> As the sound of the playgrounds faded, the despair set in. Very odd what happens in a world without children's voices.

This film powerfully illustrates the wonder, transcendence, and gritty reality of the newborn Christ; as the Christ child is born on that first Christmas, his cry echoes out into the world bringing an end to wars, transforming despair to hope, breathing the fragrance of life into the stench of death. *Children of Men* is a modern tale that reminds us that the birth of Jesus is woven so deeply into the fabric of our existence and societies, that the texts of today are but parables of the significance of what it means for the Word to be made flesh, and therefore the hope and expectation that Advent brings; the God who has come, and the God who will come again. This moment of a crying baby in the film, the soldiers ceasing at the sound of the cry of this baby, is a glorious representation of the Prince of Peace,[28] the One who will makes wars to cease, who will shatter the spear and break the bow,[29] the One who will turn swords into ploughshares,[30] who disarms Peter and therefore every Christian thereafter,[31] who declares peace at his resurrection,[32] forgiveness not retribution from his cross,[33] the One who demands off his followers that they speak prayers and blessing over their enemies.[34] Indeed, there is coming a time when this Prince of Peace will bring the *Shalom* of God to every conceivable realm of the whole cosmos, a time when time itself will be utterly transformed through the power of the resurrection. This

---

28. Isa 9:6.
29. Ps 46:9.
30. Isa 2:4.
31. "... still the Lord afterward, in disarming Peter, unbe**d every soldier." Tertullian, *On Idolatry*, 19, in *Ante-Nicene Fathers*, 3:61–78.
32. John 20:19.
33. Luke 23:34.
34. Matt 5:44–45.

is the rumor that has surfaced, and it has indeed disturbed the world as we are invited into a Way of life that militates against our violent desires, and demands of us the dangerous and narrow path of peace.

There is little doubt that the screaming cry of a baby does not always evoke wonder and awe within us, and yet, for any parent of a newborn, the very first thing they listen for, the thing that brings untold joy, is that first cry. Within an apocalyptic world like that imagined in *Children of Men* despair would be our only option at the loss of the sound of that cry, or the laughter of children playing, or the inquisitiveness of a child's questions. But in many ways the parable told through this film is a parable of the reality of the human condition without the birth of Jesus; we were dead in our sins, without hope, until the Word became flesh and made his dwelling among us, the One who becomes what we are in order to bring us to what he is. At the sound of the cry of the newborn Jesus, hope is born, and the powers of death and sin are sent reeling, forced towards their oblivion, towards a time when all will be well and all manner of things will be well.[35]

Advent, then, is a time of waiting and anticipation, of celebration and patience, a time of hope and pain, a time of embrace and waiting to be fully embraced, a time when we are reminded of how within our own time there stands the One who is present and yet felt as absent. So we celebrate the One who has come, and we anticipate how this One will come again "to judge the living and the dead."[36] Into the darkness of that first Christmas night the Christ child screams out, born into a world of sin, death, and decay, his cry piercing the darkness and echoing out into eternity, a cry of vulnerability and fragility, a cry that represents the reality of a cosmos broken and wounded by sin. Here in the birth of Jesus we encounter a God of self-emptying love, who enters our world in order to bring humanity and all of creation into the divine life, to usher in healing, hope, and peace. Here we encounter a God of total vulnerability, One who has utterly emptied himself, and becomes like us in every way; here we encounter a God who will die if he is not embraced by the warmth of his mother, who will die if not fed at his mother's breast, who is utterly and totally dependent on the care and attention of Mary, for without her, this fragile and vulnerable baby will certainly die.[37] So here

---

35. Echoing the words of Peter in Acts (Acts 3:21), Paul's words in Colossians (Col 1:20), and the famous phrase by Julian of Norwich.

36. 2 Tim 4:1.

37. "Christians both forbade the ancient pagan practice of the exposure of unwanted infants—which is almost certainly to say, in the great majority of cases, girls . . . Christian husbands, moreover, could not force their wives to submit to abortions or to consent to infanticide; and while many pagan woman may have been perfectly content to commit their newborn daughters to rubbish heaps or deserted roadsides, to become

in this Christ child we encounter the God who comes to us, who "became flesh and lived among us"[38] and will come again as this same One who was revealed in the flesh to us. God is who God is to us in the gospel story; there has never been a time when God has not been like Jesus. This same Jesus will return, the One from who we have received grace upon grace, with Advent thus a time of hopeful expectation and anticipation where we wait for humanity to move beyond seeing "in a mirror, dimly"[39] but be fully known. It is a work of divine love, a work of grace.

Grace is that we are utterly and totally vulnerable, unable to help ourselves, unable to rescue ourselves, unable to do anything to redeem our situation, and into the midst of this horror God meets with us, embraces us, and draws us to the breast of Divine Life. The incarnation is a "tear of divine pity" as Barth puts it, the means through which God is redeeming humanity and the cosmos, reorienting the cosmos away from sin's road of destruction on to the Way of Life, with all that *is* being reconciled to the One who Is.[40] And this cosmic redemption happens precisely through that which God has created, in no way bypassing it, nor rejecting it for another model like the god of modern, Western consumerism, but taking that which has been corrupted, broken, and made to be "sin-sick,"[41] with the Great Physician healing and transforming "all things" on the earth and in the heavens. Creation and redemption are a Trinitarian affair, with all that God *is* involved in the act of resurrection glory that awaits creation, a creation that is "groaning," a groaning that is not for destruction but is eager for a birth[42] made possible by the God who declares all that he has made to be "good and "very good" yet marred by a chaos and ungodliness unchosen by God.[43] The incarnation is the revelation of the God who dwells among us in the reality of the

---

carrion for dogs and birds or (if fortunate) to become foundlings, we can assume a very great many woman were not." Hart, *Atheist Delusions*, 160.

"It is [the Christians'] philanthropy towards strangers, the care they take of the graves of the dead, and the affected sanctity with which they conduct their lives that have done most to spread their atheism." Julian, Epistle 22, Letter to Arsacius, High-Priest of Galatia, AD 430, quoted in Hart, *Atheist Delusions*, 154.

38. John 1:14a.

39. 1 Cor 13:12a.

40. Col 1:19–20a.

41. "Following Augustine, and with remarkably few exceptions, the Christian tradition witnesses that we sin because we are sinners rather than that we are sinners because we sin; that our sin is an outworking of a deeply rooted disorientation of our nature; that, to use the terminology adopted by Stanley Hauerwas, we are 'sinsick.'" Colwell, *Promise and Presence*, 199.

42. Rom 8:22a.

43. Barth *Church Dogmatics* III/1, 101–9.

created cosmos, who becomes part of his own creation by taking on flesh, the Son who comes to us, lives and breathes in our neighborhood in a body fashioned by the Father, through the work of the Spirit; the Son "was born amidst the shit and stench of the stables, like a lotus flower arising out of the mud, a symbol of beauty set against hardship and pain."[44] And it is good for us to remember this, for "in many ways we have forgotten the trauma of the incarnation, thus resulting in an unrealistic, safe, and sterile version of events."[45] Colwell has consistently challenged theological sentimentality of a God who arbitrarily intervenes in the world, but much more than this, has directly confronted any theological account of God's action within his creation that suggests a God who acts in a way that is unmediated; the God who has been revealed through Jesus of Nazareth is the God who meets with and acts within and through his creation whilst never being consumed by nor indistinguishable from creation;[46] God is wholly other to all created "stuff," not "one of a kind" or defined in any way according to the categories of creation, yet through the incarnation of the Son becomes part of his own created reality, taking upon himself the fullness of the brokenness of that created reality, and ushers in a cosmic peace through this same Son, by the Spirit:

> Had it been a case of a trespass only, and not of a subsequent corruption, repentance would have been well enough; but when once transgression had begun, men came under the power of the corruption proper to their nature and were bereft of the grace which belonged to them as creatures in the Image of God. No, repentance could not meet the case. What—or rather Who was it that was needed for such grace and such recall as we required? Who, save the Word of God Himself, Who also in the beginning had made all things out of nothing? His part it was, and His alone, both to bring again the corruptible to incorruption and to maintain for the Father His consistency of character with all.[47]

This Advent God of hope calls us, with hopeful expectancy, to be aware of signs of his coming through the strangeness of his creative presence, to never cease in "telling the story," a story rumored to be about a crucified, peasant King, a story that continues to disrupt our lives with the promise of

---

44. Pound, *Theology, Psychoanalysis and Trauma*, xiii.

45. Haward, *Ghost of Perfection*, 28–29.

46. See Colwell, *Promise and Presence*, for an extraordinary account of John's sacramental theology in which he argues that God's action within creation is one that is mediated *through* creation.

47. Athanasius, *On the Incarnation*, 2.7.

bringing the "corruptible to incorruption," of the light that dawns with healing in its wings. It is this hope, this story, this God that John Colwell has so faithfully spoken of, to which so many of us want to simply say, "thank you."

8

Christmas
Eternal Humanity at the Heart of God

E. Anne Clements

Beckoning God, your child in a manger invites us
To lean close and bow down.[1]

OF ALL THE SEASONS of the Christian year it is Christmas and the Christmas story that captures the hearts and minds of people. Try as I might, the celebration of Easter is eclipsed by Christmas every year in my congregation. It is the one time of the year the families from our mums and toddlers group will come to see their little ones in the nativity play and the one time of year we always get outsiders coming along to our carol service. Christmas continues to be celebrated in churches where many have almost lost sight of the liturgical year. So what can we learn about our Christian faith, our thinking, our doctrine, as we reflect on the Christmas story?

Even in its most romanticized and distorted form, at the center of the Christmas story is the birth of a baby in a manger, a baby who brings new life and new hope. Having just become a grandmother for the fourth time I have experienced afresh the sense of wonder and joy that the birth of a baby brings, not just to their parents, but to extended family and friends. Giving

1. OBM Daily Office—Wednesday and Christmas—Incarnate Lord.

birth to a baby is messy, excruciatingly painful and strenuous, one of the most physically demanding things a woman can do. The sheer physicality of a birth and the physical demands of a new baby are lost at Christmas under the tinsel, stars, and angels. But materiality matters. This is not just a story on a par with the tales of gods and goddesses in other cultures. As Christians we affirm the birth of God himself into our world at a point in our human history as the Word becomes flesh and Christ takes on our humanity. That God did this "incomprehensible thing,"[2] becoming one of us, becoming human, is, as John comments, definitive of who God is, who we are and of God's relatedness to creation.[3]

Using these three headings: who God is, who we are, and God's relatedness to creation, I wish to sketch out and comment on some of the details of John's incarnation theology, finishing with a short reflection on creation at Christmas. Having been one of John's students over a number of years, I am indebted to him for widening my theological understanding, challenging some of my long held views and for opening a number of new "windows" into the theological world. I would also like to acknowledge John's encouragement and friendship over the years I worked on my part-time PhD. But for John I would never have embarked on it and although at times I rued the day I ever started, I am grateful that he pushed me to continuing study. Now that I am no longer in academia but continue as a Baptist minister, I would like to briefly reflect on aspects of John's theology and what this might mean for faithful ministry as a Baptist pastor and for my congregation as I encourage them to live in coherence with the gospel story.

WHO GOD IS

Any attempt to describe God without reference to the human life of Jesus is at best incomplete and at worst a fatal distortion of the God we worship as Christians. The OBM Christmas daily office includes the opening words of the epistle to the Hebrews, "Long ago God spoke to our ancestors in many and various ways by the prophets, but in these last days he has spoken to us by a Son" (Heb 1:1). Through the wonderful Hebrew stories, poems, and prophecies of the Old Testament we are given a vital and foundational but nevertheless partial revelation of the God whom we worship. It is only as we come to the Word made flesh that we are confronted by the fullest reality of who God is.

---

2. Colwell, *Rhythm of Doctrine*, 32.
3. Colwell, *Rhythm of Doctrine*, 34.

Notwithstanding God's transcendent otherness, the materiality of God's birth as a baby in Bethlehem negates any attempt to describe God in purely ethereal terms or to favor the spiritual above matter. The gnosticizing tendency to divide this material world from a higher spiritual realm or the secular from the sacred is, sadly, deeply embedded in Christian consciousness. I remember the shocked response when I pointed out to a member of my congregation that Jesus as a human baby would have dirtied his nappy (diaper). Surely God as Spirit could not have lowered himself in this way? Yet it is precisely that God did this "incomprehensible thing" in becoming human that marks us out as Christians and makes our faith distinct from that of other faiths. The free and loving action of the Creator coming to his creation and taking on our humanity is central to our faith as Christians because it is here, and nowhere else, that God fully reveals who he is. To quote Colwell:

> It is not merely that this baby born at Bethlehem is truly God; it is also and more fundamentally that God is truly defined in this Christmas story . . . in the vulnerability of this infant life.[4]

For Colwell, the doctrine of the incarnation is far more significant than most Christians recognize. In the last century it was Karl Barth who drew attention to the importance of the incarnation; it was the climax of God's eternal purpose as God uniquely and ultimately revealed himself in and through his Son. Following Barth, Colwell states:

> For Christian theology . . . the central and defining significance of the Incarnation cannot be overstated: God is revealed to us ultimately, not in some unmediated epiphany, but in and through the flesh of a Nazarene carpenter.[5]

The importance of God coming to us, not in some individual's vision, nor in the form of secret knowledge obtained only by a spiritual elite, but coming to us in flesh and blood, as one of us, as a baby for all to see, cannot be overestimated. The "all" of course includes not just the wise men but the working shepherds from the hills. The ordinariness of his life as a carpenter in Nazareth is one of the reasons people from the locality could not accept him. "'Is not this the carpenter, the son of Mary and brother of James and Joses and Judas and Simon, and are not his sisters here with us?' And they took offense at him" (Mark 6:3).

---

4. Colwell, *Rhythm of Doctrine*, 32.
5. Colwell, *Promise and Presence*, 56.

Although our focus here is Christmas, we must not forget that "the story of Christmas does not define God simply and solely as the baby in the manger; the story of Christmas leads into the unfolding gospel story, celebrated in the Christian Year."[6] In his character and relationships, in his teaching and actions: in healing the sick, caring for outcasts, challenging the societal elite, and ultimately in his death and resurrection, God speaks to us about who God is.[7] As the writer to the Hebrews describes Christ, "He is the reflection of God's glory and the exact imprint of God's very being" (Heb 1:3a). Colwell reiterates Barth's contention that "to be wrong in respect to the person of Christ is to be wrong everywhere else."[8] Sound Christology is the key not only to theological discourse but also to authentic ministry as a pastor. We sing, "Jesus be the centre," but I wonder whether we really take this on board as Christian ministers? Maybe we feel that familiarity with the gospel story means we should look elsewhere in order to engage our congregations? However, I believe both Colwell's commitment to biblical preaching and to the importance of keeping Christ central as we celebrate Word and Sacrament is vital. As a Christian minister whatever biblical passage or topic I am preaching on, while respecting the integrity of the text or topic, I need to hold onto this thought, "that God is truly defined in this Christmas story" and all that it encapsulates. Whoever I am spending time with, whoever I listen and talk to, I need to remember that our God became an utterly vulnerable, dependent human baby and that "it is not just the virgin's womb that he abhors not, it is the entire materiality of creation in all its present messiness."[9] A minister is constantly faced with the messiness of people's lives, the endemic breakdown of relationships, the anxieties and stresses of twenty-first-century life, but because of the incarnation we can celebrate the presence of God in amongst all this messiness. The challenge is discerning where and how God is at work in the pain and difficulties of people's lives, but because of the incarnation we know that Christ does not stand on the outside looking in, he is right here with us.

We must also remember Colwell's insistence that it is not just the eternal Son who is revealed in Jesus' life, death, resurrection, and ascension but

---

6. Colwell, *Rhythm of Doctrine*, 32.

7. As a female minister I have had to come to terms with the scandal of particularity, of God being revealed to us in a first-century Jewish man. Both pronouns for our metaphorical God-language and the revelation of God that has been given to us in Christ are masculine, but emphatically this is not saying God is male nor that Christ did not embrace all people. As Janet Soskice notes, "Christ is the Saviour not because he is male but because he is human." Soskice, "Trinity and Feminism," 140.

8. Colwell, *Living the Christian Story*, 131.

9. Colwell, *Rhythm of Doctrine*, 36.

the triune God: Father, Son, and Spirit. Jesus the carpenter as well as Jesus the Messiah lives out his life in obedience to the Father by the power of the Spirit. So what does the incarnation teach us about who we are as we live out our lives today?

WHO WE ARE

The question of identity is a vexed one in our current society. Nothing is a given and young people face the huge burden of having to define themselves in many different ways. At the other end of the spectrum of life the elderly, once they can no longer work or even do everyday jobs unaided, also struggle with their identity and feel worthless.

N. T. Wright comments, "Faced with a strident, sometimes even bullying, modernism in which humans are just naked apes or even just random bundles of atoms and molecules, it is important to protest."[10] How do we protest? With so many alternative identities, presented in countless different narratives, the challenge to present the Christian story in a way that speaks and communicates to people who they are in God's eyes is a challenge every minister faces. Yet as Colwell reminds us, our faithfulness to both the recounting and obedient indwelling of the gospel story is crucial to our Christian identity, to our being church.[11] Central to that story is the incarnate life of Christ. It is because his humanity is not just exemplar but defines our humanity that we must understand and constantly be reminded by Word and Sacrament of who Christ is.[12] Biblical preaching and the regular celebration of communion in its simple materiality of bread and wine is part of the lifeblood of our congregational spirituality and draws us time and again into Jesus' death and the depths of his humanity.

In the past docetic tendencies within the Christian tradition have presented Jesus to us as fully divine in his perfect human life without really coming to terms with the full reality of his humanity. Colwell emphasizes that "he truly comes to the place, context, and humanity that is ours."[13] Jesus laughed and cried, and got tired and hungry. He was tempted as we are, yet remained sinless. In looking at Rom 5:12–17, Colwell argues that it is Jesus's perfected humanity and not Adam's sinfulness that is defining for who

---

10. Wright, "Mind, Spirit, Soul and Body."

11. Colwell, *Living the Christian Story*, 165.

12. "The humanity of Jesus is definitive and determinative for our humanity." Colwell, *Living the Christian Story*, 131.

13. Colwell, *Promise and Presence*, 64. Here Colwell presents a full discussion of the temptation, sinlessness, and perfection of Christ.

we are. Hearing sermons as I grew up that emphasized our sinfulness and fallenness meant that although I had become a Christian, unconsciously, perhaps, I defined myself by Adam and, notably as a woman, by Eve's fallenness. But Colwell is right to point out that there cannot be two rival and distinct definitions of humanity (in Adam and in Christ). Following Ireneaus's view that Adam was modeled on the invisible Word, Colwell argues that both noetically and ontologically our identity in Christ is *prior* to our fallen identity in Adam. This is an important point. So often the gospel is presented in terms of our human identity originating in the culpability of our first parents. Subsequently, Christ saves us and we are redeemed. But what if originally it was not Adam and Eve but Christ who is defining of who we are as humans?[14] Both first and last I am defined not by fallen humanity's sinfulness but by the grace and truth of Christ. This is not to negate our sinfulness but to recognize that "the ultimate definition of the Fall and of 'original sin' is the story of Jesus, of his Cross, of the place he takes on our behalf."[15] Jesus died my death, experienced my lostness and abandonment, took on my sinfulness and judgment, so I can live, be "re-born into this authentic humanity identified in Christ."[16]

If the incarnate Jesus is defining of who I am, then I am called to a life of Christlikeness which involves obedience and dependence. "In this *real* humanity Jesus lived in dependence upon the Spirit and in obedience to the Father and, consequently, *true* humanity was perfected in him."[17] So we too are called to a similar dependence on the Spirit and obedience to the Father. Dependence and obedience are counterintuitive virtues in today's society. Society prizes autonomy, independence and self-determination. This is what makes one meaningfully human. Yet the gospel story tells us otherwise. It is as we live in dependence on the indwelling Spirit and in obedience to our heavenly Father that we truly become human as Christ was truly human. We discover what it means to be human not by constant introspection or self-promotion but by dependent obedience. Is this all unrealistic, an unobtainable goal?

John Stott comments that as Christians we are selective in our discipleship and that consequently we so often don't look like the Christ we proclaim.[18] As Christians we are called to live a Christlike life, live out a

---

14. Colwell, *Promise and Presence*, 69.
15. Colwell, *Promise and Presence*, 69.
16. Colwell, *Promise and Presence*, 72.
17. Colwell, *Living the Christian Story*, 148. Colwell here is following Barth's distinction between the real and true humanity of Christ.
18. Stott, *Radical Christianity*, 39.

true humanity shaped by the indwelling Holy Spirit, since we are not only justified but also sanctified. It is the promise of the Spirit that enables us. As Colwell puts it, "Through the Spirit's indwelling, our lives can become an echo of the perfect obedience of Christ."[19] If we understood more fully that "the gospel is re-creation as much as rescue"[20] and that the Spirit of Jesus indwelling our lives is transformative, enabling us to live in obedience, then maybe we would learn greater dependence not on ourselves but on the Spirit. God in Christ not only overcomes death but seeks to restore his image in us. Colwell muses whether the more recent accounts of the atonement, with their focus on the cross and resurrection at the expense of the incarnation, is a reflection of the marginalizing of sanctification in today's Christian discourse.[21]

I have to ask myself as a Christian minister, can I trust God to be at work by his Spirit, changing me and the lives of my congregation, sanctifying and re-creating? Sometimes this seems a painfully slow process! Of course, this involves a willingness on our part to be changed, to live in obedience. It also involves taking decisions on how we live in line with the gospel story. But, as Colwell points out, Jesus's humanity wasn't some kind of idealized humanity floating above the struggles and pain and contradictions we face as humans, but it was in the very context of humanity as we know it that Jesus lived in close relation to his Father by the Spirit.[22] And we can live that life too!

What we will become determines what we are. We will never fully attain Christlikeness in this life, but one day we shall see him as he is and be like him, purified even as he is pure. As Colwell puts it, "This goal will be reached, that what has been provisional will be perfected."[23] Ultimately it is Jesus's risen, ascended, divine, but nonetheless real, solid humanity that defines what fully realized humanity is. Though scarred, it is a healed humanity that relates within the loving triune life of God, a participation that we are called to since our life is now hidden with Christ in God (Col 3:3). All this might seem rather "other worldly," but in actual fact it is intensely practical. In seeking justice for the exploited and caring for others, all Christians are called to start to realize God's reign on earth. Although our lives can be no more than an anticipation of the final resurrection, nevertheless they can

---

19. Colwell, *Living the Christian Story*, 134.
20. Colwell, *Living the Christian Story*, 117.
21. Colwell, *Living the Christian Story*, 117.
22. Colwell, *Living the Christian Story*, 124.
23. Colwell, *Living the Christian Story*, 147.

be a genuine anticipation.[24] It is this hope that sustains me in ministry and every newborn baby reminds me of the hope to be found in the life of the baby born in Bethlehem.

> You call us to be part of your healing:
> to make peace, pursue justice,
> and love mercy;
> to bear witness to Christ
> anticipating the day
> when tears are wiped away
> death, mourning, crying and pain
> are no more,
> and you are at home
> among all people.[25]

GOD'S RELATEDNESS TO CREATION

I have always loved nature and the created world. It speaks to me often of the triune God. I know that this is true also for many in my congregation who appreciate a sunset or simply a rose in their garden, for whom animals can play an important part in their lives as pets, especially if they live alone. What does the birth of Jesus as a baby into our created world have to teach us about God's relatedness to this world? In reaction to the traditional emphasis on the transcendence of God, Colwell notes that there is often what he considers to be a blurring of the distinction between the Creator and creation.[26] This can be seen, for example, in the eco-feminist movement that sees mother earth as God's body.[27] Sallie McFague suggests that we should dare to think of our plant and indeed the entire universe as the body of God and therefore care for it accordingly. Attractive as this may seem, this is to collapse the Creator into creation and succumb to a form of panentheism.[28] Although upheld by the Spirit moment by moment, creation maintains its own freedom and identity apart from God. As Colin Gunton points out, a Trinitarian theology of creation makes it possible to understand that the creation remains in close relation to God and yet is free to be itself.[29]

24. Colwell, *Living the Christian Story*, 134.
25. OBM Daily Office—Wednesday and Christmas—Incarnate Lord.
26. Colwell, *Rhythm of Doctrine*, 33.
27. See McFague, *Body of God*.
28. Panentheism is the position that the universe is in God, that he permeates every part of nature, is part of nature, extends beyond nature, and is also distinct from it.
29. Gunton, *Triune Creator*, 10.

Nevertheless, at Christmas we celebrate the amazing fact that God the Creator becomes the creature, God comes to his creation as a baby. This is truly an "incomprehensible thing." God in his gracious freedom comes to his creation not by becoming one with it as a whole, but by being born into this world as a human baby; "God takes a body uniquely here."[30] Colwell argues that the eternal Son becoming flesh implies an openness in the nature of God to the ontological possibility of creation, "an eternal openness in God's being . . . to the possibility of the flesh assumed by the Son, and thereby an openness to the possibility of creation."[31] From this point, more controversially, he goes on to argue that "ontologically, though not temporally, the material flesh assumed by the Son is prior to the materiality of creation."[32] If it is allowed that God in his triune being is "simple"[33] and unchanging, and that his incarnation does not alter or modify his eternal being, then it is logical to argue that the humanity of Christ exists eternally in and with God. It is not just the risen and ascended Christ who retains humanity, there has always been humanity at the heart of God. Furthermore, the possibility of the whole of creation is predicated on the created flesh of Christ held in the eternal life of God.[34] I find Colwell's assertion compelling since once and for all it repudiates any gnostic notions that devalue the material world and our bodies. It confounds the misbegotten idea that one's physical body is inherently sinful and has to be subdued. It confounds the false dualistic thinking that only souls, not bodies, are important to God, or the over-evaluation of the mind with the implicit devaluation of the body which has been a major problem in the West for generations.[35] For too long, in strands of Christian theology, women's bodies have been represented in relation to men as objects of temptation and therefore shameful or, because of their monthly menstruation, as impure. This has deeply affected both women's attitude towards their sexuality and their body image. We need to be able to celebrate our bodies not only as temples of the Holy Spirit, but as

---

30. Colwell, *Rhythm of Doctrine*, 32.
31. Colwell, *Rhythm of Doctrine*, 34.
32. Colwell, *Rhythm of Doctrine*, 35.

33. God *is* what he *has*, as Augustine argues in *City of God*, XI, 10. As identical to each of his attributes, God is identical to his nature, for example God is love. This is the doctrine of divine simplicity. Colwell argues, "It is precisely as the one who is named as Father, Son and Spirit that he is both one and simple." Colwell, *Promise and Presence*, 20.

34. "This flesh which is eternally in and with God is itself the eternal possibility of that which is other than God, the eternal possibility of creation." Colwell, "In the Beginning Was the Word," 52.

35. Wright, "Mind, Spirit, Soul and Body."

formed from an anterior richness in God centered on Christ. None of this undermines the importance in time and in history of the Spirit's formation in Mary's womb of a body for the Son and the redemption and renewal that Jesus' incarnate human life achieves.

But what is the nature of Christ's redemption and renewal? Is it, in the words of a carol, "to save our souls from Satan's power," or does it involve the salvation of not only our souls but also our bodies? Is it to "fit us for heaven," to transport us out of this world of sin and sickness to a heavenly paradise? What of the wider creation of which we have been formed from the dust of the earth, a creation of which we are inescapably part of as created beings? Is this created world simply the disposable backdrop to the human story of fallenness and redemption? Does creation need to be included in our Christmas proclamation of good news, of the baby who came to save?

CREATION AT CHRISTMAS

Let me start our consideration of the implication of the incarnation for creation by quoting Colwell more fully:

> The celebration of God's act of creation as integral to a celebration of God's act of Incarnation is therefore a celebration of the purposefulness of creation and of the personal identity of that purposefulness . . . Christ himself is the source and purpose of creation . . . That there is a material creation is because this, the true God, invites and destines us together with all creation to participate in his glory in and through Christ by the Spirit.[36]

Colwell is thoroughly christocentric in his doctrine of creation. Following both Irenaeus and Gunton, Colwell argues that God's "project" of creation was never a creation of static perfection. It was "very good," but the created world, including humanity, needed to grow and mature in order to reach completion. Creation has its own *telos* and purpose; to participate in and be the means of God's glory. Disrupted by Adam's sin and its fallenness this *telos* is only made possible in and through Christ, through whom not only was the world made but through whom it reaches its fulfilment. *All things have been created through him and for him* (Col 1:16). In Christ's perfected humanity fallen humanity is perfected and the whole of creation is restored and reaches its goal of participating in and being a means of God's glory.

If this is the case, the redemption Christ effected, therefore, has a far broader scope than we often acknowledge at Christmas. Recognizing that

---

36. Colwell, *Rhythm of Doctrine*, 36.

humans are the problem, not inappropriately, Christians at Christmas have celebrated their Savior coming into the world, but little has been has been made of the wider creation. As Romans 8 makes clear, creation's liberation from its bondage to decay is intimately tied up with the liberation and freedom of the children of God brought about by Christ's reconciling work on the cross. N. T. Wright, in his book *Surprised by Hope*, has been at pains to stress the biblical New Testament view that salvation is not *out* of this world but *in* and *with* it, a view also endorsed by Colwell. This material world is not going to be abandoned but re-created and renewed and brought to a glorious fulfillment as heaven comes down to earth. We, together with all creation, are destined to participate in God's glory. In recognition of this I suggest that at Christmas we need to widen our horizons.

Where the confession in one of the OBM's daily offices for Christmas says "where we have acted as though your coming was only for me and mine,"[37] this can be extended to refer not only the neglect of wider humanity but also to the created world. Our eschatological future is intimately bound up with the whole of creation. Our glorious destiny in Christ is a shared one with all life, both animate and inanimate.

What are the implications of this for our Christmas liturgies and worship? There is a decided lack of liturgical or hymnal material that links Christ's incarnation to creation. Chris Voke comments, "In Christian theology the relationship of God to the material world is expressed and enabled by the incarnation of the Son. But there is a lack of attention to this idea in liturgical use."[38] The two reasons he gives for this are that, first, liturgical material understandably draws on the rich poetry of the Old Testament that celebrates God creating and sustaining the world but has no reference to Christ, and second, because the creedal statements about the creation and sustaining of the world are attached to the action of the Father but not to Christ as the agent of that creation. So Voke concludes:

> The incarnation as an aspect of the doctrine of creation is not easily illustrated from the text of traditional liturgies . . . we find very few Christological references that specifically associate the incarnation with creation as a whole.[39]

---

37. OBM Daily Office—Wednesday and Christmas—Incarnate Lord.
38. Voke, *Creation at Worship*, 63.
39. Voke, *Creation at Worship*, 63.

We need new carols and prayers that reflect this wider understanding of salvation that the baby born at Christmas came to redeem the whole of this created universe of which we as humans are a part.[40]

CONCLUSION

In the light of Colwell's theology I have briefly explored some of the implications of the doctrine of the incarnation for who God is, who we are and for God's relatedness to creation. The celebration of Christmas reminds us that Christ took on human flesh in the incredible physical vulnerability of a human baby. That this child is defining of who God is, that God became one of us in Jesus, is in some sense beyond our understanding and yet in another sense accessible to all who lean close to see the baby in the manger. Not only is this child God in all his fullness, but he is also defining of who we are as humans made in the image of God. Our identity in Christ is prior to our fallen identity in Adam and, as such, fundamentally defines who we are. As we open our lives to the indwelling Holy Spirit we receive the help to live like Jesus in obedient dependence on God. In turn we reach out to others in the knowledge that Jesus is Emmanuel, God with us, and in the anticipation and hope for the future that the Christ child brings. Along with Colwell I have argued that the Word of God made flesh has existed as an eternal possibility in the life of the Godhead, thereby utterly dispelling any notions that bodies are unimportant to God, since there has always been humanity at the heart of God. Finally, I have encouraged all who celebrate Christmas to celebrate the birth of a Savior who brings redemption not only to humanity but to all of creation, since it is through Christ and for Christ all things were made and to whom, all things, by the Spirit, are purposefully directed.

---

40. The popular carol that comes to mind, that is the exception, is *Joy to the World*.

9

Epiphany
The One Who Is Revealed

Ian Randall

Radiant God, in Jesus, your Son, you have made yourself known
to those who are near and those who are far off.[1]

Lord our God,
who anointed your only Son
with the Spirit at the river Jordan,
and so hallowed the waters of new birth
to bring us forth to salvation:
keep us strong in the life of grace,
direct the ways of your people,
and open the door of your Kingdom
to all who stand upon the threshold of faith;
through Jesus our Messiah and Saviour. Amen.[2]

THIS IS THE QUOTATION from *Celebrating Common Prayer*, with which John Colwell introduced his chapter on Epiphany, entitled "The One Who Is Revealed," in *The Rhythm of Doctrine*. My own copy of this richly theologi-

---

1. OBM Daily Office—Thursday and Epiphany—Revealing Lord.
2. *Celebrating Common Prayer*, 114.

cal book, which is structured around the liturgical pattern of the Christian year, is signed by John and expresses his gratitude for our friendship. I am very pleased to be able to contribute to a volume in which I can express similar appreciation for John as a close friend and for a considerable number of years a valued colleague at Spurgeon's College. This chapter reflects on Epiphany (with its understanding of God as manifest or made known), a liturgical season which John notes is "a little ambiguous, having rather different significance and rather different focus in the Eastern tradition than in the Western tradition."[3] Here my main focus is on the Eastern Christian tradition and towards the end I offer some thoughts about possibilities in liturgical practice.

THE SIGNIFICANCE OF EPIPHANY

Thomas Talley, in his magisterial work on the origins of the liturgical year, presented a case for the origins of the celebration of Epiphany which is derived from a system of Bible reading.[4] For Peter Bower, in his *Handbook for the Revised Common Lectionary*, one crucial aspect of Talley's work was that it showed how the Bible shaped the calendar and its preaching.[5] Thus the early Christian celebration of Epiphany in Alexandria, Talley argued, was derived from Alexandrian devotion to Mark and had as its focus the way the beginning of Mark's Gospel told the story of the baptism of Jesus.[6] Clement of Alexandria made reference to a very early Egyptian celebration on January 6 of the baptism of Jesus, a celebration which took place among Basilidians, whose views were gnostic. It was in the fourth century that the wider church embraced this and Talley drew from the *Canons of Athanasius* as evidence that in Egypt the baptism of Jesus became the primary theme of the liturgical celebration of Epiphany.[7] As a further possibility, Ledwich suggested that Epiphany became the primary baptismal day in the Eastern church.[8] Although this does not seem to have been the widespread practice which Ledwich considered to be the case, baptisms did take place at

---

3. Colwell, *Rhythm of Doctrine*, 47.
4. Talley, *Origins of the Liturgical Year*, 129–34.
5. Bower, *Handbook for the Revised Common Lectionary*, 16.
6. Talley, *Origins*, 129–34.
7. See more in Bradshaw, *Search for the Origins of Christian Worship*; Talley, *Origins*, 121; cf. Crum and Riedel, *Canons of Athanasius of Alexandria*.
8. Ledwich, "Baptism, Sacrament of the Cross," 209.

Epiphany. It is possible that some of those baptized at that time did not have the extended period of preparation which was normal with Easter baptisms.[9]

Significant developments also took place in Syria. Merja Merras, who developed the idea that Epiphany was a Christianization of the Jewish Feast of Tabernacles (her thinking in this area is still being discussed), drew attention to two hymns attributed to Ephrem the Syrian (306–373) as apparently being among the earliest writings that elaborated on the feast of Epiphany celebrated on January 6.[10] Over the course of several decades, Sebastian Brock has brought early Syrian Christianity to the attention of a wider English-language readership. He has explored, for example in *The Luminous Eye: The Spiritual World Vision of Saint Ephrem* (1992), the way in which Christ's baptism was for Ephrem part of a process of "mingling in," as Ephrem put it, of God with human experience. Christ assumed a body and later "puts on the waters of baptism." In baptism—in Ephrem's vivid picturing of the event—Christ "dived down" and then "raised up from the water the treasure of salvation for the race of Adam." Ephrem saw a close connection between Christ's baptism and Christian baptism. In a hymn on Christ's baptism he portrayed the river as a place of birth and illumination. Christ "dazzled as He went up from the river, gave illumination at His Ascent."[11] In his *Fire from Heaven*, Brock notes the tradition of a "great" or "mighty" light at the baptism of Jesus, linked with the Spirit.[12]

It seems that in the period under consideration, celebrations of Epiphany were emphasized to a greater degree in the Eastern as compared with the Western Church. Jan Willem Drijvers, in a study of Cyril (c. 313–386), Bishop of Jerusalem, drew from a narrative written by Egeria, who visited Jerusalem in the final years when Cyril was bishop. She was a young woman who travelled from her home in Spain on pilgrimage and spent three years in Jerusalem. She speaks in her account of the striking liturgical celebration of Epiphany, of an Epiphany procession from Bethlehem to Jerusalem and of church decorations at this season that were, as he put it, "too marvellous for words."[13] It was not that Epiphany was played down in the West. Indeed Augustine, in an Epiphany sermon preached in 412, made a case against the Donatists in part on the grounds that they did not celebrate Epiphany. In

---

9. Talley, "Liturgical Time in the Ancient Church," 29.

10. Merras, *Origins of the Celebration of the Christian Feast of Epiphany*, 1.

11. Brock, *Luminous Eye*, 90–92. For an earlier study, see Brock "Studies in the Early History of the Syrian Orthodox Baptismal Liturgy," 16–64.

12. Brock, *Fire from Heaven*, 234.

13. Drijvers, *Cyril of Jerusalem: Bishop and City*, 65.

the sermon Augustine clearly had in mind the visit of the magi, rather than the baptism of Jesus, as what was being celebrated at Epiphany. Nonetheless, he refers to unity with the Eastern Church. "With good reason," Augustine pronounced, "have the heretical Donatists never wished to celebrate this day with us: they neither love unity, nor are they in communion with the Eastern Church where that star appeared."[14]

Sermons by two Fathers of the Eastern Church, Gregory Nazianzus and John Chrysostom, illustrate how Epiphany was presented in preaching. Gregory's sermons—three, on the subject of the Christian mystery of salvation—were delivered in the Basilica of the Holy Apostles in Constantinople. The first was "On the Theophany," with "theophany" (manifestation of God) often being used in the East with reference to Epiphany. The other two were "On the Holy Lights" and "On Baptism." These sermons, Brian Daley comments, "offer a comprehensive vision of the Christian Gospel of salvation and renewal, through Christ and in the Church, that has rarely been equalled for the richness of its theological imagination."[15] Concurring, Christopher Beeley describes the sermons as containing Gregory's "most comprehensive treatment of Christian theology and spirituality."[16] Daley concludes that they were probably preached on January 5, 381, the day before the main feast of Epiphany, then on January 6 at a night vigil ("holy lights"), and then again on January 6 when baptisms were probably performed.[17] A famous Epiphany sermon was preached six years later, on January 6, 387, at Antioch, by John Chrysostom. He referred to the celebration of the day on which Christ was baptized, "that is called Theophany," and continued: "For this is the day on which he was baptized, and made holy the nature of the waters . . . Why then is this day called Epiphany? Because it was not when he was born that he became manifest to all, but when he was baptized; for up to this day he was unknown to the multitudes."[18] Job Getcha makes the important comment that the sermons by Gregory and Chrysostom had what he terms "an apologetic purpose." They were not essentially to celebrate the anniversary of Christ's baptism but to enable "the manifestation of God in Jesus."[19]

---

14. Augustine, *St. Augustine: Sermons for Christmas and Epiphany*, 170.

15 Daley, *Gregory of Nazianzus*, 22.

16. Beeley, *Gregory of Nazianzus*, 43. For further analysis, see McGuckin, *St Gregory of Nazianzus*, 336–47.

17. Daley, *Gregory of Nazianzus*, 198. Others think the first sermon was preached on December 25, 380.

18. White, *Documents of Christian Worship*, 30.

19. Getcha, *Typikon Decoded*, 127–28.

At the same time, there was emphasis on the baptism of Christian believers. Everett Ferguson has emphasized that registration for instruction of those to be baptized at Easter took place not long after Epiphany, and the proximity of the celebration of Christ's baptism and the enrolling of baptismal candidates "made the time around Epiphany a propitious time for preaching sermons on baptism."[20] Other liturgical elements became standard, such as the "Great are you" prayer, as it is denoted, which became an integral part of the Eastern service at Epiphany. Armenian tradition assigned its composition to Basil of Caesarea, while Syrian sources assigned it to Prochus, the fifth-century Archbishop of Constantinople. The account of the Epiphany celebration given by a sixth-century pilgrim, Antoninus of Plaisance, at the place of Jesus's baptism in the Jordan, makes it clear that baptism was being conferred. Liturgical blessing of the water was incorporated and this was often done outdoors, with dramatic effect. The first such blessing is ascribed in some sources to Peter the Fuller (his former trade was as a fuller, cleansing cloth, in a monastery), the Monophysite bishop of Antioch, in the fifth century.[21] However, it seems that there were earlier liturgies for blessing of water for spiritual purposes, which were in process of revision.[22] What Epiphany did in the East was to focus attention on the significance of water for the baptism of Jesus and Christian baptism.

CELEBRATING EPIPHANY: EASTERN DEVELOPMENTS

The baptism of Jesus came to be seen as the dominant model for Christian baptism in Eastern Orthodox thinking and practice, with connections being made between water sanctified by Jesus and water used when people were baptized. This is despite the fact, as Ferguson notes, that there are no texts in the New Testament which link Christian baptism with the baptism of Jesus.[23] Looking for texts would not have been the natural way liturgy developed. Rather there was a desire to experience the manifestation of God in Christ. In early baptismal theology there is little evidence that a classical baptismal text such as Rom 6:4 ("we have been buried with him by baptism into death") played any role. Only at a later stage did the Pauline view of

---

20. Ferguson, "Preaching at Epiphany," 1–17.

21. Talley, *Origins*, 125–26.

22. Brock, "Consecration of the Water," 317–32; Bradley, *Water: A Spiritual History*, 63.

23. Ferguson, *Baptism in the Early Church*, 115. See Wilken, "Interpretation of the Baptism of Jesus," 274–76.

baptism begin to be discussed in the Antiochene area.[24] In Syrian and Armenian Churches the baptism of Jesus was more influential than it was in either the Latin or Greek Christian traditions. Gabriele Winkler, known for her close analysis of the wording of early texts that are not given the attention they warrant, has shown that the baptism of Jesus was an essential article of faith in the early creeds in Syria and Armenia. The Armenian Creed reads: "We also believe in the Holy Spirit, uncreated and perfect, who spoke in the law, the prophets, and the gospels, who descended into the Jordan, and proclaimed the Sent One, and dwelt in the saints." Winkler argues that the presence of this wording in the Armenian Creed represents an ancient theological stratum.[25] Epiphany themes are evident.

The Orthodox tradition also invested Epiphany or Theophany with considerable theological meaning. Ephrem shaped an understanding in Syria of "fire and Spirit" in Jesus's birth, in his baptism, in "our baptism" as Christians and in the Eucharist. This hymn, making these links, was attributed to him: "See, Fire and Spirit in the womb that bore You; see Fire and Spirit in the river in which You were baptized; Fire and Spirit in our Baptism; in the Bread and the Cup, Fire and the Holy Spirit."[26] Similarly vivid terminology, this time speaking of unparalleled "beauty" and "treasures," was applied to the celebration of Epiphany in a hymn to be sung at the feast: "All of the feast days derive their beauty and are adorned, from the treasures of this feast day. Greater is this day than every day, for on it the Compassionate One came out to sinners."[27] Lev Gillet wrote of the Orthodox tradition that it "surrounds the feast of the Baptism of our Lord (Epiphany or Theophany) with a quite special veneration." In accordance with ancient Christian tradition, he continued, the Orthodox Church "rates Epiphany above Christmas, which she regards as a comparatively private event."[28] In the *Menaion*, the liturgical book used by the Orthodox Church, there is a full liturgy for Theophany which covers seventy pages of text. The major theological themes have to do with how Christ has "appeared and *enlightened* the world." The emphasis in the whole liturgical sweep is on manifestation, illumination and renewal.[29]

24. Ratcliff, "Old Syrian Baptismal Tradition," 142.

25. McDonnell, "Jesus' Baptism in the Jordan," 211, citing Winkler, "Eine bemerkenswerte Stelle im armenischen Glaubensbekenntnis," 130–62; Winkler, "Remarkable Shift in the 4th-Century Creeds," 1396–401.

26. Brock, *Luminous Eye*, 94.

27. McVey, *Ephrem the Syrian*, 91.

28. Gillet, *Orthodox Spirituality*, 41.

29. Ware and Mother Mary, *Festal Menaion*, 57. The full Theophany liturgy is 314–87.

The *troparion*, a short hymn, which is sung during the Orthodox celebration of a feast, has these words for Epiphany, expressing a fully Trinitarian vision of God revealed when Jesus was baptized:

> When You, O Lord, were baptized in the Jordan
> The worship of the Trinity was made manifest,
> For the voice of the Father bore witness to You
> And called You His beloved Son.
> While the Spirit, in the form of a dove,
> Confirmed the truthfulness of His word.
> O Christ, our God, who has revealed Yourself
> And has enlightened the world, glory to You![30]

This is repeated and is then followed by a brief *kontakion*, a thematic hymn.

> Today You have appeared in the world, O Lord,
> and your light shines forth on us who sing your praises with understanding.
> You have come, you have revealed Yourself to us,
> O inaccessible Light.[31]

Other customs may and have been added. In Russia, for example, where Theophany is celebrated according to the Julian calendar—on 19 rather than 6 January—the *troparion* and the *kontakion* are sung, and the tradition in some places has been that the Orthodox priest visits local homes with a cross and with holy water, while the local cantor draws a cross on a wall in the house, along with a drawing of a sword and a sponge, indicating details of Jesus' crucifixion.[32]

One widespread Eastern custom at Epiphany is the blessing of the waters. During the *Ektenia* (litany) of Peace, there is a long prayer of consecration of the water, a prayer now generally ascribed to Sophronius of Jerusalem in the seventh century. This is a poem in praise of the mysteries of Theophany and the regeneration of all creation through Christ. During this prayer, when the celebrant comes to the words: "Great are You, O Lord, and wonderful are Your works, and our words are insufficient to praise Your wonders," he blesses the water—which might be outdoors—dipping the cross into the water three times. Then the cross is often set on a platform. Baptism and the cross are thus brought together.[33] Nicholas Denysenko has

---

30. Mathewes-Green, *Open Door*, 122–23. See also Louth, *Introducing Eastern Orthodox Theology*, 23.

31. Evdokimov, *Light from the East*, 25.

32. Friesen, "Missionary Priests' Reports from Siberia," 258.

33. For this, see Dalmais et al., *Liturgy and Time*.

examined the historical development and the theological significance of what is done in this ritual. He has particularly offered greater understanding of the history of the blessing of the waters throughout the centuries. Water has been consistently seen as a source of healing, purification, and communion with God. In the context of that approach, the gifts requested from Christ at each Epiphany, Denysenko argues, are the same as those requested at baptism. "They include redemption, freedom from the slavery of sin; spiritual growth towards holiness through the gift of sanctification; the removal of sin; a source of healing for bodily illness; and protection from evil forces, bolstered by angelic activity."[34]

At least three major themes can be identified in Eastern spirituality in relation to Epiphany. The first is that a full-orbed spiritual life is one lived in fellowship with God as Father, Son, and Spirit. Sergius Bulgakov speaks about the way in which the "power of the Holy Trinity was manifested in the baptism of Christ," celebrated at Epiphany, and "human baptism is conducted, according to Christ's direct command, in the name of the Holy Trinity," to be lived out in the light of Epiphany.[35] A second theme is being aware of creation. For Orthodox spirituality, "all our individual baptisms are a sharing in the baptism of Christ—they are the means whereby the 'grace of Jordan' is extended, so that it may be appropriated by each of us personally." All created things can therefore be made holy.[36] The "harmony between creation and the incarnate Word" is clear in the Orthodox Epiphany.[37] Finally, this spirituality has within it humility and glory. Lev Gillet writes: "What does this manifestation consist of? It is made up of two aspects. On the one hand, there is the aspect of humility represented by the baptism to which our Lord submits: on the other hand, there is the aspect of glory." He speaks about every manifestation of Christ, in history and in "the inner life" of each person, as "a manifestation of humility and of glory." Epiphany, the feast of baptism, "not only of Jesus's baptism, but also of our own," is for Gillet "a wonderful opportunity for us to renew in spirit the baptism that we received, and to revive the grace which was conferred on us."[38]

---

34. Denysenko, *Blessing of Waters and Epiphany*, 128.
35. Bulgakov, *Churchly Joy*, 57–58. Originally published in Russian in 1938.
36. Mother Mary and Ware, *Festal Menaion*, 58–59.
37. Gillet, *Year of Grace of the Lord*, 82–83.
38. Thompson, *Spirituality in Season*, 52–53.

PROTESTANT EMPHASES AT EPIPHANY

The differing emphases at Epiphany in the Western and Eastern Churches are clearly described in *The Rhythm of Doctrine*: "The focal narrative for the Western tradition at Epiphany is the presentation of Christ to the Magi as significant of Christ as the light of the world, the light to the nations." By contrast: "Within the Eastern tradition, Epiphany tends to be granted greater emphasis and significance than Christmas and, as the name of the season implies, there is similar celebration of Christ as the light to the nations, of the making visible of God's saving presence in Christ, but here the focal narrative is the story of Jesus baptism, of the declaration of his sonship, of his making public his identity." In the East, and increasingly in the West, there is also some focus on baptism itself and prayer for those who "stand upon the threshold of faith."[39] Richard Trexler has investigated the powerful influence in the West of the journey of the magi: "In the West, the magi eclipsed the baptism of Jesus as an occasion for celebration . . . The magi—their journey, gifting and adoration—became the centre of Epiphany celebrations in an explosion of fifth-century sermons and treatises on their story."[40] The distinction in traditions, however, was not always clear-cut. In the eighth century, in Gaul, January 6 was celebrated as a feast of the magi, the baptism of Jesus and the turning of the water into wine. Baptisms were held.[41] Ludolph von Suchem described in 1350 visiting an Eastern monastery at Epiphany when the Gospel was read in Latin, suggesting East-West connections.[42]

With the Protestant Reformation in the sixteenth century, the tendency in celebrating Epiphany was to adopt the (Western) Catholic Church's emphasis on the magi. But in contrast to this, Martin Luther expressed his own preference that Epiphany be celebrated as "the Baptism of Our Lord," as in the Eastern Churches.[43] In a sermon preached on January 6, 1534, "This Is My Son, the Beloved," a sermon on the baptism of Jesus, he stated: "The most important thing about today is that Jesus was baptized." Luther referred to the wise men, but then said he wished the day was called "The Baptism of Christ." He connected this with Christian baptism: "Even if it [baptism] offered us nothing at all," he said, we should honour baptism "simply for Christ's sake." But something is indeed offered: "God in heaven

---

39. Colwell, *Rhythm of Doctrine*, 47.
40. Trexler, *Journey of the Magi*, 10.
41. Bradshaw and Johnson, *Origins of Feasts*, ch. 17; Johnson, *Rites of Christian Initiation*, 168.
42. Stewart, *Luloph von Suchem's Description of the Holy Land*, 119–20.
43. Senn, *Christian Liturgy: Catholic and Evangelical*, 343.

poured himself out when Christ was baptized."[44] One study of Luther and baptism, by Scaer, sums up the heart of Luther's view: "Baptism was a death by drowning and a rebirth, patterned after the death and resurrection of Jesus. Still the sign or the outward form did not exhaust the meaning of the sacrament but pointed to God as the greater reality hidden within it." Scaer argues that for Calvin "reality and symbol are joined by divine command, but with Luther there is an actual *perichoresis*, so that one is in and with the other in an organic unity."[45] This coheres with the high Eastern view of God as present in the water. The link is rightly made in this commentary on Luther's baptismal theology with the death and resurrection of Jesus. What is not highlighted is the connection with Jesus's baptism.

In his sermon on "the Baptism of our Lord," Luther explained that the festival of Epiphany received its name because of the revelation of God: Father, Son, and Holy Spirit. As Christ himself was baptized by John and the dove came and God spoke, the message for Luther was that "the Holy Spirit comes in a friendly form; the Father has a friendly voice."[46] Luther here, as often elsewhere, used the language of "appearance, epiphany, presence, action, and speech" in relation to God's role in baptism.[47] Also Luther could not resist making an application to his time of reform: "Formerly, we knew nothing. The heavens were still closed. We had to hear, in the devil's name, what the monks said about purgatory, poltergeists, and the like. But now the indescribable gift of God is being taught so that we can learn it." The church should, Luther insisted, look again at the meaning of Epiphany. "To some degree it is about the wise men. But there is something much, much more important here." The real "three kings," he posited, are the Father, Son, and Spirit. On the power of the water of baptism Luther noted that some were saying baptism was "plain water." This he repudiated. His dog, Tölpel (often mentioned in Luther's *Table Talk*), knew about ordinary water. But baptism is "water in which the Son of God bathes, over which the Holy Spirit hovers, over which God the Father preaches." To baptize in the name of the Trinity was to know the actual presence of the Trinity: "the Son, who sanctified baptism with his body, the Holy Spirit, who sanctified it with his presence, and the Father, who sanctified it with his voice." Luther hoped that the subject of Christian baptism would be addressed by preachers on Epiphany.[48]

---

44. Luther, "This Is My Son," 7–8.

45. Scaer, "Luther, Baptism and the Church Today," 262.

46. Luther, "This Is My Son," 8.

47. Trigg, *Baptism in the Theology of Martin Luther*, 32. This is a full and satisfying treatment of the subject.

48. Luther, "This Is My Son," 9–10.

Luther's views on this subject had some influence. He introduced a long prayer at baptism, the *Sindflutgebet*, or Great Flood Prayer, and this prayer, which has been seen as a masterpiece, was taken up by Philip Melanchthon and other Lutheran leaders. As with Eastern prayers, the *Sindflutgebet* spoke about the water of baptism being sanctified. God, through the baptism of Jesus, "consecrated and set apart the Jordan and all water as a salutary flood and a rich and full washing away of sins."[49] Martin Bucer, the leading reformer in Strasbourg, who moved to Cambridge to be Regius Professor of Divinity, was one of those asked to critique the Church of England's *Book of Common Prayer* of 1549. The "Blessing of the Water of the Font" was heavily modified in the Prayer Book 1552 revision. No blessing of the water was thought of as needed: Luther's view, that sanctification had already taken place, was influential.[50] Other Protestants moved a long way from Luther's thinking. John Calvin preached a sermon on January 6, 1551, as part of a series of sermons on Micah. In the course of preaching he asked how many people "still regard Epiphany with high reverence." He did not know "where they came up with this festival." His view was that "we must divest ourselves of all silly superstitions and frivolous inventions," with Epiphany being placed in that category.[51] Following Calvin's lead, the 1560 Church of Scotland *Book of Discipline* pruned the calendar of saints and deleted Christmas and Epiphany. They appeared in a list of things that "neither have commandment nor assurance" in Scripture.[52]

The eighteenth century, which saw the Evangelical Revival, and as a crucial part of that the impact of John Wesley, might have been a time when fresh engagement with Epiphany as a powerful "manifestation" of God's presence could have taken place. Wesley certainly had a deep interest in the Eastern Fathers of the Church.[53] However, it is striking that this interest did not seem to affect Wesley's celebration of the Christian year. A connection could have been made between the "Renewal of the Covenant" in Methodism, which from the 1760s took place at the beginning of each year, and Epiphany. It is true that the covenant service did not begin as a January event. It was on May 11, 1755, that Wesley introduced a service which he saw as having been practised in the past with significant blessing. In the service, those present joined in a covenant to serve God with all their heart

---

49. Spinks, *Reformation and Modern Rituals*, 12.

50. Spinks, *Reformation and Modern Rituals*, 69.

51. *Sermons on the Book of Micah*, 362–64. For analysis of the sermons, see Parsons, *Calvin's Preaching on the Prophet Micah*.

52. Johnson, *Sacraments and Worship*, 398.

53. Maddox, "John Wesley and Eastern Orthodoxy," 29–53.

and soul. Wesley quoted from the Puritan Richard Alleine on covenanting: *Directions to Penitents and Believers for Renewing Their Covenant with God*. Approximately 1,800 people attended the first Methodist covenanting service, in the French church in Spitalfields, London.[54] When the covenant service moved to January, there were occasions when it coincided with Epiphany. Wesley recorded in his *Journal* for Sunday January 6, 1765: "The whole society met in the evening. The service lasted from five till near nine; and I do not remember so solemn a season since the first time we joined in renewing our covenant with God."[55] A communal approach to covenant has been important in Baptist thinking and practice.[56] However, with early Baptist life having been strongly influenced by Calvinist thinking and then later by the Evangelical Revival, it is perhaps not surprising that Epiphany has not been a significant celebration within Baptist churches.

LITURGICAL POSSIBILITIES

In *The Rhythm of Doctrine*, John Colwell has offered consistently engaging insights into Christian thought and practice through a journey with the Christian year.[57] In considering "The One Who Is Revealed," he writes: "Epiphany is a celebration of a light that has shone and is shining—it shone in Christ, and it shone into our lives—and as a celebration, Epiphany is a response of gratitude and of trust, we have seen this light and we have confidence in this truth; we have come from darkness to light."[58] Part of the Daily Office of the Order for Baptist Ministry has these words for Epiphany:

> We give you thanks
> that your light shines
> in all places and towards all peoples
> and that your light
> has shone in our hearts.
> Help us this day
> to walk in the light of your Spirit
> as we seek to live for your glory.
> In Jesus' name we pray. Amen.

---

54. Tripp, *Renewal of the Covenant*, 15.
55. Ward and Heitzenrater, *Works of John Wesley*, "Journals and Diaries IV," 21:498.
56. See, e.g., Fiddes, "Walking Together," 47–74.
57. Here I am not able to engage with other books by John. His *Promise and Presence* I regard as an outstandingly creative exploration of sacramental theology.
58. Colwell, *Rhythm of Doctrine*, 56–57.

Gathering for Worship, has three prayers which relate specifically to the baptism of Jesus, and it is significant that they come in the Epiphany section of the Christian year. The first of these, entitled "Dedication," is explicit in linking the baptism of Jesus with the baptism of believers.

> Lord Jesus,
> you did not need to repent,
> but still you came to be baptized,
> immersed in the Jordan
> and showing us the way.
> Help us to be penitent
> and, by your grace, to walk the new path life.
>
> Lord Jesus Christ,
> you are the anointed one, God's messiah,
> commissioned for service and empowered by the Holy Spirit.
> Fill us with your Spirit
> that we might live to serve and praise you,
> proclaiming your love in word and deed.
>
> Saviour Christ,
> you call us through the waters of baptism
> and promise that, as we are united with you in death,
> so we shall be united with you in resurrection life.
> Help us to keep saying "yes" to your call,
> that in trusting your faithfulness we might live faithful lives.
> In your name we ask it.[59]

This is a prayer which could fruitfully be used by Baptist communities at Epiphany, with those in the congregation being encouraged to remember their baptism and to renew their "yes" to God and their desire to be filled with the Spirit. The Orthodox theologian Alexander Schmemann, who noted that the form of baptism in the Eastern liturgy reflected adult baptism, wrote: "The proper celebration of Baptism is indeed the source and the starting point of all liturgical renewal and revival. It is here that the Church reveals her own nature to herself, constantly renews herself as a community of the baptized."[60]

The second prayer in the "Baptism of Jesus" section of *Gathering for Worship* is entitled "Living Our Baptism."

---

59. Ellis and Blyth, *Gathering for Worship*, 367. The prayers before these three refer to the magi.

60. Schmemann, *Of Water and the Spirit*, 38. For Schmemann, who was born in Estonia and who later moved to Paris with his family, see Louth, *Modern Orthodox Thinkers*, 194–210.

> Almighty God,
> who anointed Jesus at his baptism with the Holy Spirit
> and revealed him as your beloved Son:
> inspire us, your children,
> who are born of water and the Spirit,
> to surrender our lives to your service,
> that we may rejoice to be called the sons and daughters of God;
> through Jesus Christ our Lord.[61]

Bulgakov, in his "Open Heavens: Oration on the Epiphany," speaks about Christ's baptism as "Christ's Pentecost," which in Orthodox celebrations "becomes a day of the manifestation of the Holy Trinity."[62] The *Gathering for Worship* language of Jesus "anointed" and "revealed" coheres with this thinking. Also, the description of believers as those "born of water and the Spirit" suggest a sacramental view of baptism, in which God is seen as active, a view promulgated by John Colwell, who expresses his indebtedness in this area to George Beasley-Murray, Paul Fiddes, Stanley Fowler, and Anthony R. Cross.[63]

The third prayer in this section of *Gathering for Worship* is entitled "Discipleship," and reproduces an Epiphany prayer found in *Celebrating Common Prayer*.

> Almighty God,
> we give you thanks for your Son, Jesus Christ,
> who was baptized in the river Jordan
> and passed through the deep waters of death.
> We praise you that you raised him to life and exalted him.
>
> Help us to follow in his way
> as disciples and faithful servants of his gospel.
> By your grace, help us,
> that being united with him,
> we may continually die to sin
> and live to your praise and glory,
> though Jesus Christ our Saviour.[64]

There is a clear call here to discipleship. In the Russian Baptist tradition, mirroring to a surprising extent Russian Orthodoxy, Epiphany has been

---

61. Ellis and Blyth, *Gathering for Worship*, 368.

62. Bulgakov, *Churchly Joy*, 57–58.

63. Colwell, *Promise and Presence*, 110. For more on Baptists and baptism, see in particular the substantial volumes by Cross, *Baptism and the Baptists*, and *Recovering the Evangelical Sacrament*.

64. Ellis and Blyth, *Gathering for Worship*, 368.

celebrated as the "Baptism of the Lord" and as part of this event there has been a call to see Christ as an example, to respond to God's summons to baptism and to enter a life of discipleship in the power of the Holy Spirit.[65]

I found that being in an ecumenical local church setting—my last local church ministry was in a missional ecumenical congregation in the Cambridge area—helped me to reflect on the possibilities of weaving into services strands from different liturgical traditions, together with contemporary styles of worship. For example, we used the Methodist covenant at the beginning of the year, and it was good in an ecumenical setting, where there were different ecclesial understandings, to unite in the covenant's wonderful Trinitarian ending.

> And now, glorious and blessed God,
> Father, Son and Holy Spirit,
> you are mine and I am yours. So be it.
> And the covenant now made on earth, let it be ratified in heaven.
> Amen.

We also had the experience of "asperges," the sprinkling with water as renewal of baptismal vows. Ruth Myers notes that in some Anglican rites this renewal may occur on the first Sunday after Epiphany.[66] Perhaps Baptists could helpfully incorporate the ideas of renewing the covenant and renewing the promises we made when we were baptized as part of the congregational worship, together with a focus on Jesus's baptism, on the first Sunday after Epiphany.[67]

CONCLUSION

This reflection on Epiphany has drawn especially from Eastern Christianity, because of the theological power of the understanding of Epiphany in that tradition and also because Orthodox celebration of the baptism of Jesus and Christian baptism in the Epiphany season seems to offer fresh possibilities

---

65. Prokhorov, *Russian Baptists and Orthodoxy, 1960–1990*, 196–97. I am indebted to two colleagues, Otniel Bunaciu in Romania and Parush Parushev in Bulgaria, who have noted that in their contexts Baptist celebration of the Baptism of Jesus on Epiphany is rare. The theme of the magi is more prominent. For an example of Orthodox-orientated Baptist life, see Songulashvili, *Evangelical Christian Baptists of Georgia*. For Christmas and Epiphany among Armenian evangelicals: Anna Ohanjanyan, "Evangelical and Pentecostal Communities in Armenia," 112.

66. Meyers, "Renewal of Baptismal Vows," 52–53.

67. The OBM daily offices for Epiphany make no mention of baptism and perhaps a daily office that picks up the theme of baptism could be written.

for Baptists. Ruth Meyers outlines the place of Epiphany and baptism in the Episcopal context and notes suggestions that Epiphany might be revitalized by "drawing it into closer relation" to substantial themes such as baptism.[68] The seminal work that has been done by John Colwell opens the way for changes of this kind. The ideas contained in this chapter draw upon deep wells of worship in the story of the church.[69] For Baptists and others in baptistic churches to remember their baptism and renew their vows has special significance, since those baptized as believers do actually remember what took place. This chapter began with a prayer from *Celebrating Common Worship* and it is appropriate to conclude the chapter with further lines from there.

> Almighty God,
> in our baptism you have consecrated us,
> to be temples of your Spirit:
> may we . . . nurture this gift of your indwelling Spirit
> with a lively faith, through Jesus Christ our Lord.[70]

---

68. Meyers, *Continuing the Reformation*, 61.
69. See Webber, *Ancient-Future Worship*.
70. *Celebrating Common Prayer*, 360: Epiphanytide.

10

Annunciation
Behold, a Virgin Shall Conceive

Paul Goodliff

Here I am, the servant of the Lord. Let it be to me according to your word.
(Luke 1:38)

Lord, we too are your servants, and we offer this day in joyful obedience to your word in the power of your Spirit.[1]

The Baptist Church in Wendover, Buckinghamshire, is remarkable for a number of ways, including the depth of its ecumenical engagement in this large village proximate to Chequers, the country seat of the British Prime Minister. However, unless you visited it, as I did on occasion when general superintendent of the Baptist area in which it sat, you would be unaware of a most unusual feature of its building. In the corner by the Lord's Table is an almost life-size statue of the Blessed Virgin Mary. I know of only one other English Baptist church that has one, and it belongs in both churches because the congregations share their building with the Roman Catholic Parish, to which the statue belongs.

---

1. OBM Daily Office—Annunciation.

Baptists do not know what to do with the Feast of the Annunciation (and most will never have heard of it), not least because we do not quite know what to make of Mary. With our Reformation roots that rejected so many of the religious accretions that had come to characterise the way the Catholic Church articulated its faith at a popular level, the first generations of Baptists had little in their statements of faith to say about Mary, even by way of denouncing what they found problematic in Catholic devotion to her. When they do speak of her, it is generally minimalist. The Second London Confession of 1677 simply refers to Mary as an organ of reproduction—"The *Son of God* . . . being conceived by the *Holy Spirit* in the *Womb* of the *Virgin Mary*, the *Holy Spirit* coming down upon her, and the power of the most *High* overshadowing her, and so was made of a *Woman* of the Tribe of *Judah*, of the seed of *Abraham* and *David*."[2] This is almost an exact repetition of the earlier Short Confession of Faith of John Smyth.[3] The 1610 Short Confession of the Helwys party describes the everlasting Word becoming flesh "in the womb of the holy virgin (called Mary) by his word, and power, and working of the Holy Ghost . . . and he is one person true God and man, born of Mary . . ."[4]

Nowhere is there an explicit denouncing of devotion to Mary, but if we include her in the category of the saints, the Second London Confession is clear that "*religious worship* is to be given to *God* the *Father*, *Son* and *Holy Spirit*, and to him alone; not to *Angels*, *Saints*, or any other."[5] Worship of Mary is absolutely absent as a valid expression of Christian living. The fullest description is in the 1644 London Confession, paragraph IX, which states that "the Lord Jesus . . . was made man of a woman of the Tribe of *Judah*, of the seed of *Abraham* and David, to wit, of *Mary* that blessed Virgin, by the holy Spirit coming upon her, and the power of the most High overshadowing her."[6] This, with its successor, the Second London Confession, is the closest the early Baptist statements of faith come to the Lucan words of the angel who announces her impending conception of Jesus. It is a small step from the minimalist creedal statements that Jesus is "born of the Virgin Mary," but very far from any developed theology of Mary as either sinless, or assumed bodily into heaven. Her conception as immaculate, and her fate as assumed bodily into heaven upon her death (known in the East as her

---

2. Lumpkin, *Baptist Confessions of Faith*, 261.

3. Lumpkin, *Baptist Confessions of Faith*, 100. It is similarly repeated in the Somerset Confession of 1656, XII, ibid., 206.

4. Lumpkin, *Baptist Confessions of Faith*, 104–5.

5. Lumpkin, *Baptist Confessions of Faith*, 281, Second London Confession, XXII.2.

6. Lumpkin, *Baptist Confessions of Faith*, 158–59.

Koimesis, falling asleep) do not feature in Baptist thought. These are, admittedly, espoused as doctrines of the Catholic faith long after the origins of the English Baptists. Promulgated by Pope Pius IX in 1854, the immaculate conception of Mary—that is, she did not inherit original sin at her conception in St Anne, her mother's, womb by an act of sanctifying grace—enabled the two-natures model of Christ's divinity and humanity articulated in the Chalcedonian definition to accommodate what the London Confessions affirm as Jesus's sinlessness ("was also in all things like unto us, sinne only excepted"—the 1644 London Confession IX;[7] "the Son of God . . . did . . . take upon him man's nature, with all the Essential properties, and common infirmities thereof, yet without sin"—the Second London Confession Ch. VIII[8]). The doctrine of the assumption is affirmed even later, defined as an article of faith by Pius XII in *Munificentissimus Deus* (1950), although it had a long prehistory as a probable Catholic opinion from the seventeenth century, and with its origins in Gnostic texts of the late fourth century. Baptists inherit Protestantism's rejection of both doctrines, essentially as absent from Scripture, but also as attempts to both provide unwarranted elements in the explanation of the two natures doctrine of Christ, and admitting elements of folk religion and Gnosticism into the rational post-Enlightenment character of Christian faith.

From a minimalist end of the spectrum, Mary being an almost unattributed womb to the more expansive ascription of "blessed" to Mary, the range is hardly forthcoming in saying anything more about her than her status as the virgin mother of Jesus. One might expect little more, admittedly, given the Baptists' desire to say nothing more than Scripture proclaims. One senses that from these early passing references to Mary as the bearer of Jesus, the later status of Mary for Baptists almost diminishes to her entire absence from the narrative, other than the reading of the Christmas story. Mary is a scarcely visible person, such is the anxiety that her inclusion might be a temptation to Catholic Mariolatry.

Yet, this part of the gospel narrative is an expression of the gospel *in nuce*. In Luke's account a woman is addressed by God's messenger, who announces God's mercy and favour, his presence to bless rather than condemn, and the way in which she might participate in the divine plan. Her response is one of humble obedience and trust, recognizing who she is in her relationship to the Lord—a servant. One might view this as the archetypical disciple, receiving mercy and pledging obedient submission to the divine will.

---

7. Lumpkin, *Baptist Confessions of Faith*, 159.
8. Lumpkin, *Baptist Confessions of Faith*, 260–61.

The main feasts of the Christian year are well-represented in the weekly rhythm of the Order for Baptist Ministry Daily Office. There are, however, missing feasts, among which is the Feast of the Annunciation. In 2017 a daily office for this one day was written, from which the quotation at the head of this chapter is taken. Too often elided with Advent or Christmas, it seemed to me that the Annunciation, the beginning of the story of Jesus, warranted such acknowledgment, even if the office is used but once a year. Previously the Order for Baptist Ministry took the opportunity at its 2015 Convocation at St Columba's, Woking, to write a daily office for Advent that might supplement the regular, alternative and shorter Advent offices that were already available. The theme that runs through this office is Advent, of course, composed as small groups each worked on a separate section of the usual office schema, but there arose separately a strong theme of Mary's role. So, in acknowledging our humanity, we say,

> God of grace
> Your favour rested on Mary
> and rests on us
> Formed life within Mary
> Forms life within us
> Dazzled and baffled Mary
> Dazzles and baffles us

and so forth. In the prayers of intercession, a recurring theme is "With Mary . . ." So,

> With Mary, God-bearer,
> we pray for all who carry the most precious of gifts . . .
>
> With Mary, Christ-birther,
> we pray for all who today utter their first cry
>
> With Mary, accepter of the wildness of God,
> we pray for all who are misunderstood

and this continues with reference to Mary's Song, the *Magnificat*. For the first time an Order for Baptist Ministry liturgy heavily referenced Mary's role in the gospel narrative, even if, quite properly, it fell far short of invoking Mary's prayers or help. The sense of this daily office is an identification with Mary as a forerunner, rather than any particular devotion to Mary as possessing a distinctive or unique human nature (free from original sin) or fate (her assumption into heaven in order to intercede for us). She is someone whose example in faith we might draw encouragement from. This goes some way to rehabilitate Mary as possessing an extraordinary role in the divine plan of salvation—no other woman bore Jesus, and given his divine nature as Son of God, even as a single-cell zygote, no other woman has, in that sense, been *Theotokos*, God-bearer.

Locating the celebration of the Annunciation in Advent places it within the secondary theme of that season, which is anticipating the birth of Jesus. The primary themes of waiting in hope for the return of Christ, and the attendant focus upon the "last things," are less palatable to a contemporary sensibility and too easily become secondary to a secularized and extended pre-Christmas season. Thus, in a typical Baptist congregational life, the more sombre themes that are referred to at All Saints' and All Souls' are entirely absent, and once Advent begins, while there may be a passing nod to the eschatological notes on the First Sunday in Advent (typically, though mistakenly, called "Advent Sunday"), from the Second Sunday through to Christmas Day itself, the overwhelming theme is that of Christmas, despite the now widespread lighting of Advent candles. Carols will be sung throughout, the Christmas tree installed from at least the Second Sunday, and the church collaborate with secular society to eviscerate the season of anything that might threaten the enforced jollity. In the middle of Advent I am encouraged to participate in the decoration of the church sanctuary so that I might "get into the Christmas spirit." However, if Advent is a season of waiting, anticipating the joy of Christmas too early is entirely consistent with the false note that our culture sounds with its avoidance of patient waiting, and the church has once again sold its soul to a secular society, even if it believes it has done so dressed in a missional robe.

Into this sorry confusion the extraordinary message of the Annunciation is too easily overlooked. If Easter is quite properly the great festival to celebrate God's vindication of the death of Jesus as the death of death and the resurrection of life, remembered weekly by the church's moving of the Sabbath to the first day of the week, then there should be a greater reminder, liturgically, of the extraordinary miracle that preceded that—indeed, makes it possible at all—that the Word became flesh, the divine became human and in the conception of Jesus announced by Gabriel the divine agent of creation (Col 1:16) takes creaturely form as do all living things, first as a single cell endowed with the potential to grow into the wonder that is a living being. If as Baptists we said or sang the *Magnificat* regularly, then that reminder would be present, but we do not, and so the imbalance between incarnation and passion remains.

Which is why I believe that there is wisdom in displacing the celebration of the Annunciation from its sole location in Advent to its traditional liturgical one, the biologically coherent date of the March 25, nine months before Christmas Day. While this does very rarely fall after Easter,[9] normally this will be in Lent, since the latest possible date for Ash Wednesday is March 10. This has some benefits in replacing some of the more romanticized elements of the Annunciation bestowed upon it by its proximity to Christmas with the more stringent Lenten tones of the cost of discipleship born by Mary in her willing obedience. That "let it be with me according to your word" (Luke 1:38), was an anticipation of a broken betrothal to Joseph, and a lifetime at the receiving end of stigma and sniggering, rejection and loneliness. That Joseph did not do "the right thing," and break off the union quietly, as he first intended (λάθρα ἀπολῦσαι αὐτήν, Matt 1:19) was not anticipated by Mary when she said "yes." If Lent is a season for reflecting upon discipleship—a penitential review of what it means to take up a cross and follow Christ—then the insertion of Mary's example is entirely appropriate. She becomes the first "cross-bearer," even as she becomes *Theotokos*, God bearer, although not in the ways she could have imagined then, as a teenage girl.

So, if the most appropriate place liturgically for the Annunciation is March 25, embedded within Lent, it is appropriate to use a daily office specifically for that day. If the Annunciation is the unique event in history that the Christian tradition believes it to be,[10] the embedding of the Word in the womb of Mary, then to use a liturgy sparingly, just once a year, somehow reflects the particularity of that event. While the response of discipleship in obedience to God's word is ubiquitous (although far from as ubiquitous as we would want) the particular context of this act of obedience is absolutely unique. In the supplementary Advent daily office, Mary's response of obedience becomes for us an example *par excellence* of obedience.

Baptist theological discussion of Mary in the twentieth century is limited. James McClendon, for instance, discusses Mary only in the context of the miraculous conception of Jesus of Nazareth, and in the process, distinguishes between the virginal conception—which, he argues, is not the reason to affirm Jesus's divinity according to the biblical narratives[11]—and the "virgin birth" and immaculate conception, which are later theological

---

9. The earliest possible date for Easter being March 22, although the last time this happened was in 1818—and it will not be until 2285 that this is repeated—and it is not until 2060 that it falls on March 23.

10. "It was an extraordinary action of God's creative power, as unique as the initial creation itself (and that is why all natural science objections to it are irrelevant e.g. that not having a human father, Jesus' genetic structure would have been abnormal). It was not a phenomenon of nature, and to reduce it to one, however unusual, would as serious a challenge as to deny it altogether." Brown, *Birth of the Messiah*, 531.

11. McClendon, *Doctrine*, 270.

accretions.[12] He almost suggests a holy and human act of coitus as the origins of Jesus: "There is no suggestion in these accounts that this beginning apart from normal coitus is the cause or source of Jesus's sinlessness, for this last notion was introduced only later, when Christians had begun to think human sexuality as such sinful."[13] He continues to argue that the virginal conception is "not a touchstone of Christian orthodoxy or a dogma to be believed on pain of damnation . . . The virginal conception is instead a sign of faith for the faithful, speaking to many . . . the full presence of God in the full story of Jesus."[14] This reflects a significant move away from the popular defense of the "virgin birth" (mistaking it for the virginal conception) by evangelical Baptists keen to both defend the historical integrity of Scripture, and the full deity of Christ in the face of theological questions about the nature of Christ that deny the two-natures definition of Chalcedon. McClendon's may not be mainstream Baptist thought, but it is present, clearly, in the breadth of perspectives that Baptists hold.

However in one recent book, *Baptists and the Communion of Saints*, Paul Fiddes argues at length for a rehabilitation of the role of Mary.[15] Not only is Mary's role unique in salvation history, and her response is that of the model disciple as she remains faithful to Jesus to the cross and beyond (citing Karl Barth, who argues that "Mary represents the whole of humanity in being the definitive hearer and receiver of the word of God"[16]) but the corporate witness of the church is that it has found "her life to be a special manifestation of God's grace."[17] Fiddes notes that in two recent theological conversations between Roman Catholics and Baptists, the Baptist participants have conceded that it is right to honor Mary as Elizabeth does, and that the title *Theotokos* is fitting for her.[18] Baptists do not agree, however,

---

12. Raymond Brown notes how to the belief in a virginal conception (i.e., without an act of penetrative sexual intercourse), which seems to have been widely believed by the early church, and reflected implicitly in the creeds ("born of the Virgin Mary"), was subsequently added a belief by the fourth century in the miraculous virgin birth—that somehow Jesus came forth from Mary's womb in a painless way by which her hymen was not ruptured (the second of the triad, "*virginitatas ante partum, in partu, et post partum*") and which became Roman Catholic revealed doctrine, even if that is now taken in a more nuanced way by, for instance, Karl Rahner in "Virginitas in Partu," 134–62, and who notes how this reflects a docetic view of the birth (162). This reflects a move from Christology to Mariology that Brown seems to reject.

13. McClendon, *Doctrine*, 270.

14. McClendon, *Doctrine*, 270.

15. Fiddes, "Praying with Mary."

16. Fiddes, "Praying with Mary," 96.

17. Fiddes, "Praying with Mary," 97.

18. "The Word of God in the Life of the Church," 28–122, para. 133, 143; *Marie*,

that Mary's redemption was effected before Christ's birth, but that, rather, she too had to grow in grace through normal human conditions.

The authors of *Baptists and the Communion of Saints* are agreed that in Christ there is a continuing role of intercession by those who are held alive in Christ but no longer alive on earth. In that role, Mary participates, with all others, but perhaps in a distinctive way, so that while we may not worship her, we may recognize that we pray *with* her—that our prayers accompany hers in being ever caught up in the intercession of the Son to the Father. It is not that Mary, the saints, or we, for that matter, have some independent existence before God or access to him, other than our being "in Christ." If we were not "in Christ," our prayers would be mere human expressions of longing, and not effectual means of participating in the divine life and mission. Nor is that Mary, in some way, collects our prayers and presents them to Christ, as if we needed her mediation between us and a rather stern and remote Christ (although there is this tendency in Eastern Christianity, with its images of Christ as Pancreator—the very image of a Roman emperor with the power of life and death). Even in her unique role as *Theotokos*, Mary's humanity is redeemed, as is ours, by Christ's sacrificial death, and not by virtue of some special role as the bearer of Jesus. Fiddes writes, "Because there is already a movement within God of a Son responding in obedience to a Father, then it is possible to discern many in our world who are leaning on that movement to say 'yes' in their own way, to the purpose of God."[19] Having gone before us on this journey of obedient living, and now alive in Christ awaiting the resurrection of all God's people, we may believe that they continue that obedient living, a perfected alive-ness, by participating in the divine life of intercession and gracious outpouring. Amongst them, surely, will be that archetypal disciple, Mary, whose response to God's "will you?" was a faithful "yes, I will." So, we might pray "with Mary, and all the saints."

What of John Colwell, in whose honor these essays are written? In *The Rhythm of Doctrine*, admittedly a sketch of doctrine rather than a full-blown dogmatics, Mary does not figure beyond a passing mention of her name in the chapter on Advent,[20] referring to her as "a light," and her presumed inclusion in the chapter on the incarnation, although she is only mentioned as "the virgin's womb that he 'abhors not'"[21] and that "it

---

comité mixte Baptiste-Catholique en France, para. 15.

19. Fiddes, et al., *Baptists and the Communion of Saints*, 100.
20. Colwell, *Rhythm of Doctrine*, 17.
21. Colwell, *Rhythm of Doctrine*, 35.

is by the Spirit that Christ is born of the virgin Mary."[22] In the chapter on the communion of the saints, Colwell takes a similar stance to Fiddes discussed above, but without ever mentioning Mary amongst the saints (and he includes a list ranging from Irenaeus to Aquinas, Calvin to Wesley). I suspect that those that came to his mind when writing this were primarily theologians, and Mary does not figure among them. However, I wonder if Colwell's conservative roots and subsequent charismatic experience, with little by way of sustained worship with any tradition that might pay greater attention to Mary, has created a lacuna in his written theology that is not entirely reflected in his private conversation. A psychologist might perhaps discern a subconscious anxiety about being seen as too "Catholic" playing into this, even though he is amongst the most catholic of Baptists. But I suspect the reason is more prosaic—*The Rhythm of Doctrine* is a "sketch," not a fully-developed systematics and Colwell had found little room for an interest in Mary beyond a tangential role in the doctrine of the incarnation. Neither his *Promise and Presence* (a book about the sacraments) nor *Living the Christian Story* (concerning Christian ethics and the gospel narrative) provide an obvious context for any prolonged discussion about Mary's role in the unfolding purpose of God, and so it is therefore not surprising that she is not mentioned in them. In this way Colwell would be a typical Baptist theologian, for whom the place for reflection on Mary never really gains traction. Perhaps more surprising, given Colwell's lifelong interest in Barth (his doctoral research was in Barth's doctrine of election) is that Barth takes an extended look at the doctrines associated with her in volume 1/2 of the *Church Dogmatics*.[23] But even here, Colwell in following Barth, perhaps, in rejecting any theology of Mary independent of the christological context, is typical. Barth writes, "It is her 'low estate' . . . and the glory of God which encounters her, not her own person, which can properly be made the object of a special consideration, doctrine and veneration . . . Along with John the Baptist Mary is at once the personal climax of the Old Testament, and the first man of the New Testament . . . she is only important as the one who receives and is blessed."[24]

What then might be the particular perspective of a celebration of the Annunciation which the Order for Baptist Ministry might pursue in its daily office for that day? A clue emerges from one of the most famous

---

22. Colwell, *Rhythm of Doctrine*, 37.

23. Barth, *Church Dogmatics*, 2/1, 138–46, 174–202. Barth adopts the title θεοτόκος but rejects Mariology as "an excrescence, i.e. a diseased construct of theological thought. Excrescences must be excised," 139.

24. Barth, *Church Dogmatics*, 2/1, 140.

depictions of the Annunciation, the third account by Fra Angelico.[25] In 1436 Pope Eugenius IV ceded the church and monastery of San Marco in the heart of Florence to San Domenico in Fiesole, Fra Angelico's monastery. Fra Angelico set about painting frescos in the renovated convent, and amongst them is his third *Annunciation*, found in the North Corridor. The fresco stands at the point of demarcation between the more public space for the lay brothers, and those using the library, and the private dormitory of the friars. This marked "the threshold to the liminal, private space."[26] From here, the friars journeyed through the passion and resurrection, and the joys and sorrows of the Virgin in murals on the walls of this private space. Everywhere Dominican saints meditate in these frescos, reminding the friars that contemplation was a surer way to God than scholarship.

This version excludes the expulsion of Adam and Eve from Eden (a feature of the two previous works) and is altogether simpler. The arms are crossed by both participants in the exchange, Mary's above her womb, the angel's in reciprocity; the setting is a loggia within a garden enclosed by a fence; and the angel's multicolored wings depicts the polychromaticism of paradise. Here is simple conversation without the aid of those visual prompts in the earlier two, more public, versions, such as the Latin script of the angel's words,[27] or the light from heaven depicting the moment of conception. These become inner moves for contemplation, rather than the more explicit depictions in the Museo del Prado or Cortona versions.

Two aspects of the Order for Baptist Ministry emerge with clarity from this painting, and could be imbedded in the annunciation theme and its office. The first is the way in which the order is self-consciously contemplative, eschewing a view of ministry that is unreflectively activist. At its heart the order understands that ministry is less about how much is done than what is offered in the doing, less about what is done than who is the agent of that activity, and most of all, a dependence upon the gracious activity of the Spirit through the life and work of the minister that has as its goal an assurance that this is God's work and not simply the minister's. This requires a contemplative approach, and a willingness to engage in that "right royal waste of time" which is prayerful waiting upon God. In Luke's account Mary can do very little except be available: she does not have to persuade Joseph to be the father, nor find another husband to impregnate her in order to fulfill Gabriel's word (and one is reminded of John's prologue in the Fourth

25. I have discussed all three in Goodliff, *Shaped for Service*, 205–8.

26. Cole, *Fra Angelico*, 137.

27. SPS S SUPVEIET I TE VIRT ALTISI OBUBRA BIT TIBI, with Mary's words upsidedown ("Here I am the Servant of the Lord . . . ," ECCE ACI LLA DO MINI . . . VBV TUUM).

Gospel where he describes all those who through faith in Christ receive the right to become children of God, "born not of blood nor of the will of the flesh, or of the will of man, but of God"), but she simply has to receive the Holy Spirit, and be willing. This is the supreme example of the person who is first a recipient of grace ("Greetings favored one! The Lord is with you . . . you have found favor with God," Luke 1:28, 30) out of which her response is willing and humble obedience. In the exercise of ministry, this is always the right direction of movement. This is not to decry all the intellectual and practical preparation for ministry that John Colwell has devoted much of his working life to instill in generations of Spurgeon's College students—all that is very necessary. However, such preparation is not the well-spring of ministry, simple the humble and obedient response to the call of God to participate in the divine mission and nature. So, the Annunciation in its contemplative and profound simplicity reminds ministers that being precedes doing, and while angelic commissions might be as rare as hen's teeth, the open Scriptures become the commissioning and saving Word that is ever available.

The second Annunciation theme from Fra Angelico's San Marco depiction is found not in the character of the work, but in its location in that liminal space between the public and private quarters of the monastery. Fra Angelico chose the Annunciation for the fresco that is both the first in the private space where the friars lived and the last in the public space that included the monastery's library. At the turn of the stair, at this hinge in the buildings habitus, it is this story that he paints. The friars had both a public and private role, unlike the entirely contemplative orders that sought remoteness and avoidance of others where possible. Here is Mary's calling, away from a simply private existence to one that will take her to the most public of deaths, that of her son on the cross. In a similar way ministry is a calling away from a merely private discipleship to one that is very public in its exemplary intentionality, and it begins with a "yes" to God's gracious invitation to become one who publicly bears the word.

But this liminal space has a second horizon, that of those moments in the Gospel narrative when history turns on its hinge and at "the top of the stair" something confronts us which is extraordinary and momentous. The first of those moments in the gospel narrative is this fulfillment of Old Testament prophecy that a virgin shall conceive and bear a son. Without that, nothing would follow. The second is the baptism of Jesus and his anointing by the Spirit, for even the eternal Son in his full humanity can only do the Father's will in the power of the Spirit. The third, the death of Jesus and the fourth, the resurrection, complete the way in which through this life of Jesus of Nazareth history has ceased to be simply "one damn thing after another."

Baptists, with their tendency to crucicentric evangelicalism, systematically underplay the significance of the incarnation, and where they attempt to redress that, it is the birth of Jesus they remember. But that is not the beginning, simply the moment of first breath—the eternal Son has taken human form some nine months previously, as the medieval lyric about Mary's bearing of Jesus, *There is no rose of such virtue*, puts it, "heaven and earth in little space."[28] The first turning point in human history in the story of Jesus is his conception, the Word become flesh, announced by Gabriel to the one who would bear that foetus, give birth to that child, and nurse him at her breast. The church remembers that on March 25, and the Order for Baptist Ministry can and should do so also.

---

28. *There is no rose of swych vertu*, "heaven and erthe in lytyl space," fifteenth-century *Trinity Roll*, Trinity College, Cambridge, MS 0.3.58.

11

Lent and Dissent
Discovering the "Poor"

SALLY NELSON

*In you, Jesus, we find solidarity with our weakness and hurting...
we find understanding of all that tempts us.*[1]

INTRODUCTION

HOW MIGHT BAPTISTS REIMAGINE a modern observance of Lent that resonates with a radical dissenting tradition?

The observance of Lent as a spiritual discipline seems to have been adopted early by the Christian community, both as a time for preparing believers for baptism at Easter, and as a time of fasting and reflection before the resurrection celebrations. Many denominations still practise such disciplines, although Baptist observance of Lent is varied—perhaps reflecting the contemporary variety of denominational origins within congregations.[2] Some Baptists may "give up" some luxury during Lent, and offer this token of asceticism to God as a recognition of our flawed humanity—although with

---

1. OBM Short Daily Office—Friday and Lent and Passiontide.
2. Jones, "Lent," 299. As Free Churches we are arguably more likely to make pragmatic adaptations provided our core ecclesiology is unchallenged.

the significant qualification that Baptists would not want to feel *constrained* to do it.[3] Others may "take up" a discipline for Lent: perhaps connected with a rule of life such as OBM offers, perhaps attending Lent study groups (often ecumenical), perhaps a new commitment to giving or to prayer. Still others will consider that, as nonconformists, we are most true to ourselves if we do not observe Lent with any great rigor.[4] Howard Williams, in a rare Baptist publication on Lent, comments: "When I was a boy in Wales we did not take Lent very seriously. Most of us had little idea when it began and no knowledge of its end. We felt no urge to fast nor to discipline our bodies with thorns. For us, the solemn progress of Nonconformity was discipline enough."[5]

While Baptists may rightly reject the imposition of practices by any authority other than Jesus Christ as revealed in Scripture (from the first part of our Declaration of Principle),[6] John Colwell reminds us that observing the seasons of the wider catholic church tradition has its own doctrinal and scriptural value. "To celebrate the Christian Year is to engage in theological reflection that is narratival, doxological, and truly systematic."[7] I would like here to explore some aspects of a dissenting theology of Lent for Baptists, based upon John's suggestion that "Christian theology appropriately attempted will take the form of an indwelling of this [gospel] story, being drawn into its dramas, identifying with its characterisations, tracing the movements of its plot . . . [and be] worshipful and prayerful,"[8] but also grounding the argument in the idea that a *dissenting* faith is one that never ceases to remain alert to structural sin, and is thus dynamic, reflexive, and deeply *faithful to the story of Christ*, above any other criterion of authority or power. Curtis Freeman, in his study of dissenting writers Bunyan, Defoe, and Blake, asserts: "To be sure, dissent entails the courage to say 'No!' But it is about more than just the 'No!' Dissent is not simply a case of whining against oppression, resisting institutional corruption, demurring against the affirmations of others . . . Dissent is also grounded in a profound

---

3. Colwell suggests that "to celebrate Lent merely as a matter of denial or abstinence is potentially distorting. Too easily self-denial can slip into a false asceticism that implicitly repudiates the essential goodness of God's creation," *Rhythm of Doctrine*, 72.

4. The reasons for this latter view are probably rooted in a suspicion of repeated rituals that may become "meaningless"; and the lack of an explicit biblical mandate for the penitential practices of Lent.

5. Williams, *Song of the Devil*, 3.

6. For example, see the first article of the Baptist Union of Great Britain's Declaration of Principle.

7. Colwell, *Rhythm of Doctrine*, 8.

8. Colwell, *Rhythm of Doctrine*, 7.

'Yes!' to Jesus Christ as Lord, to God alone as sovereign over the conscience, and to the gathered community where Jesus Christ reigns and is discerned together."[9]

When the Berlin Wall came down in 1989, my own Baptist church in the UK immediately engaged in a process of mutual encouragement with Baptists in one of the former Eastern Bloc countries. These Baptist Christians formed a tiny Christian minority (there existed also a powerful state church), and under Communism our friends could find themselves summarily taken to the police cells on very flimsy grounds—their main crime being that they were perceived to be free thinkers. Quite simply, being on the margins was for them, and is for us, a necessary element of dissent. Once we stop asking primary questions about how our practices reveal Christ, once we become absorbed into the broad culture of church or society, we are no longer holding a necessary prophetic and critical mirror to mainstream practice.

This is our role, but it is not a comfortable place in which to live. The marginal ground of the wilderness, whatever its precise contextual form, is a liminal space that is never particularly friendly or well resourced—but it is precisely (perhaps only) in the wilderness that we begin to see exactly what Jesus' mission is about.

The argument of *The Rhythm of Doctrine* is that the Christian year offers us a way of doing theology that is Christ-centred, life-giving, and concrete rather than theoretically abstract. The gospel is delivered to us as a narrative, not a set of propositions, and we learn best by indwelling that narrative, rehearsed annually and helpfully in the Christian seasons: we can "do" our theology by living it. Indeed, "an abstract Christology, a doctrinal system . . . are essentially inimical to the whole conception of following Christ," argues Bonhoeffer in *The Cost of Discipleship*.[10] As our contexts change and our lives evolve, we can cyclically revisit the essentials of the gospel and reexamine our faithful inhabitation of them. To this end, the offices of OBM offer one way (though not the only way—we are Baptists, after all!) of recalling and indwelling the story. The prayer that features in every OBM daily office described as "Reflecting on Our Roots" summarizes the challenges of this lived doctrine:

> Living God,
> enable us this day to be pilgrims and companions:
> committed to the way of Christ,

---

9. Freeman, *Undomesticated Dissent*, 5. See also Thomas Merton's introductory chapter to *The Wisdom of the Desert*.

10. Bonhoeffer, *Cost of Discipleship*, 50.

faithful to the call of Christ,
discerning the mind of Christ,
offering the welcome of Christ,
growing in the likeness of Christ,
engaging in the mission of Christ,
in the world that belongs to Christ.

With this prayer and the OBM Lenten offices in mind, and with the narrative of Jesus's time in the wilderness in Luke 4:1–13 as a biblical reference point, this essay will explore something of what it means to live as a disciple within the Baptist tradition.

John challenges us to explore the "authentic" life, suggesting that repentance—a feature of Lenten reflection—can be understood as the move away from "inauthentic" living, towards a deeper commitment to Christ.[11] Our question here is how can Lent, often seen as a practice of the ecclesial establishment, serve our faithful dissent? Perhaps by exploring truthfully our understanding of our status as outsiders: biblically, the "poor."

CALLED INTO A DISSENTING SPACE

Earlier, we asserted that being a Baptist has always meant dissent: to be a marginal, edgy, prophetic, wilderness people who are not in the centre of things, but who offer an external critique.[12] Whether we are truly happy with occupying this space in the success-oriented, resource-poor, growth-focused twenty-first century is another matter! Yet the narrative of Scripture offers us numerous examples of voices "crying in the wilderness": patriarchs, judges, prophets, kings, disciples, apostles, young men (and even some women!); unafraid to speak the word of the Lord into an unsympathetic situation. To say this is *not* to assert in a partisan manner that all mainstream practices are corrupt or idolatrous, but merely to state that those occupying any majority carry a responsibility to be self-critical and to make themselves vulnerable enough to hear others, for there is always truth to be spoken bravely from another perspective.[13] Jesus said, "You always have the poor with you" (Matt 26:11; Mark 14:7), and we can be sure that however many injustices or exclusions we consciously address or eliminate, new ones

---

11. Colwell, *Rhythm of Doctrine*, 69ff.

12. This idea is also explored from a disability perspective in Nelson, *Thousand Crucifixions*.

13. Freeman's *Undomesticated Dissent* explores this dimension of religious non-conformity and argues that dissent and democracy are necessarily yoked together in a healthy society.

will emerge as culture evolves and changes. The poor will be sociopolitically reconstituted until the eschatological renewal of all creation: as Williams explains, the world's problems do not have a political solution for "the gift of community and brotherhood [sic] [is not ours] to give."[14] As Baptists, one of our core commitments is to be alert to dimensions of structural injustice,[15] and prophetically to challenge them where we can.

What does discipleship entail? In the words of Jesus, "If any want to become my followers, let them deny themselves and take up their cross daily and follow me. For those who want to save their life will lose it, and those who lose their life for my sake will save it. What does it profit them if they gain the whole world, but lose or forfeit themselves?" (Luke 9:23–25). Interestingly, in the light of the earlier warning about unreflected asceticism, there *is* a place here for denial, but one that is explicitly for the sake of Christ.[16] The key dynamic of authentic living is to follow Jesus, and the assumption must be that the authentic life means pursuing the way of Calvary—used metaphorically, for the events of the cross were once for all, but in our following of the Way of Jesus some form of crucifixion experience will be contextualized for each of us.

During Lent we are given a privileged insight into the authenticity of Jesus's own life as the Son of the Father. If we are also to live authentically by indwelling the narrative, as Colwell suggests, then our journeys will also adopt this Christ shape. We may or may not recognise or respond to the call to the wilderness, but there *will* be an invitation for each of us, and this invitation will be a call to a dissenting space, where truth is named and evil is rebuked.

The narrative of Lent begins with the baptism of Jesus; and our denominational commitment to believers' baptism signifies a promising beginning for this journey of authentic discipleship. When total immersion is possible, together with a personal testimony of faith and commitment, we have a dramatic example of this indwelling of the gospel that is more than reenactment—it is inhabiting the archetypal narrative for oneself. Committing ourselves to Christ in believers' baptism requires of us a public threefold promise: to confess Christ as Lord; to repent of sin; and to live as part of the community of the baptized.[17] This promise encapsulates (though does not prescribe) the authentic life—one that is directed towards Christ

---

14. Williams, *Song of the Devil*, 22.

15. See *Five Core Values*, identified by the Baptist Union of Great Britain in 1998 as follows: we are called to be prophetic, inclusive, sacrificial, missionary, worshipping communities.

16. Also known by Jesuits as "indifference" and explored later in this essay.

17. See Ellis and Blyth, *Gathering for Worship*, 70–71, for suggested forms of words.

in all its aspects. The focus is deliberately dynamic and reflexive, for we are called to indwell a narrative, to live in a certain Way, not to embrace a status. Baptism for us is a visible Word of the Lord in the story of a life, a transformative declaration.

> To be baptised is to abandon an inauthentic humanity with all its vain attempts to dominate, to exploit, to transcend; it is to be re-born into this authentic humanity identified in Christ; it is to accept the way of the Cross.[18]

Baptism is to declare that our allegiance has changed, to throw down the gauntlet to inauthentic living. For Jesus, baptism was followed by time in the wilderness during which he is tempted *in extremis* to abandon the authenticity to which he has just committed. The temptation narrative is full of allusions to the comparison between faithless (inauthentic) Israel, and the obedient Son of God;[19] primarily the devil is exploring the boundaries of Jesus's Sonship. But for us and for now, let us note that entering the wilderness is a necessary requirement of our commitment to authenticity—and the wilderness is a marginal place, a place on the edge of culture, a dissenting space in which the Word of the Lord is proclaimed by authentic disciples. This, I would argue, has enormous resonance for Baptist identity in a post-Christendom Western world. We may not be large; we may not be powerful; we may not have resources; but we are called to travel through a dissenting space, by virtue of our baptism and our commitment to this narrative of Christ.

In this wilderness, outside the mainstream, "the poor" are to be found. Our question for Lent becomes this: if the wilderness is the place of the poor, then where—and who—are we?

THE PROPHETIC TASKS OF ATTENTION AND INDIFFERENCE

For each of us, the wilderness will look different. It may be that we decide to go on retreat in the midst of life, to be alone and to be challenged by our own demons; it may be that we find ourselves isolated by circumstances—bereavement, redundancy, illness, cultural displacement. Jesus's humanity was real and not assumed, and he was "in every respect tested as we are, yet without sin" (Heb 4:15). Jesus's temptations have a universal dimension (he was fully human) and a particular one (as God's Son in first-century

18. Colwell, *Rhythm of Doctrine*, 72.
19. See, e.g., Green, *Gospel of Luke*, 186–87.

Palestine):[20] we, too, are tempted by power and personal or physical satisfaction, but the form of our temptations will be different. Temptations and sins arise opportunistically within our contexts, and it is for this reason that we need to indwell Christ, rather than to "know the rules" of Christian living. The devil is nothing if not subtle and creative in his testing. Our faith in, and response to, Jesus can only withstand such diverse and unpredictable testing by having a narrative, flexible, responsive character. Our deepest desire must be for God, or we are lost to temptations.

One of the characteristics of modernism (whose cultural influence has not yet departed the Western world) has been a somewhat indiscriminate empiricism, and a tendency to approach all manner of problems and difficulties reductively and forensically. While this approach has delivered unparalleled success in many areas of life—examples being improvements in healthcare, technology, and even the communal exercise of justice—it cannot provide satisfactory solutions to all life's problems. For example, the experience of suffering frequently cannot be commodified, evaluated, or rationalized, and thus suffering represents a seriously discontinuous experience within modernism.[21] "Why?" is the human cry; and if no answer is forthcoming, the person who suffers "for no reason" is even more anomalous. Yet, which among us does not suffer?

In *The Nazareth Manifesto*, Sam Wells explores a significant aspect of this modernist philosophy, arguing that, for too long, Christians have been responding to the key problem of the human condition as *mortality*, whereas in fact it is *isolation*. This argument has profound implications for theology: if we accept that isolation is the problem (and therefore *relationship* rather than *solution* is the answer), we begin to foreground "God with us" as opposed to "God for us" (Wells' phraseology); and consequently our mission is focused less on "salvation from" and more upon "traveling with" (crucially, not "doing for").[22]

For those who *know* they are "poor," the power play within "doing for" is part of their everyday experience. News bulletins are peppered with references to those who "receive care" or "get benefits." We like to "give to" charity or mission for the "less fortunate," and we embrace the concept of "showing God's love" to our communities by giving things away—food,

20. Colwell explores this in *Rhythm of Doctrine*, 63.

21. See Wells, *Nazareth Manifesto*, ch. 16. Viktor Frankl, in *Man's Search for Meaning*, identifies the human desire to ascribe meaning to suffering; I explore the idea with reference to terminal illness in *Confronting Meaningless Suffering*.

22. See Wells, *Nazareth Manifesto*, particularly ch. 3. The same ideas about the value of a person being reduced by demoting someone to the role of permanent receiver are articulated in Vanier's exploration in *Becoming Human*.

Scripture, maybe even time (though often only as convenient within our own schedules). The recipients indeed need all these things—but being a "receiver" all the time is diminishing to any human person because it fails to see that other person as "gift," as Jean Vanier explores so elegantly in his books about L'Arche.[23] Mission that is based on giving, however we interpret that giving, does not see *persons*,[24] only "the poor"—so can it ever be truly transformational? Wells notes that "the conventional way of 'doing good' is based upon a false premise."[25] This is because it (often unintentionally) reinforces the divisions between people: the "haves" and "have-nots."

I agree heartily with most of Wells's analysis, except that I would *not* make a key distinction between mortality and isolation but would see them as different facets of the same stone: simply, human being. While working in hospice chaplaincy, I noticed that serious distress could arise from the extreme isolation that attends terminal illness in a society that is disastrously untutored in the holding of pain and loss. Dying, or being bereaved, places a person in liminal space, a place in between life and death, and if we are not dying or bereaved we do not normally choose to go near, lest we be contaminated by the "unholiness" of this unboundaried space.[26] Without resurrection faith, death and dying are indeed the ultimate isolation of a person, and this loneliness adds significantly to his/her pain. In a society that has forgotten about living well in anticipation of Christ's return to renew the earth, we now try instead to live for as long as possible; and to ignore the discomfiting reminders of mortality that surface in the deaths of our loved ones.[27]

Suffering, pain, and death (or isolation) evade a causal analysis that satisfies the modernist agenda.[28] If, then, our response is such that we seek to "answer" such "problems," we will always be both dissatisfied and pastorally inept. The patient whose cancer has no apparent cause—no genetic history, no lifestyle triggers, no exposure to toxins—is condemned by the buoyancy of modern culture to bear an additional burden: that his/her suffering has no meaning or significance.[29] It just *is*—but this is culturally

23. For example, *Becoming Human* offers an extended discussion of true, dialogical relationship.

24. In the sense of other relational and dialogical beings *like me*, created by God, equally beloved.

25. Wells, *Nazareth Manifesto*, 33.

26. Mary Douglas explores this in *Purity and Danger*.

27. See McNamara, *Fragile Lives*, 7.

28. See Nelson, *Confronting Meaningless Suffering*, for a fuller exploration.

29. Signification and meaning are technically not identical. I understand Paul Ricoeur to argue that meaning is about what we understand, think, and feel (an

unsatisfactory, and we ask: to what can this suffering be attributed? Put so bluntly, it is obvious that this is a crass analysis—yet it happens over and over again, and marginalizes those who are dying. There is not space here to do more than hint at the possible toxic underlying moral assumptions about the deserved or undeserved nature of someone's sickness—or poverty or disability or sexuality: indeed, the poor *will* always be with us, if we cannot be more compassionate than this.

It is precisely the identification and indwelling of such marginalized places that should interest dissenters. Just as Thomas Helwys was able in 1612, long before the formal concept of racial discrimination, to express a belief in the religious freedom of "heretics, Turks and Jews,"[30] so should we be able to *identify* (not superficially to sympathize) with the outsiders (the poor), wherever we find "them." But we are also enculturated, and structural oppression is so very hard to identify when we are part of that structure (even at its margins). How can we pay attention to the poor, while remembering that our call is to *accompany* and not to *solve*? Here the wilderness can truly be a blessing to us in identifying our mission.

The generic concept of the wilderness, or desert, has a long history in classical Christian spirituality. In recent decades there has been enormous interest in rediscovering the wisdom of the desert through contemplative practices and studies, and to examine not only the biblical temptation narratives but also to revisit accounts of the desert fathers and mothers in early Christianity.[31] How does this help our pursuit of authenticity? What is the value in wilderness and abstinence?[32]

I have a child with a severe hearing loss that is combined with other learning, sensory and physical disabilities. Having received hearing aids at two years of age, she is a competent and habitual hearing aid user in spite of her learning problems, so the physical receipt of sounds is not an issue. However, put her into a shopping centre or busy café and she slowly shuts down, ceasing to respond to external stimuli. This is the result of chaotic overstimulation, which she cannot control in the way that a fully hearing person does—my brain can filter out the background noise, but her hearing aids are not so intuitive.

What my daughter has unintentionally shown me is that the amount of "white noise"—physically, socially, and spiritually—that we deal with

---

embodied response), while signification is about that of which it is a sign (directing one to the transcendent dimension, see *Rule of Metaphor*, 57).

30. Helwys, *Short Declaration*, 53. Of course, we should not presume to impose a twenty-first-century inclusive agenda onto Helwys.

31. For example, the writings of Thomas Merton, John Main, and Rowan Williams.

32. Which need not, of course, just be from food.

daily is toxic to the human soul. It prevents us from listening and noticing what we should hear and see. As a result, ironically, we focus on preformed agendas of action and thought, and deliberately shut out the cacophony around us, because we know we cannot deal with it all—and then perhaps miss the particular thing that God places before us.

The wilderness is a place in which such white noise is largely removed. There is little in the way of superfluous stimulation, and so our attention is caught by and will be focused on things that might otherwise seem insignificant—or "poor." A cabbage in a field of cabbages is uninteresting, but a cabbage in the Sahara is a miracle. Belden Lane, in a study of wilderness spaces, discusses how the desert elicits both *attentiveness* and *indifference*.[33] Attentiveness arises from a heightened level of vulnerability or openness. The desert is truly hostile, and our survival is not guaranteed: our bodies are under threat from inside (physical challenge from hunger, thirst and exhaustion) and outside (predation and exposure). We pay attention to our surroundings as never before, and thus we *see* things we have never seen before.

This is our wilderness imperative as dissenters: to see the "poor" clearly—and to recognize ourselves truly *among* them. Rowan Williams put it like this: "We are still refusing to look at certain other human beings in the trust that we shall see them in Christ's image," calling it a failure to contemplate (or to be attentive): "Contemplation . . . is looking and listening and being moulded by what is other. It is recognizing that you are created."[34] As Wells identifies, the difference that we so often (ab)use in our marginalization of the other is actually built into us by virtue of being *created*:[35] we are not the same as God, however much we would like to be so (this is the disordered human desire revealed in the biblical creation narrative of Gen 3:1–7).

The other experience of the desert is *indifference*—a term also used (and often misunderstood!—it does not mean "uncaring") in Ignatian spirituality. Ignatius makes it clear in the First Principle and Foundation of the Spiritual Exercises that indifference is about realizing that men and women are created to praise and serve God, and all other things can be for our use *in order to attain the end for which we are created*—so we do not want things for their own sake, but for the purpose of living a godly life.[36] Being indifferent is about *learning to ignore what does not matter*, to see what we should leave behind. In the light of the gospel, what else *is* eternally important? We

---

33. Lane, *Solace of Fierce Landscapes*, 188.
34. Williams, *Truce of God*, 41–42.
35. Wells, *Nazareth Manifesto*, 56.
36. Puhl, *Spiritual Exercises of St Ignatius*, 12.

know that we are called to subordinate everything to this truth. Bonhoeffer expressed this as follows:

> The cross is laid on every Christian. The first Christ-suffering which every man must experience is the call to abandon the attachments of this world. It is that dying of the old man which is the result of his encounter with Christ. As we embark upon discipleship we surrender ourselves to Christ in union with his death—we give over our lives to death. Thus it begins; the cross is not the terrible end to an otherwise god-fearing and happy life, but it meets us at the beginning of our communion with Christ. When Christ calls a man, he bids him come and die.[37]

Lane explains that a combination of attention and indifference is the unique gift of the desert. The harsh terrain pushes us into a state of desire: we badly want what is scarce and thus valuable. But, crucially, if desire is combined with indifference (so that we can identify—and dismiss—what does not really matter), then desire becomes a focused love for God, as we see in the life of Jesus.[38] "It is here [the desert] that one drives out everything that is not God," offers Foucauld.[39] Of course, we still need bread and breath and human love, but God is the deepest need. This realization is the indifference that is the goal of Ignatius's Exercises. Rowan Williams concurs, saying that impure desire is about needing things to fill us—"I *consume* things—to stop myself being consumed by real desire [for God] . . . Real desire is about recognizing that I have no resting place . . . my journey only 'ends' when it reaches God . . . Real desire can live with an unlimited horizon—which religious people call God—while unreal desire stumbles from moment to moment trying to gratify an immediate hunger, without accepting that 'hunger' is part of being human."[40]

And so, having entered the dissenting space of the wilderness through following Christ in our Lenten discipline, we can pay attention to our revealed disordered desires (prioritizing things above our desire for God), and to the structural injustices with which we may be colluding (but which we can see more clearly when the white noise is removed). By occupying the space of the "poor" we may begin to realize that in our shared humanity we also are "poor," and perhaps this is the greatest potential revelation of Lent.

---

37. Bonhoeffer, *The Cost of Discipleship*, 79.
38. Lane, *Solace of Fierce Landscapes*, 199.
39. Foucauld, *Meditations of a Hermit*, 137.
40. Williams, *Truce of God*, 85.

QUESTIONS FOR THE DISSENTING SPACE

As disciples in pursuit of the authentic life, then, perhaps we have entered the dissenting space and we have submitted to the discipline of the desert. But the work cannot stop there. Just as the overflow of true contemplative prayer must be compassionate action, so the spiritual work of the desert must lead to prophetic proclamation and praxis (interestingly, not the other way round: action should not precede contemplation). What next?

The temptations of Jesus are indeed those of the Son of God, but we can interpret their form as model temptations for every (wo)man, which could provide the framework for personal self-examination in the wilderness of Lent:

- the temptation to turn stones into bread (Luke 4:3-4) can be interpreted for us as the temptation to consume without discrimination;
- the temptation to take power over all the world (Luke 4:5-8) is for us the temptation to use and abuse the other;
- the temptation to test God (to be preserved supernaturally from death, Luke 4:9-12) is for us the drive to seek resolution of tension at all costs: we believe we have the godlike power to fix the world, and want to do so because we are uncomfortable with its raggedness.[41]

It is against these inauthenticities that Jesus takes his dissenting stance. The baptism of Jesus was marked by a Trinitarian epiphany: the Spirit appearing as a dove and the voice of God (the Father) speaking words of grace: "You are my Son, the Beloved; with you I am well pleased" (Luke 3:22b). This knowledge of being loved is prior to, and undergirds, the whole ministry of Jesus. Rooted in this affirmation, Jesus wrestles with the temptations to abandon his authentic Sonship.

Our own starting point for Lent, if we are to indwell the Jesus story and explore our authentic humanity in solidarity with him, has to be based upon our prior acceptance by and beloved status in God—who in Christ stands beside us in solidarity, but who also, in the Spirit, undertakes a relentless journey (let us resist the idea of Lent as a static and boundaried experience) that may include confronting danger, desolation, and testing (see Luke 4:1-13).[42] Three fundamental anxieties of every human being are

---

41. An example might be a church social action project; we can be so busy doing the big things that we do not see the individuals who need our time and love. Jesus could have healed the world, but instead gave his attention to the smaller number who came one by one for healing. The *significance* of our actions is eternally important.

42. Green helpfully clarifies the action as "Jesus, full of the Holy Spirit, *withdrew*

challenged here: the related fears of pain and death; of loneliness; and of disempowerment—but we should also note that one of the key characteristics of suffering, from which Jesus is not exempted either here or on the cross, is not knowing when it will end.[43] The devil comes to Jesus not once, but multiple times (with the promise in Luke 4:13 that he will return when the opportunity arises); food and companionship do not supernaturally appear over this extended period; and indeed, there is no Savior for Jesus, except his deep trust in the power of the Word of God and in the prior affirmation of his eternal and beloved Sonship.

For Jesus, giving in to Satan's offers must have been a real possibility; yet it was simultaneously impossible that he should do so, since Jesus's perfection is helpfully understood in the sense that he is never anything but himself: the beloved Son, in all eternity in full and perfect relationship with the Father, through the Spirit. Whatever happens, he is never other than this. Howard Williams offers this: "Jesus, when nearly maddened by the wilderness experience, wins the victory *because he cannot be isolated*" [italics mine].[44] If he had accepted the devil's offers, then Jesus would have been inauthentically human. If he had given in, then we could be certain of nothing because even God would have a price. In the context of global consumerism, this promise of the real and ultimate existence of unconditional love, narrated to us through the story of Jesus' temptations and his ability to resist them, is profoundly liberating.

What does it mean for us to indwell this story, and not merely to read it? Temptations—which will take the generic, if personally contextualized, form of the biblical temptations—are very real in each human life, and we are free to respond entirely from our inauthentic humanity and to take the devil's shilling. Our dissent comes from our resolute refusal to do this, even in small things. If our discipleship consists of following and serving Jesus as revealed in the wilderness, then there is a certain shape to our prophetic calling which we are encouraged to reimagine each Lent, our annual rehearsal for the inevitable but unpredictable challenges to our authenticity. As the community of the baptized, each of us is now in Christ, and can stand on that prior affirmation of love to energize our own resistance to sin. Will we dissent as Jesus dissented? There are no other ways truly to live than the Way, setting one foot after another, after Jesus.

---

from the Jordan and was led *around* by the Spirit in [not 'into'] the wilderness," *Gospel of Luke*, 193n29.

43. Paul Fiddes explores the significance of this aspect of suffering in *The Creative Suffering of God*, 91. If we know when and if our suffering will end, it is mitigated. It is not knowing the duration of suffering that is a key feature of pain for human beings.

44. Williams, *Song of the Devil*, 9. Jesus cannot be isolated from his Sonship.

Although this narrative gives us three paradigmatic temptations to ponder, perhaps the root of all our own temptations is the same: it lies in the Genesis sin of forgetting our created status, that we are all equal, yet other than God.[45] Deep within each of us may lie the suspicion that we are different from—perhaps superior to—the "others," and our life task is to confront honestly this inauthenticity. It is fundamental to relational being—with God, with others, with the environment. None of us is an exception—and what it tells us (if we will listen) is that every one of us is numbered among the "poor." The poor are not the ones living in sleeping bags in the city centre, dying of treatable diseases in equatorial countries, struggling under economic repression. The poor are simply—ourselves.

Vanier has explored the dynamics of life with those who are deeply physically and cognitively impaired and his insight that their question (which is also our question) is "do you love me?"—for deep down we *do* know our deepest desire: it is nothing other than Augustine's restlessness of the heart without God. To come to someone with disabilities and to assume that I, with my able body, can "help them" is the core of this problem: I am not recognizing that I, too, am poor. I am not recognizing that I am an equally inauthentic creature unless I occupy fully my baptismal status in Christ. To think that I am enabled to "help them" is what Wells would call "being for," the inauthentic version of the divine model of "being with."[46] Vanier summarizes: "We must not get caught up in the need for power over the poor. We need to be with the poor."[47]

To be for without being with is to exercise power over the other, to diminish his/her personhood, and to forget our own poverty. At its worst, it reduces our interactions to transactions, understands life as a problem to be solved rather than a journey to be embraced, separates and isolates rather than embedding relationship. The devil's final temptation (Luke 4:9–12) is that Jesus should appeal to his divine status and be lifted out of suffering. That Jesus refused tells us that suffering, wilderness, poverty, are neither negotiable nor avoidable, but the only way to authenticity, and to enter the wilderness is the way to life.

An analysis by Dorothée Sölle can help us here. Deeply committed to justice and peace, Sölle explores the notion of "death by bread alone," which means "being alone and then wanting to be left alone; being friendless, yet distrusting and despising others; forgetting others and then being forgotten;

---

45. "When, therefore, man lives according to man, not according to God, he is like the devil," Augustine, *City of God*, bk. 14, ch. 4.

46. Wells notes that he is not saying that it is never right to be "for"; only that God is first "with" us.

47. Vanier, "Vision of Jesus," 75.

living only for ourselves and then feeling unneeded . . . Death is what takes place when we look on the other not as gift, blessing or stimulus but as threat, danger, competition."[48]

This is where we finally make the intimate connection between isolation and death. "Death is the wages of sin, the consequence of inauthentic life," says Sölle,[49] and argues that Jesus resisted this kind of "creeping" death, both in his life and in his resurrection. Jesus refused *life dominated by death*, not death as the end of physical life. We do not usually notice the creeping death that so compromises our humanity—a structural death that exists through acquisition, power and domination—for we are wrongly preoccupied and distracted by the physical kind, which is in fact natural for mortal beings, and has been defeated by the resurrection.

"The greatest perfection of a person is also his deepest need: to need God," says Sölle.[50] The pursuit of God in the place of desert prayer is the door to authentic life, and indeed, it is also the answer to the fear of death: the creeping sort and the final sort. And it is in the place of desert prayer that we recognize our deepest desire to be God and then pursue it relentlessly, to be in a state of consolation, as Ignatius would term it, knowing that the ultimate consolation is physical death, when our pursuit of God comes to fruition.

Our Lenten dissent can be no less than this: willingly to enter a marginal space without a promise of resolution; to attend to small things and see our shared state of poverty; to learn what really matters (God); and to stand with courage against the fear of death, wherever we should find it.

> Suffering Lord,
> you knew the pangs of hunger,
> the agony of thirst,
> the burning heat of the noonday sun,
> the chill of a desert night,
> and the power of temptation
> through forty days in the place of testing.
> Come to us now and deliver us from evil,
> that with you we may watch and pray. Amen.[51]

---

48. Sölle, *Inward Road*, 3–4.
49. Sölle, *Inward Road*, 6.
50. Sölle, *Inward Road*, 133.
51. OBM Alternative Daily Office—Friday and Lent with Passiontide—Suffering God.

12

Passiontide
Soteriology and the Prayers of Passiontide

Stephen R. Holmes

Gracious Lord, the crown you wear as King of all is a crown of piercing thorns; your brow bears the marks of your passion.[1]

LEX ORANDI LEX CREDENDI: BY WAY OF INTRODUCTION

JOHN COLWELL WAS NOT quite the first to teach me theology—that was Nigel Wright—but his teaching was the most formative of my early career by some distance. He arrived to teach doctrine at Spurgeon's College when I was in my third year of study there, pursuing an MTh in Christian Doctrine under his and Nigel's guidance.

I have many memories of John in those early years; one is that he was self-consciously *systematic*: the questions of how the doctrines (and practices) of the Christian faith related to each other, and why that mattered, was something that he reflected on repeatedly and generatively. To take only one example, he redesigned the theology curriculum in those years at Spurgeon's

---

1. OBM Alternative Daily Office—Friday and Lent and Passiontide—Suffering God.

to an explicitly Trinitarian pattern: God the Father, the doctrine of God, the doctrines of creation, providence, and predestination in year 1; God the Son, Christology, and soteriology in year 2; God the Spirit, eschatology, and ecclesiology in year 3. Of course, curricula are redesigned regularly in all sorts of ways, but so intentional a theological shaping remains unique in my experience, at least.

When John came to write a sketch of Christian dogmatics, however, he adopted a different approach. *The Rhythm of Doctrine* proposes a systematic theology structured according to the seasons of the Christian year. John confesses in the book that he knows no one who has attempted such a thing before, although he then owns a suspicion that this is a result of his ignorance rather than his inventiveness;[2] I know no other example either, and I suspect John modestly underestimated his own originality here. He hints at what may well be the reason for this: he identifies (rightly of course) the flow of the liturgical seasons as a narrative structure.[3] This turn to narrative as an organizing feature of dogmatics brings to mind the proposals of the Yale School, and perhaps John's sketched programme might be seen as belonging within this post-liberal turn. (The facts that the closest previous example he can find is Wainwright, and that he acknowledges Hauerwas as a key inspiration for the move, might both support this reading.[4]) If we read *Rhythm* as a post-liberal proposal, then it is perhaps not surprising that it was novel: the movement was relatively young.

John cites Hauerwas's own pedagogical decision to structure his ethical teaching around the eucharistic liturgy as a key inspiration for *Rhythm*;[5] with this in mind, John's proposal might be read as a bold application of Prosper of Aquitaine's ancient maxim, *lex orandi lex credendi* ("the rule of prayer is the rule of faith"); in the book, however, this is worked out only at the level of organisation. Although each chapter begins and ends with a prayer (all, I think, collects taken from the SSF office *Celebrating Common Prayer*), the development of the doctrines in the chapters between those prayers is structured narratively rather than liturgically. The chapter that encompasses passiontide, for example, entitled "The One Who Journeys to the Cross,"[6] begins with reflection of the developing self-knowledge of the infant Christ, and moves through baptism and temptation and then straight to Gethsemane. The doctrinal questions discussed might be classed

2. Colwell, *Rhythm of Doctrine*, vii.
3. Colwell, *Rhythm of Doctrine*, 7–8.
4. Colwell, *Rhythm of Doctrine*, viiin2; 1.
5. Colwell, *Rhythm of Doctrine*, 2.
6. Colwell, *Rhythm of Doctrine*, 60–74.

as "christological anthropology": the discussion is about what it means for Christ to be truly human, and therefore what it means for any one of us to be truly human. These doctrinal proposals draw from the narrative of Christ's life that forms the proper reflection of the season of Lent, not from the prayers and liturgical acts proper to that season.

I make these points not to criticize, but rather to expose an alternative possibility, which I intend to explore in this chapter: what if (taking our cue from Hauerwas's practice noted above) we let the liturgical details of the seasons shape our account of doctrine, rather than the underlying narrative to which the seasons bear witness? Would such a procedure be interesting and/or generative? In what follows, I intend to offer some reflections on soteriology through a close reading of liturgical texts and practices traditionally associated with Passiontide, to test the possible value of such a methodology.[7]

Two notes of caution are necessary to begin. First, it is of course not possible to do this as if previous theological reflection has not happened. In writing about the theology of salvation, I cannot pretend that I have not written several times on the subject before. As with John's narratival sketch, I am not pretending to come to the question *ab novo*, but to explore whether the change of methodology leads to shifts of emphasis, surprising juxtapositions, or creative rereadings of this or that aspect of the doctrine. Indeed, I trust that the result will not be too far away from earlier treatments: it would be rather discomforting to find that attention to the implied and expressed theology of the liturgy led to significant material differences from the traditional doctrine of the churches: theologians and liturgists alike surely assume—and hope—that the beliefs expressed in Christian confession and the beliefs expressed in Christian prayer are not at significant variance.[8]

Second, we cannot idealize the liturgy. There are different Christian traditions, with different liturgical practices. Local variations (sanctioned or

---

7. Such a methodology is not new, of course; it represents a form of the "liturgical theology" of Alexander Schmemann (see, e.g., "Task and Method of Liturgical Theology"). Christopher Ellis's *Gathering* offers a Baptist version of this. If what I am proposing goes beyond Schmemann and Ellis in any way, it is in borrowing Colwell's suggestion that such a procedure might structure a full systematic theology, rather than provide occasional essays such as this one.

8. I might note that a version of this worry first led me to write on the atonement. I was at a conference on "Theologies of the Cross" where paper after paper assumed, often mockingly, that the old doctrine of penal substitution was no longer credible. This did not worry me particularly—I had not thought about the doctrine, and had no particular commitment to it—but it began to dawn on me that the prayers and songs of the local church I was then leading would need significant revision if this were true, and so the question became live for me.

unsanctioned) are common, and so an anthem (say) that is felt by one local community to define a season might well be unknown to a different local community, even within the same ecclesial communion. I have been asked to write about Passiontide, which already provides a perfect example of this historical contingency: as a named season, it was removed from the General Roman Calendar by the 1969 revisions which implemented the proposals of Vatican II and were authorized by Paul VI in *Mysterii paschalis*.[9] It is a season that persists in memory, but has no particular liturgical standing today, a profound example of the mutability through history of the liturgical calendar. To speak of "the liturgical texts and practices of Passiontide" is therefore inevitably to engage in a work of selection and construction. Nonetheless, there are practices and texts that are, or once were, iconic, widespread, or both, and that might thus be argued to capture something of the broad liturgical mood of the season. I will simply pick three.

VEILING THE CRUCIFIX: THE ATONEMENT HIDDEN IN PLAIN SIGHT

"Passiontide" used to refer to the two weeks before Easter, beginning on the fourth Sunday in Lent and continuing through Palm Sunday and Good Friday to Holy Saturday. It was, in effect, the second half of Lent, and was kept as a second season, with different symbolism (the old Sarum rite had the liturgical color changing from Lenten purple to crimson for Passiontide, for example) and a different focus.[10] In the new Roman Calendar the focus on the Easter triduum (the three days from Good Friday to Easter Sunday), which takes first precedence amongst all liturgical commemorations, has displaced it.

The commemorations of Passiontide varied, but they were generally muted. An old tradition, which apparently began in the papal chapel, but spread across the Western church under Charlemagne,[11] has all statues and images veiled for the season (possibly excepting statues of St. Joseph, if the season falls in his month of March). This practice has been discouraged since 1969, although it is permissible at the discretion of the local bishops' conference, with the advice that it should be abandoned unless strong pastoral reasons suggest otherwise.[12] The Roman liturgy lost the *Gloria Patri* from various points, again suggesting solemnity. Lent 4 is commemorated

---

9. See Sheppard, "New Calendar," 13–14, for an account of this.
10. On this, see Hardison, *Christian Rite and Christian Drama in the Middle Ages*.
11. See Hardison, *Christian Rite*, 110–11.
12. Sheppard, "New Calendar," 13.

fairly ecumenically as "Passion Sunday"; the Friday following was, until 1969, a commemoration of the seven sorrows of the Blessed Virgin in Roman tradition (a commemoration dating back to the high middle ages, at least); Palm Sunday and the more familiar days of Holy Week follow, and are again ecumenically recognized.

Veiling was common in the Western church by the ninth century; despite recent official discouragement, the practice is still current in Roman Catholic parish churches today,[13] so it may be regarded as a relatively lasting practice of Passiontide devotion. I will therefore take it as my first example of a liturgical act that may suggest theological themes to us. The practice was historically linked to the gospel reading for Passion Sunday, John 8:46–59, which includes the line "Jesus hid himself";[14] statues would be veiled as the deacon read this line.

This seems an odd practice, however, particularly in previous centuries when congregations would have not been universally literate. To hide every crucifix from congregational view at the very moment the focus of liturgical commemoration turns to the passion seems at least counterproductive, if not actively perverse. Durantis (c. 1237–1296)[15] wrote to explain the practice: statues of Christ are veiled because his deity was hidden as he suffered and died; statues of the saints are veiled because it would be inappropriate for servants to appear when their Lord is hidden. What are we to make of this?

The liturgical practice appears to propose that we will commemorate Christ's passion better if visual reminders of his death are veiled. They are, we should note, veiled, not removed: the presence of a large black or purple cloth covering something in the sanctuary is inevitably an obtrusive presence, particularly given its novelty. Hiding the crucifix like this might well draw conscious attention to it—but it remains unseen. It is, so to speak, the obtrusive presence of an absence, a powerful visual reminder that something is now unseen.

---

13. I can offer one amusing witness to this: an academic colleague in Cambridge who worships in a Roman Catholic parish in one of the nearby towns told me of an ecumenical walk of witness one Good Friday recently; on entering the Catholic parish church for refreshments after the conclusion of the walk, he overheard a Baptist deacon exclaim to a friend "Isn't that thoughtful? They've covered all their idols so we won't be offended!"

14. Hardison takes it as obvious that the practice arose in direct mimesis of this dominical act: "The action is a simple and obvious instance of copying." *Christian Rite*, 110. I am less convinced of the obviousness of this link, but the origins of the practice are not relevant to my argument here.

15. Nilles, *Kalendarium manuale utriusque ecclesiae orientalis et occidentalis*, II.188, citing Durandus [*sic*, Gulielmis Durantis], *Rationale diuinorum officiorum*.

Karl Barth wrote a profound reflection on the hidden nature of the resurrection in the gospel narratives: it is an event which is everywhere presupposed, but nowhere observed or described. He proposed that this was because it is in an important sense not a historical event: not that it did not happen—of course Barth thought it did—but it does not fit into any of the normal patterns and theories of history, and so is not susceptible to historical investigation.[16] Paul Fiddes has argued that there is a sense in which the crucifixion should be understood similarly. Of course, as he acknowledges, the crucifixion is observed and narrated and in a sense explicable historically, because of Jesus's attitude to the Jewish law and/or his conflict with the imperial power; in that sense the crucifixion of Jesus is no different from thousands of other crucifixions. Considered as a divine saving act, however, the crucifixion is indescribable and unobservable in just the same way that the resurrection is. Inasmuch as it is *sui generis*, it is not accessible to historical investigation, which relies on identifying repeating patterns in human affairs.[17]

Might we read the Passiontide veilings as a liturgical witness to a theme like this? To understand the passion in any adequate way we need to look away from the mere fact of suffering, even unjust innocent suffering, which is after all common enough in human history. Covering images of commonplace torture might help us to turn our minds away from the mundane and quotidian fact of death to the unique and unrepeatable significance of this particular death. It is not (as we shall see) that it is wrong to find in Christ's patient bearing of pain a model for our own response to our own suffering—the statues are unveiled fifty weeks of the year, inviting us to connect Christ's suffering to the broader mass of human suffering—but there is a moment, as we meditate on the passion, when it is necessary to turn away from that continuity to a deeper discontinuity, to that which Christ accomplished once for all on the cross.[18]

The veiled crucifix points us, that is, to the mystery of Christ's passion, to the deeper reality of divine action in this particular death that is not accessible to observation or to historical investigation. How, then, do we know it? Through revelation, and through faith, which is our trusting acceptance of revelation. Like the veiled crucifix, at Calvary divine saving

---

16. Barth, *Church Dogmatics*, IV/2, 118–32.

17. Fiddes, *Past Event and Present Salvation*, 52–56.

18. To forestall misunderstanding, despite its Reformed pedigree, I do not use this phrase here in a polemical sense. The Reformation debate turned on the possibility of the re-presentation of Christ's sacrifice in the mass; I have my views on that question, of course, but both sides of it preserve the truth I am pressing for here, that Christ's suffering is of unique salvific value.

action is hidden in plain sight. The mere sight of the suffering is contextless and so in danger of being meaningless; it is only with interpretation that it can be properly understood.

STABAT MATER DOLOROSA: REFLECTING ON REFLECTION

As noted above, for a long period until 1969 the first Friday of Passiontide was a Marian commemoration in the Roman calendar, on which the faithful were called to remember the seven sorrows of the Blessed Virgin. The great thirteenth-century hymn *Stabat Mater*, set for the first Friday of Passiontide from 1727 until 1969 in the Roman rite, is perhaps the most famous liturgical expression of this. It invites us to meditate on the sorrows of the Virgin mother, and to share her suffering and pity for her dying son.

The call to be transformed by meditation on Christ's sufferings aligns fairly straightforwardly with the "moral influence" theory of the atonement, which is regularly traced back to Peter Abelard's great commentary on Romans,[19] but finds its clearest expression in various nineteenth- and twentieth-century theologies.[20] On this account, the event of the cross brings change in our lives through inspiration: the example of Christ's patient bearing of unjust suffering on our behalf leads us both to reflect on, and then to repent of, our own failings, and to be inspired to live lives of self-sacrificial love ourselves. This point, it seems to me, is uncontentious: there is a significant theological argument to be had over whether it is, on its own, an adequate doctrine of atonement, or whether it should be seen as an aspect of something broader, but surely no-one would deny the transformative power of meditation on the suffering of Christ?[21]

It is possible, although certainly not necessary, to read the *Stabat Mater* through this lens: the intense focus on meditation on the wounds of Christ and the sorrow of the Virgin invites the reading—clearly, whatever power the event of the cross has for the hymn, it is made real by such contemplation. That said, a more natural reading of the hymn suggests that participation in, or perhaps imitation of, Christ's suffering is somehow the (efficient)

---

19. For an account of recent re-appraisals of Abelard which distance him significantly from the subject/moral influence model of atonement see Williams, "Sin, Grace, and Redemption," 258–78.

20. For one of the clearest statements in English, see Rashdall, *Idea of the Atonement*.

21. To take only one example, Isaac Watts would certainly have wanted to go further, but his "When I Survey" is a pure and profound expression of this theme.

cause of our salvation.[22] Christ's crucifixion, and Mary's weeping observance of it, become together the ultimate example of penitential suffering, which, if we share in and imitate, will lead us to salvation at the last—although even then, the need for mediation (not just meditation) remains explicit in the hymn, with a plea that the Virgin will defend us on the day of judgment,[23] and two variants of stanza 19, one speaking of the cross and death of Christ as (respectively) a "guard" and a "weapon,"[24] and the other again looking to the mediation of the Blessed Virgin.[25]

There is an interesting vicariousness in the hymn. Mary truly—immaculately—loved Jesus, and so her empathetic sorrow is perfect. We are invited to observe her sorrow as a way to learn to meditate on Christ's sufferings as she did,[26] and indeed a substantial portion of the hymn is a prayer to the Virgin that we would learn to feel as she has felt.[27] The heart of the desire expressed in the hymn is to stand beside the weeping mother at the foot of the cross, and to weep with her.[28] The hymn calls us to meditate on her meditation, to reflect on her reflection on Christ's sufferings.

This is interesting. If we believe Ritschl and the nineteenth-century theologians who most fully developed the "moral influence" theory, one of its great strengths is that it is purely Protestant, it removes any account of priestcraft, any need for mediation. Salvation becomes a direct interaction between the individual and God. The *Stabat Mater*, however, suggests to us that we cannot adequately meditate on Christ's passion without someone acting as both exemplar and helper. Of course, it would be possible to reject the hymn as simply wrong—and as a Baptist I would have a great deal of sympathy with such a rejection.[29] My stated aim, however, is to explore the theological suggestions, particularly the striking or arresting ones, of the passiontide liturgy to discover if there is anything generative or helpful in them. Let me therefore pause on this point to explore it.

I ended my examination of the veiling of the statues with the comment that only revelation, and our trusting acceptance of revelation, can enable

---

22. There are variant texts of stanzas 16–18, which complicates this theme somewhat. However, all speak of "bearing the death of Christ" (Fac ut portem Christi mortem) and being "wounded by his wounds" (plagas recolere / Fac me plagues vulnerari).

23. Per te, Virgo, sim defensus [fac, defendar in one variant] in die iudicii.

24. Fac me cruce custodiri morte Christi praemuniri . . .

25. . . . da per matrem me venire ad palmam vicoriae.

26. Quis est homo qui non fleret, / matrem Christi si vidéret / in tanto supplício?

27. Almost the whole hymn from the stanza beginning Eia, Mater, fons amóris circles around this theme.

28. Fac me vere tecum [or tecum, pie] . . . Luxta crucem tecum stare . . .

29. On this as a specifically Baptist theme, see my *Baptist Theology*, 130–32.

us to grasp the reality of divine action in the passion of Jesus. If that is right, then meditation on Jesus's suffering is likely to be misdirected without guidance. Dillistone understood Abelard as standing within a mystical tradition, through which transformation came through understanding of, and then emotional engagement with, Christ's passion;[30] in the tradition of Christian mysticism, of course, there is considerable reliance on guidance—spiritual direction, or canonical obedience to a superior, or similar—to ensure that the practice of prayer is not fruitless or damaging (by promoting spiritual pride, for example).

In the Order for Baptist Ministry we find one of the most developed attempts amongst Baptists to reclaim some of the wisdom developed in the Catholic monastic tradition. Precursors, such as the Baptist Union Retreat Group, rapidly rediscovered the importance of spiritual direction, if occasionally drawing back from the language (even the OBM "Dream" statement speaks of "spiritual accompaniment" rather than "spiritual direction"). "Canonical obedience" is hardly the language of Baptists (the OBM "Dream" begins with "a community of equals"), but perhaps we do need to pause and reflect on the extent to which we do need to put ourselves in the hands of another to do this work of contemplation well.

Of course, even Peter Abelard was hardly the most patient with such notions of canonical obedience, as Bernard of Clairvaux bad-temperedly pointed out, but that does not invalidate the point. In Christian terms, to meditate properly demands a guide, one who themselves is practiced in the art and so can model and teach it. The Blessed Virgin in the *Stabat Mater* fulfills—perfectly—the role of spiritual guide, enabling the believer to meditate well on Christ's suffering, and so to be transformed in good, not vicious, ways. Perhaps the authentic Baptist model locates this guiding and directing role in the community of the local church, which covenants to "walk together and watch over each other"; might we find "canonical obedience" to our local church meeting a palatable idea that encompasses this vicariousness, this need for guidance and direction?

I do not know of an account of a moral influence theory of the atonement that makes space for such guidance, but it is not hard to see how one might be constructed. It would emphasize the fellowship of the church—perhaps pointing to liturgical aids, perhaps to personal relationships, perhaps fairly equally to both—as the proper context for making sense of our emotions and experiences as we reflect more and more deeply on the passion of Christ. Several writers have noticed the appeal of some sort of moral influence theory to an anabaptist/believers' church theology—particularly

---

30. Dillistone, *Christian Understanding of Atonement*, 324–29.

in the focus on a profound personal ethical reorientation as the primary result of atonement/conversion.[31] A communitarian moral example account might align with baptistic theologies even more directly.

PALM SUNDAY: THE ASHES OF THE KINGDOM

Many forms of reenactment of the triumphal entry of Jesus into Jerusalem are known to liturgical history, but most have involved the use of palm branches, or other branches in climates where palm trees did not grow. In Russian orthodoxy pussy willow is traditionally used; in England Palm Sunday was for some centuries known as "Yew Sunday," because yew branches were typically employed for the enactment of the procession.

The development of international trade has now made palms available more or less worldwide, and in many churches palms will now be used. One common practice bears some reflection: Palm leaves will be blessed, and then folded into the shape of a cross, and these palm crosses will be distributed to the congregation, to be retained as quasi-sacramental objects until just before the beginning of the following Lent. On Shrove Tuesday they will be collected and burned, and the ashes from their burning will be used in the customary penitential ceremony of "ashing" on Ash Wednesday.

There is a fascinating collision of metaphors here, both in the variant branches employed and in the practice of making palms into crosses and then into ash. The palm is an ancient symbol of victory, symbolism surely intended by the writer of the fourth gospel in specifying (uniquely) that the branches waved were palm. (The association of palms with victory is present in Jewish tradition, not just Greek and Roman, in, e.g., 1 Macc 13:51.) The yew, by contrast, is associated in Northern European tradition particularly with mourning. In Poland, at least, the pussy willow has similar connotations to the daffodil in the UK—the first plant to bloom in spring, and so a marker of the end of winter, associated no doubt with an Easter and springtime message of re-birth. The symbolism of the reused palms run from victory through suffering and death (the palm folded into a cross) to penitence and the call to repentance (ashing).

Both the variant plants used in Palm Sunday ritual and the practice of re-using the palms in a series of liturgical acts, then, point towards a complexity of symbolism. Triumph is intertwined with death and repentance, and the whole falls within a broader Easter promise that death will be followed by resurrection. Of course, it is not news that, in the gospel narratives, the triumphal entry was rapidly followed by betrayal, suffering, and

---

31. See van Hulst, "Abelard on Atonement," 14–23, and references there.

death, but the deliberate recycling of the same sacramental[32] objects calls us to reflect on an entanglement of meaning, not just a happenstance temporal nearness. This complex of rites would tell us that cross is already present in the triumphal entry—as are the penitential ashes of Lent.

The triumphal entry has the nature of a coronation, an identification made clear by the appeal to the composite prophecy (Isa 62:11 and Zech 9:9) in Matt 21:5. Kingdom intertwines with cross, and the branches used to celebrate the coming kingdom become the penitential ashes. Two theological themes are suggested by this liturgical practice, one common but disputed, the other more creatively suggestive.

First, the deliberate liturgical linking of the coming kingdom and the cross in the weaving of the palm branches into crosses demands that we do not separate kingdom and cross. J. Denny Weaver is only one recent writer to suggest that we should re-narrate the atonement in such a way that the death of Jesus is not intended by God.[33] Indeed, Rashdall had already insisted on as much in 1919, in his engagement with James Denney.[34] The weaving of Palm Sunday branches into crosses is a liturgical act which declares that such separations of cross and kingdom are theologically wrong. Now, Weaver and Rashdall would of course be unsurprised to discover that traditional liturgical acts support the link they argue against; they both give an account of how the church has fundamentally misunderstood the work of Jesus for most of its history, but the theological point is nonetheless there in the liturgical practice.

Second, making the penitential ashes out of the Palm Sunday branches points to a significant theological linkage that bears reflection. Our exuberant celebratory worship at the coming of the King, it suggests, is in some deep way at one with our commitment to public penitence for our sins. The implicit claim is not just that both are a part of a full-orbed Christian life, but that within that life they share a particular closeness of relationship. The proper liturgical response to our own cries of "Hosanna!" is to groan "miserere mei Deus . . ." How might we make sense of this?

---

32. In Roman Catholic tradition, the palm leaves are blessed and are considered to be "sacramentals."

33. "While Jesus' mission for the reign of God may have made his death inevitable . . . neither the purpose nor the culmination of his mission was to die. God did not send Jesus to die, but to live," Weaver, *Nonviolent Atonement*, 74. Unsurprisingly, Weaver references Girard in this connection.

34. "To use a parallel from which some of us might have shrunk had not Dr Denney forced it upon us, the truer representation of the matter would not be to picture Christ as saying, 'To show my love for you, I will jump into the sea,' but, 'To show my love for you, I will allow myself to be thrown into the sea,'" Rashdall, *Idea*, 442.

There are, I think, two sides that are both necessary. First, to welcome Christ as King is to accept his judgment, to accede to his account of what is real. From his self-identification with us in baptism on, his persistent witness is to the sinfulness of broken humanity. Therefore penitence is precisely the right response to the welcoming of Christ as King. If we did not repent in dust and ashes, we would be denying his sovereign proclamation. Second, however, we need to remember that the celebratory branches become crosses before they become ashes. Jesus is King for us, and his conquering reign is devoted first to overcoming the powers of sin and death for us, in us, and through us. So our penitence is hopeful, looking forward to the cycle beginning again as Lent moves from ashes to palms once more—and looking forward to the final culmination of the reign of King Jesus, when "there will be no more mourning or crying or pain."

This theme points to (what I, as an outsider, regard as) the most difficult aspect of the various OBM liturgies: the introduction of the penitential acts with the heading "Acknowledging Our Humanity." We need to repent of sinfulness, not of humanity. This is inevitably particularly problematic in the Friday/Lent/Passiontide offices, with their penitential focus. The "shorter office" does not fall into this trap, affirming weakness, hurt, and temptation as aspects of the human condition. Both the "daily office" and the "alternative daily office," however, invite us to "acknowledge our humanity" by confession of sin and recitation of some form of the Kyrie Eleison, suggesting some irreducible connection between being human and being sinful. There can be no hope in such penitence.

LEX ORANDI: BY WAY OF CONCLUSION

It may seem strange for an essay by a Baptist, in celebration of another Baptist, in a book that will probably largely be read by Baptists, should turn on three practices/texts that are very Roman in origin, and have hardly ever featured within any Baptist church. My justification for such oddity is in part being asked to write on passiontide, which was only ever a Roman season. In part, however, my justification is also pragmatic. Roman, Anglican, and Presbyterian worship is both well regulated by easily available texts and well investigated by competent historians, and so is readable in a brief essay like this. The law of prayer in Free Churches, in Baptist Churches, is less accessible to investigation—and less noticed by history. To do this investigation properly in Baptist life would require extensive ethnographic work to discover what the churches actually do.[35]

35. On this, see (extensively) Ellis, *Gathering*.

In the first sentence of the previous paragraph I was forced to correct "never" to "hardly ever" after being informed by the editors of one British Baptist congregation that has indeed burnt the previous year's palm crosses to provide penitential ashes. Baptist worship, and Free Church worship, is more open to symbol and ritual today than perhaps it has ever been. Some would decry this as a symptom of a theological crisis: we reach for seemingly-meaningful rituals when we have lost the transformative power of the gospel preached. No doubt there are places where this is an accurate description, but I think more often the explanation is more positive. Others would point to the continuing influence of the twentieth-century liturgical movement on Baptist life, which again is not wholly wrong, but I think we are seeing a second stage of liturgical renewal, which recaptures practices and symbols, not just texts. Beyond even this however, we have to acknowledge that we live in a culture that is rediscovering the power of symbol, of art, of ritual—the explosion of public art, much of it iconic (Falkirk's "Kelpies" or "The Angel of the North"), in our time is striking. (It replaces a celebration of "great men" by statuary, which was a very different thing.)

So should Baptists be making ashes of palm crosses, veiling statues, and singing the *Stabat Mater*? Well, no to the last—it makes claims about the role of the Blessed Virgin in salvation that we should be uncomfortable with—and the middle one might be difficult; most of us lack statues to veil. More pointedly, I think we should take seriously the conciliar decision to eliminate Passiontide as a liturgical season—not because we should be bound by Vatican II, but because the reasoning, that the marking of Passiontide in practice detracted from the proper focus of the events of the Easter triduum, should be one we find very convincing. We should emphasize the death and resurrection of Jesus, and practices which have been found by experience to detract from that are not practices that we should look to adopt.

As Baptists, however, we have always felt the pull of the eschaton at least as powerfully as the push of tradition. We were born in the confession that more light and truth may break forth from the Word. If we will not sing the *Stabat Mater* or veil our statues, we can still be intentionally open to recovering, proposing, and disseminating other ritual and symbolic actions that will help us, as the people we are, formed by the culture we inhabit, to be creatively faithful to our triune God's revelation and call. Sometimes—when a Baptist church does burn palm crosses—this might involve reaching back across a thousand years of tradition; sometimes it might involve doing something previously unimagined that may, in God's good providence, inspire a thousand years of tradition.

13

Easter
Constructing Resurrection Narratives

Nigel Wright

Life-giving God,
with gladness we acknowledge that in the death and resurrection of Jesus Christ
you have interrupted our lives with your grace:
a new beginning has been announced and the world will never be the same.[1]

In an article for the *Guardian* online during Easter 2017, Simon Gathercole of the University of Cambridge responded to the question, "How confident can we be that Jesus Christ actually lived?" His short article reviewed the evidence and then concluded, "These abundant historical references leave us with little reasonable doubt that Jesus lived and died. The more interesting question—which goes beyond history and objective fact—is whether Jesus died and lived."[2]

No Christian, of course, doubts that the resurrection of Christ is the fundamental conviction of the Christian community. What continues to surprise is that the prior fact of his historical existence is still contested. The

---

1. OBM Daily Office—Sunday and Risen Lord.
2. Gathercole, "What Is the Historical Evidence."

reason is plain: If there never was a Jesus there never was a resurrection, and if there never was a resurrection then, given its own claims, there ought never to be a Christianity. Rendering Jesus a myth disposes in one swoop of that troublesome religion. Yet on the basis of supposedly objective, disinterested scholarship, the fact of Jesus as an historical figure remains beyond serious question.

To demonstrate this Gathercole refers to two nonreligious scholars whose expertise in New Testament scholarship is beyond dispute. Bart Ehrman is no friend of Christian belief in general and inimical to certain of its manifestations in particular. Yet in his book *Did Jesus Exist?* he takes aim in the name of historical integrity at the "mythicists" and comprehensively refutes them. His position is plainly stated: "Jesus existed, and those vocal persons who deny it do so not because they have considered the evidence with the dispassionate eye of the historian, but because they have some other agenda that this denial serves. From a dispassionate point of view, there was a Jesus of Nazareth."[3] Ehrman then acutely, and fairly, points out how Christians make Jesus attractive today by reinterpreting him in terms that are meaningful to us rather than true to a first-century Jew with "outdated" ideas, and so "transform the historical Jesus into a creature that we have invented for ourselves and for our own purposes."[4] Rather than assert the Jesus of history to be a myth, secular humanists should do the opposite: to expose the fact that the real, first-century Jesus was an apocalyptic prophet who as such remains profoundly *unattractive* to right-thinking people today: "Jesus did exist. He was simply not the person that most modern believers today think he was."[5] Good reason for not believing in him.[6]

Ehrman's portrayal of Jesus should be contested. Jesus is much more attractive than he allows and fits no simple formula. He is doing that of which he accuses Christians, only to opposite effect, extrapolating an unattractive image of Jesus in order to render him unbelievable. Interestingly, Ehrman has little to say in this book about the resurrection.

The same cannot be said of Gathercole's second New Testament scholar, Maurice Casey, formerly professor at Nottingham University, and his monumental work *Jesus of Nazareth*.[7] Casey's work mirrors Ehrman's in the quality of its scholarship. The view that Jesus did not exist "is demonstrably

---

3. Ehrman, *Did Jesus Exist?*, 7.
4. Ehrman, *Did Jesus Exist?*, 334.
5. Ehrman, *Did Jesus Exist?*, 336.
6. Ehrman, *Did Jesus Exist?*, 263–64.
7. It is also well worth consulting Amy-Jill Levine's delightful *The Misunderstood Jew*.

false. It is fuelled by a regrettable form of atheist prejudice."[8] In contrast to Ehrman, Casey deals directly with the resurrection in his chapter "Did Jesus Rise from the Dead?" Unconvinced of the resurrection himself, concluding that at the root of this belief were bereavement visions[9] (to which subject we shall return), he nonetheless generously commends the "outstanding scholarly defences of (the) tradition, the standard works of William Lane Craig, and of Bishop Tom Wright,"[10] and even after many penetrating criticisms concludes with the judgment (as an independent historian): "There should be no doubt, even on the most rigorous of historical criteria, that some of the first followers of Jesus had genuine visions of him after his death, and that they interpreted these as appearances of the risen Lord. In other words, the historical evidence is in no way inconsistent with the belief of the first disciples, and of many modern Christians, that God raised Jesus from the dead, and granted visions of the risen Jesus to some of the first disciples and to St Paul on the Damascus Road."[11] So we return to the "more interesting question": not whether Jesus lived and died—this should be beyond doubt—but whether Jesus "died and lived."

Resurrection studies are alive and well, yet they are by no means without complexity. Writing in the 1980s, Peter Carnley discerned three approaches.[12] The first sees the resurrection as an event to be accessed through the exercise of historical reason. Although falling short of proof, it does nonetheless point to the reasonableness of resurrection belief as the argument to the best explanation. This approach gives an impetus to apologetics and there are examples of those whose journey to faith has begun at this point. It might be added that even here there remains a wide range of interpretation concerning what counts as "historical," where the weight of evidence lies and how historical event and editorial interpretation are to be understood.

A second approach is equally convinced of the resurrection as an objective event in the past but far more pessimistic about the ability of critical-historical research to access or substantiate it through argument. It is rather an eschatological event perceived by faith as "a gift of God with its own *sui generis* claims and beyond the need to set out its credentials," an event of a unique kind that does not yield to the techniques of critical historical

---

8. Casey, *Jesus of Nazareth*, 499. See 499–508 for an excellent summary.

9. Casey, *Jesus of Nazareth*, 488–98.

10. Casey, *Jesus of Nazareth*, 455, referring to Craig, *Assessing the New Testament Evidence*, and Wright, *Resurrection of the Son of God*. Comparably thorough works include Licona, *Resurrection of Jesus*, and Lorenzen, *Resurrection and Discipleship*.

11. Casey, *Jesus of Nazareth*, 498.

12. Carnley, *Structure of Resurrection*, 12–15.

enquiry. In this sense it cannot be "man-handled." Human research cannot capture such a transcendent happening or possess and exhaust what it is essentially "an otherworldly event, defiantly awesome and inscrutable."[13] Carnley suggests Karl Barth as representative of this tendency.

The third category comprises those who reject the idea of resurrection as a post-mortem occurrence in any form. It is rather a response to the life of Jesus in its entirety, the product of faith and not its ground. Easter faith is an "after-effect" of the life of Jesus, a religiously significant myth affirming the general truths that death does not have the final say, or that innocent sufferers will be vindicated, or justice will ultimately prevail.[14] This approach, that Carnley labels "modern reductionist," clears out of the way the difficulties attached to the resurrection accounts, removing the embarrassment of having to justify them as historical happenings. Resurrection becomes the unwillingness to let Jesus or his "values" die. Christian faith escapes the scandal of particularity and is evacuated into hopeful, or fictional symbolism. It is quite literally a "nonevent."

Further categories might be added. What of those who remain agnostic or disinterested in bodily resurrection and yet wish to assert that the exalted Christ lives in God with his identity intact: he is risen indeed, but not bodily so? Carnley's own eventual position appears not far removed from this. The third approach he outlined looks like the refuge of those who have lost confidence in the Christian faith but are unwilling or afraid to let it or its mythology go. By contrast, what is worth saying in the third approach can be substantiated more robustly by the first and second. Any value in the third is undermined by the fact that Christ and what he stood for has been defeated and destroyed, a counter-indication to naive ideas of the triumph of love or justice.

Were I to place John Colwell within Carnley's framework he would fit firmly within the second approach. On the one hand, as an orthodox believer he affirms that Christ was raised, that his tomb was found to be empty. Christ is risen in a way that could never be said of Lazarus, the widow of Nain's son or Jairus's daughter. He is the one who lives and reigns,[15] and unites doctrine, worship and ethics in himself for those who believe. On the other hand, nowhere does Colwell attempt to justify these claims before the bar of historical reason since such reasoning has no purchase on the truths that are at stake. In this sense Colwell stands firmly in the camp of Karl

---

13. Carnley, *Structure of Resurrection*, 24, 73.
14. Carnley, *Structure of Resurrection*, 11–12, 148–82.
15. Colwell, *Rhythm of Doctrine*, 75–91.

Barth in having no interest in apologetics to establish "points of contact" with unbelief.

In keeping with his Barthian formation, Colwell is deeply suspicious of modernist, Enlightenment claims to "pure" objectivity and supposed access to neutral criteria of rationality. He opposes the kind of foundationalism that sets itself up as the neutral arbiter between truth or falsity on the basis of criteria independently determined apart from revelation. The Enlightenment assumption of a detached vantage point from which to judge ethics or determine meaning is proud, overly optimistic and illusory.[16] There can be no detached reason because there are no detached reasoners. Even "secular" reason requires its own kind of faith. Everything is undertaken within the context of existing perceptions and presuppositions.[17] Following Trevor Hart, Colwell rejects the presumptions of both secular thought and liberal theology that they can make "unrelenting appeal to 'reason' as an independent authority to be set advantageously over against both scripture and tradition."[18] Any perspective assuming its superiority over Christian revelation and thereby presuming to negate or fundamentally modify its content is unacceptable from a theological perspective. Such claims are in fact both totalitarian and illiberal.[19] This does not make it wrong to seek for a foundation, simply that Enlightenment thought seeks it in the wrong place.[20] The true foundation for sure knowledge is rather to be found in God's Trinitarian engagement with the world through creation, redemption and revelation. Colwell is no foundationless postmodernist, although he understands the challenges and the opportunities of postmodernity. He finds in the gospel not a metanarrative the powerful might use to oppress, but rather a "sub-narrative" that underlies reality, "the narrative that undergirds rather than overrules, every other narrative."[21] Colwell's hesitation concerning apologetics derives from the reluctance to allow Christian claims to truth to be made subject to external criteria that are themselves poorly grounded.

These are chastening insights. Colwell's suspicion of secular reasoning and of the liberal theology that follows in its wake is further evident in his caution concerning Jesus studies and what is regularly known as "the Jesus of history." There is no such thing as a "purely factual" account of the history

16. Colwell, *Promise and Presence*, 89–90.
17. Colwell, *Living the Christian Story*, 21.
18. Hart, *Faith Thinking*, 168, cited in Colwell, *Living the Christian Story*, 11, 21.
19. Colwell, *Living the Christian Story*, 12.
20. Colwell, *Living the Christian Story*, 22.
21. Colwell, *Living the Christian Story*, 245.

of Jesus because no account can avoid being colored by the significance it finds, or fails to, in the account itself. Attempts to reconstruct the historical Jesus on a supposedly purely factual basis are therefore doomed to failure. Critics cannot avoid bringing their own creative and artistic inclinations into their attempts. This is not to deny the factuality that underlies the Gospels, without which the significance of Jesus would be lost. Yet those facts are not related in a disinterested way. They are inseparable from their interpretations which are inevitably proclamatory and artistic.[22] The reference to the artistic dimension of biblical history is valuable. It serves both to question the self-perception of the skeptic and to remind even the most orthodox believer that in biblical interpretation we cannot avoid the presence of the "artistic" dimension.

John and I entered training for Christian ministry at the same time and have kept pace ever since, including working closely together on the staff of Spurgeon's College and sharing a common field of interest in systematic theology. Our theological journeys have been in parallel and with much shared conviction, despite differences of temperament and approach. Sometimes our interactions have been clouded by the mists of mutual incomprehension and there are aspects of his theology that, while clear to him, remain opaque to me. It has always been evident to me, and equally so to him I suspect, that he is the better theologian and is able to think consistently at levels that come only sporadically to me. Perhaps I do not possess the same propensity for agonizing as does John. Theological wrestling is an emotionally costly business, not least because of what is at stake. I am full of admiration for his theological passion and integrity. At the same time I am convinced he overstates his argument from time to time. Some of his lines of thought I am inclined to pull back from with a respectful "Yes but." His critique of the supposed search for "pure objectivity" seems to me not to invalidate a more modest, self-critical and chastened attempt to exercise honest, free and fair reasoning. The employment of God-given reason is consistent with the New Testament appeal to witnesses and aims at knowledge and insight into the acts of God.[23] Although historical science often deals with probabilities rather than absolute certainties, it is unreasonable to suppose that it cannot also deliver assured results. Where I affirm his analysis is in its rejection of the kind of intellectual effort, whether in secular reasoning or liberal theology, that finally believes itself superior to the Word of God and claims the right to stand in judgment on it. Good methodology should not be elevated to the status of overweening ideology. Patently, this

22. Colwell, *Living the Christian Story*, 71–75.
23. Note the extended argument in Carnley, *Structure of Resurrection*, 132–43.

does not obviate the need for patient and respectful scientific, historical, philosophical, and theological questioning of Scripture and its message, but *under* the Word of God not over it.

Within its limits such thinking is appropriately applied to the resurrection, the cardinal datum of Christian theology, as is implied in Paul's statement, "If Christ has not been raised, your faith is futile" (1 Cor 15:17). In the incarnation God has entered into history and therefore into the realm of historical questioning. As noted, the historical evidence has been exhaustively investigated in a number of recent works. I simply offer some modest reflections.

Objections to the resurrection immediately present themselves, not necessarily irreverently so. Indeed, the dead do not rise, but this is precisely the point: the claim that there is one who *has* been raised marks him out as uniquely significant for humankind given the previous history of which his raising is deemed a vindication. A key decision is whether resurrection faith was created by a prior, objective event or whether resurrection faith simply substantiated *itself* as an event, in which case "resurrection" was not an event at all but a subjective occurrence, a leap of imagination on the part of the disciples. Yet belief that the crucified Jesus had been raised must have been caused by something that was large and substantial enough to give rise to everything that ensued from it. Resurrection was something that first happened to Jesus before anything happened to the circle of his followers.[24] And yet weighing that evidence is no simple matter.

Most thoughtful Christians will be familiar with a way of arguing that took a relatively naive position, the kind of reasoning employed by Frank Morrison in his famous book *Who Moved the Stone?* Whatever the apologetic impact of this work, Carnley is surely right to say, "It cannot be assumed that the various New Testament writers are rightly treated when they are thought to have preserved a set of more or less contemporaneous and complementary but independent reports of the one event, similar to the several reports of the witnesses of a road accident, each of whom describes what happened in a slightly different, but essentially congruent way."[25] Such an approach fails to reckon with the wide and irreconcilable differences between the various resurrection accounts,[26] their sheer "narrative mayhem."[27] Even given the tendency of New Testament scholars to elevate differences to

---

24. Lorenzen, *Resurrection and Discipleship*, 184.

25. Carnley, *Structure of Resurrection*, 18.

26. Carnley, *Structure of Resurrection*, 17. Attempts to reconcile the differences are made by Wenham, Ladd, and Walker. Whatever plausibility is achieved, the amount of conjecture involved jeopardizes the project.

27. Bockmuehl, "Resurrection," 111.

the status of contradictions, those differences remain startling. Nor does it take account of the development of tradition over the period of some sixty years before the final editions of the Gospels.

We might reasonably expect from an historical point of view that the original witness to the resurrection undergoes a degree of adaptation and redaction, even elaboration, for kerygmatic, apologetic and theological reasons. Among the earliest testimonies to the resurrection is Paul's account in 1 Corinthians 15. This appeals to the modern reader because of its ordered and factual account, free of obvious legendary accretion, and remains resilient against attempts to reduce its reliability. It is inevitable that from the beginning[28] that bare outline should be filled out with narratives such as we find in theologically developed form in the Gospels. Here in particular we encounter the kind of artistic construction (not to be confused with fabrication) born of theology to which the title of this chapter refers. "The Gospel narratives and some of the Epistles in the New Testament were in part written to protect the reality of the resurrection and defend its message against denials and inadequate explanations."[29]

Matthew 28:2–4 serves as an example of artistic elaboration and the dramatization of truth. According to Mark 16:4, which redaction critics might argue is itself an elaboration of pre-Marcan traditions,[30] the women come to the tomb, find the stone rolled back and are spoken to by a young man in a white robe sitting to the side. In Matthew, the women come to the tomb, there is a violent earthquake, an angel of the Lord then descends from heaven, rolls back the stone and sits on it. His appearance is like lightning, his clothes as white as snow, and all this happens in the presence of the guards who shake in fear and become like dead men. Later the guards are handsomely bribed and told to say that the disciples removed the body (vv. 11–15). It is difficult not to see in this narrative an elaboration of the tradition for dramatic and apologetic purposes.[31] Does this invalidate the historical core, or is it what might reasonably be expected to develop over a period of time as "an inevitable by-product of the attempt to communicate and defend resurrection belief in different contexts to different people with different preoccupations and concerns"?[32] Despite the differences within the range of resurrection narratives, there is still a basic coherence to the

---

28. Allison, *Resurrecting Jesus*, 234–36, 288.
29. Lorenzen, *Resurrection and Discipleship*, 1, 82–83.
30. Catchpole, *Resurrection People*, 4–9, 196.
31. Levine's amusing comments on the guards are worth nothing: *Misunderstood Jew*, 113–14.
32. Carnley, *Structure of Resurrection*, 67–68.

underlying testimony.[33] This resolves into two sets of traditions, one centering around appearances of the risen Lord and the other around the empty tomb. These two comprise the historical core of what is at stake. However both need to be understood in the context of continuing experience of the presence in the first and subsequent church of "the Lord, who is the Spirit" (2 Cor 3:18).[34] It is, after all, because of the latter that believers are disposed to affirm the resurrection: "Most who believe in Jesus' resurrection . . . have as little need for modern historical criticism as birds have for ornithology."[35]

To suggest that the total New Testament witness to the resurrection comprises a historical core elaborated for theological purposes over a period of time does run certain risks. The first of these is that even the historical core might be dismissed as nothing more than an elaboration, even an "idle tale" (Luke 24:11). This would be the fear of those whose prior commitment to biblical inerrancy, or something like it, disposes them to interpret Scripture to the maximum degree in terms of facticity. Yet the second is that in the drive to take everything as factual history we depart from common sense. It is entirely coherent, and appropriately reverent, to insist that there is a solid core to the resurrection accounts and that that core is elucidated and elaborated over time to expound its drama and its significance. This is particularly the case when there is a disposition to communicate in terms of narrative. In fact this event-and-interpretation approach is consistent with the nature of the Scriptures as we have them which are predominantly testimonies in narrative form to events that are perceived to be acts of God. Scripture is unashamedly and explicitly interpreted history with a theological goal in view (e.g., John 20:30–31). Elsewhere I have applied the same mode of thought to the birth narratives,[36] and it is to be noted that the narratives of womb and tomb that enclose the Gospels of Matthew and Luke have similarities in witnessing to events that are theologically significant but mysterious in nature. Here we have the fusion of history and interpretation, of form and content, the triumph of "portrait" over "photograph" in capturing "the surpassing greatness of Jesus."[37] As Colwell is at pains to assert, the Bible is "a book full of stories."[38] What I propose therefore is that the various resurrection accounts should be read across a span of possibilities ranging

---

33. Note the sequential parallels to 1 Cor 15 in Acts 10:39–43 and 13:28–31.

34. Highlighting this element is the major contribution of Carnley, *Structure of Resurrection*. Despite significant differences note also Lampe, *God as Spirit*.

35. Allison, *Resurrecting Jesus*, 352.

36. Wright, *Real Godsend*, 97–102.

37. Carnley, *Structure of Resurrection*, 352–68, 353.

38. Colwell, *Living the Christian Story*, 69–70.

from the legendary to the factual. What lies between these two poles may be harder to discern than what lies at either end.

Conservative readers of the Bible are as allergic to the idea of legend as they are to the category of "myth," yet unnecessarily so. Despite their popular usage, neither category need denote something that is untrue but rather particular forms in which truth is conveyed. We may imagine these as examples of Christian *midrash* or commentary. Matthew 27 contains what appear to me quite obvious legends in which theology is portrayed as event. At Jesus' death two events occur: "At that moment the curtain of the temple was torn in two from top to bottom. The earth shook, the rocks split and the tombs broke open. The bodies of many holy people who had died were raised to life. They came out of the tombs after Jesus' resurrection and went into the holy city and appeared to many people" (vv. 50–53). Now should it ever be shown that the temple curtain was indeed torn in two I would be delighted. However, the truth that this report stands for does not depend upon whether this actually happened. It would be true either way. In the death of Christ as an atoning sacrifice, the way into God's presence is laid open. The following account of "holy ones" being raised is surely much more difficult to credit as fact. Why is such an astonishing event only reported in Matthew; why is it not referred to as substantiation of the resurrection elsewhere; why are those who were raised not brought forward as witnesses; why were they not numbered within the early Christian community; and what eventually happened to them? Perhaps there is some kind of visionary experience underlying this narrative, but it is more straightforward to see it as a way of interpreting the meaning of Christ's death through legend: he opens the gate of resurrection life to those who have preceded his coming as for those who come after.

To admit such artistic theological constructions permits us to understand other narratives. In Mark's and Matthew's accounts the earthquake and the rolling aside of the stone are indications that a mighty act of God with earth-shaking consequences has taken place; the glory of God shines through the event and makes it luminous; the angels act the part of preachers who interpret that work of God; and the presence of guards refutes the charge that the disciples removed the body of Jesus from the tomb. Such a charge by itself is credible, given what happened in the case of John the Baptist (Mark 6:29); but it also indicates that the emptiness of the tomb was, for whatever reason, beyond refutation. This is communication in narrative form. Yet it does focus the mysterious question of what lies at the historical core. As Diarmaid MacCulloch has it, "The New Testament is thus a literature with a blank at its centre; yet this blank is also its intense focus."[39]

In what is widely regarded as the best "life of Jesus," E. P. Sanders asserts, "That Jesus' followers (and later Paul) had resurrection experiences is, in my judgment, a fact. What the reality was that gave rise to the experiences I do not know . . . Nothing is more mysterious than the stories of his resurrection, which attempt to portray an experience that the authors could not themselves comprehend." Sanders rules out deliberate fraud on the grounds both that several of the disciples would die for their cause and that calculated deception would have produced greater unanimity.[40] In fact, the most secure historical point in the whole debate is that, right or wrong, the first disciples firmly believed that Christ had risen and appeared.[41] "One does not normally give up one's life in defence of one's own fraud."[42] As with Casey, some commentators now advance that behind this conviction was a series of "bereavement visions." This leaves the question open as to whether such visions were "viewer-dependent" or "viewer-independent," that is whether they had an objective or solely subjective nature.[43] If the latter it must be accounted extraordinary in the extreme that, even were bereavement visions understood, they should happen at that exact time, on a temporally and geographically dispersed basis, to those people, concerning that particular crucified person, giving rise to such far-reaching consequences. Yet the appearances must indeed have had a visionary element to them if the experience of the apostle is anything to go by (Acts 9:1–9; Gal 1:15–16), and given the paradoxical notion he developed of a "spiritual body" and a "glorious body" made of light (1 Cor 15:42–57; Phil 3:21). It is also worth

---

39. MacCulloch, *History*, 94.

40. Sanders, *Historical Figure of Jesus*, 279–80.

41. Licona regards this as part of the "historical bedrock," *Resurrection of Jesus*, 372–73. See also Carnley, *Structure of Resurrection*, 89, 90–94, and Allison, *Resurrecting Jesus*, 269.

42. Carnley, *Structure of Resurrection*, 149.

43. Licona, *Resurrection of Jesus*, 564.

considering that visions may have auditory and tactile dimensions.[44] N. T. Wright advances the concept of "transphysicality" to capture a transcendent reality that is both physical and spiritual and that gives the indication of our own future resurrection (Rom 8:9–11).[45]

In a very moving discussion, Dale Allison gives extensive attention to the nature of the resurrection appearances and the phenomenology of visions,[46] in the course of which he offers an extended account of his own, and of several members of his family's, visionary experiences of first a recently-deceased friend and then a relative. The former experience he describes as "ineffably beautiful," "beautiful, and brightly luminous and intensely real," and draws parallels with the resurrection appearances and the consequent accounts.[47] Beyond this he draws no firm conclusions (his exploration is heuristic not dismissive), but the appeal to bereavement visions, or any other kind, does leave us with an ambiguity and a choice, an "item of business yet to be resolved."[48] In the resurrection we are dealing with something mysterious. We may choose the reductionist option and seek "to explain it away." Or we may accept the witness (and evidence) presented us by those first disciples who understood their experience as encounter with a risen, transformed, and transforming Lord, present to them in reality and with decisive clarity and force. Rather than explaining what we do not understand by visionary mechanisms that we also do not understand, we might rather argue from the lesser to the greater: if a bereavement vision can be so powerful, how much more so the raising of the Son of God?

There is a boundary beyond which historical science cannot travel. As Gathercole indicated at the head of this chapter, here we journey beyond history and objective fact. Earlier I located John Colwell in the second of the approaches to the resurrection identified by Carnley and associated with Karl Barth. There is that which is not accessible to historical-critical reasoning. The resurrection is an objective event, but it is not objectifiable. It was eschatological, an event *in* history rather than an event *of* history. As an act of God it remains inscrutable. It was inexplicable but undeniable, real but not public.[49] Historical criticism only takes us so far, but it can indeed take us that far if the historical and the eschatological are seen to be comple-

---

44. See for instance John Cornwell's observations on the twentieth-century visions at Medjugorje in *Powers of Darkness Powers of Light*, 101–5. Consider also Isa 6 and Ezek 2–3 and Allison, *Resurrecting Jesus*, 291–99, 347.

45. Wright, *Resurrection of the Son of God*, 476–79.

46. Allison, *Resurrecting Jesus*, ch. 6.

47. Allison, *Resurrecting Jesus*, 275–83, 275. See also 364–75.

48. Carnley, *Structure of Resurrection*, 245.

49. Lorenzen, *Resurrection and Discipleship*, 139.

mentary.[50] Beyond that the resurrection is to be "perceived by faith as a gift of God with its own *sui generis* claims." The exalted Christ appeared to his disciples as one who had been exalted into the life of God and future glory (Luke 24:26), "a generative event of irreducibly colossal magnitude."[51] As the liturgy for the *Order of Baptist Ministry* expresses it, "a new beginning has been announced and the world will never be the same." Christ is the "Radiant Lord" whom we worship as such not simply at Easter but throughout the year; and as we accept the witness of those first disciples so it is our calling to extend that witness joyfully by word and deed into our world. I am confident Dr. Colwell would agree.

---

50. Carnley, *Structure of Resurrection*, 143–47.
51. Bockmuehl, "Resurrection," 111.

14

Ascension
"Rich Wounds Yet Visible Above"

Anthony Clarke

> Risen and ascended One, your body bears still the marks of your passion,
> taking our humanity into the heart of the Godhead.[1]

My sense is that Baptists are, in general, not very good at remembering—the spontaneous, the new and the extempore easily dominate. Unless a Baptist church follows the lectionary, then even aspects of the Christian year that fall on Sundays tend to be forgotten; so the celebration of Ascension Day, which by necessity always falls on a Thursday, has little hope of being remembered. The same can be true for the work of theologians. It is an easy jump from Easter to Pentecost with perhaps only the most cursory of nods to the reality of the ascension, and John's post-crucifixion account that brings into a single focus the resurrection, ascension and coming of the Spirit can encourage this.[2] John Colwell's own book *The Rhythm of Doctrine* includes a chapter on "The One Who Lives and Reigns" in which he ad-

---

1. OBM Alternative Daily Office—Friday and Lent and Passiontide.

2. Authors who have paid particular attention to the ascension are Farrow, *Ascension and Ecclesia*; Farrow, *Ascension Theology*; Dawson, *Jesus Ascended*.

mits that while the ascension deserves its own chapter it has been slightly squeezed into a seven-chapter framework.[3]

Something similar is true of the liturgy of the Order for Baptist Ministry—at least so far. An Ascension Day liturgy may yet be added in its own right. Where there are clear references to the ascension it is in the orders for Friday morning and passiontide, and Sunday morning and Easter. On Friday morning as part of the opening responses, of becoming present to God, we recall:

> Risen and ascended One,
> your body bears still
> the marks of your passion,
> taking our humanity into the heart of the Godhead.
> In your passion you reveal what it is to be God;
> in your resurrection
> what it is to be human;
> in your glory,
> what it is to make all things new.
> Come to us afresh, dear Lord Christ.[4]

Here are words in whose poetry there is a surfeit of meaning, that offer deep opportunities to explore who Jesus Christ is for us.

Reflection on the texts that relate to ascension in the Gospels and Epistles, tend to begin with more exegetical questions: where, when and how did Jesus go? Further theological reflection might then pursue questions around the presence and absence of Jesus, his continual lordship—now at the Father's right hand—and his ongoing work of intercession.[5] But, taking up two themes combined in the above prayer this paper will take a different route. The prayer offers an image to ponder—"the marks of your passion"—and then a corporate response that recognizes this as revelation.

This image is one which has been taken up particularly by visual art and hymnody. Perhaps the most well-known line comes from Matthew Bridges in "Crown Him with Many Crowns": rich wounds, yet visible above, in beauty glorified.[6] Alongside this we find lines from Wesley, "those dear

---

3. Colwell, *Rhythm of Doctrine*, 80.

4. Order for Baptist Ministry, Friday Morning and Lent with Passiontide—Suffering God an Alternative Daily Office.

5. See Wright, *Surprised by Hope*, 120–27.

6. This is the original wording from verse 2 written in 1851. Godfrey Thring later wrote six further verses with most modern hymnbooks choosing verses from both authors. See Morgan, *Then Sings My Soul*. 125.

tokens of his passion still his dazzling body bears,"[7] and in contemporary hymnody, "he pulls me close with nail scarred hands, into his everlasting arms."[8]

Two of the Gospels, Luke and John,[9] depict the risen Christ bearing the marks of crucifixion, not surprisingly the two Gospels that speak most about Jesus' resurrection encounters with his disciples. These two writers, perhaps reflecting different traditions, point to different aspects of Jesus's resurrection body: Luke records that Jesus showed them his hands and feet, while in John it is his hands and side. In both these accounts it is Jesus who takes the initiative to reveal himself in this way (Thomas only asks to see his hands and side because of the reports of the other disciples) as evidence of both his identity as the crucified Jesus and of the reality of his resurrection. This image continues in Revelation with the worship of the Lamb who had been slain.[10]

The prayer uses careful yet provocatively balanced poetry to combine the image with revelation. Divinity, perhaps surprisingly, is revealed in the passion, humanity in the resurrection, and the possibilities of the new creation in glory, which presumably could be taken as a reference to the ascension. The ascended risen Christ who stills bears the marks of passion is the revelation of divinity and humanity in its eschatological perspective.

The aim of this chapter, then, is to explore further the significance of the ascended Jesus in the revelation of humanity and deity; that is, it will ask what an understanding of the ascension might have to contribute both to an anthropology and a theology more narrowly conceived, to how we understand who we are and who God is.[11]

TRULY HUMAN

The most significant text that deals with the identity of Jesus is the definition from the Council of Chalcedon. Putting firmly aside the continuing traces of the Apollinarian heresy, it insists that, with the exception of sin, Jesus is fully human like us. In its carefully balanced statements it draws on the key philosophical descriptor of "homoousios" to prescribe the boundaries for

---

7. Charles Wesley's version of "Lo He Comes in Clouds Descending."
8. Rend Collective, "Boldly I Approach (The Art of Celebration)" ©2014.
9. Luke 24:36–43; John 20:19–29.
10. Christ is described as the Lamb twenty-seven times in Revelation and the first, surely formative, vision of the Lamb in Rev 5:6, is of one looking as if he had been slain at the centre of the worship of heaven.
11. Colwell offers a similar focus in *Why Have You Forsaken Me?*, chs. 5 & 7.

ongoing christological reflection. Whatever else is said, Jesus Christ must be understood as of the same nature as God and as human beings. The Chalcedonian definition draws on two other Greek terms, again deliberately ascribed equally to Jesus's divine and human natures: "alethos" and "teleios." A key aspect of the ongoing interpretation of the settlement from Chalcedon has been that in this christological formula Jesus is not only described as fully human but also as true humanity, perfect humanity, humanity as it was meant to be; and by implication, of course, true and perfect divinity. As Karl Barth wrote,

> We do not need to engage in a free-ranging investigation to seek out and construct what God truly is, and who or what man truly is, but only to read the truth about where both resides, namely in the fullness of their togetherness, their covenant which proclaims itself in Jesus Christ.[12]

If Chalcedon insisted, against theological pressures to the contrary, that the incarnate Jesus had a fully human soul or mind, the theological tradition since has equally insisted that the ascension should not be understood in the opposite way, as the ascension of the soul or mind *without* the human flesh. There are some, for example, among the patristic writers who toy with the ascension of the soul,[13] among whom Origen adopts most fully a spiritualized interpretation of the ascension,[14] yet the majority of the witness is to insist on the ascension of Jesus in a resurrected human body and so the continuing incarnation of the Son of God. The questions of incarnation and ascension are thus deeply linked; the intention and direction of Chalcedon might then be extended to insist that the body of the one and same Jesus Christ, of the same nature as us, continues in the ascension as much as the human soul or mind was present in the incarnation. What begins as a christological statement has, following Barth above, clear anthropological implications.

In many ways the christological and anthropological questions posed by the ascension are similar to those posed by the resurrection, but they are presented in a more profound and challenging way, because the witness of

---

12. Barth, *Humanity of God*, 47. See Colwell, *Why Have You Forsaken Me?*, 88: "The suffering of Jesus, as the one who uniquely is truly human, is significant and perhaps definitive for an authentically Christian understanding of human nature."

13. Farrow, *Ascension Theology*, 22–24, points to Maximus and early writings from Augustine as other examples.

14. Origen, *First Principles*, 2.3, 2.6, 2.10, in *Ante-Nicene Fathers*, 271–75, 288, 293–96. See Farrow, *Ascension Theology*, 20, for a fuller discussion.

the ascension is that this resurrected human body was not just briefly encountered by the disciples, but is taken up to be with God for all eternity.[15]

The challenges of addressing anthropology christologically include, of course, the particularity of the incarnation. Jesus was not human in a generic sense but was a Jewish, free, first-century man; such particularly is part of what it means to be truly human since there can be no humanity that is not particularized. Colwell tackles head on the challenge of particularity, especially from feminist theologians, and argues clearly that there can be a modern concept of representation that connects a particular and universal and that therefore Jesus can represent and contain all humanity, not just those who are Jewish, male free people.[16] But there is a further aspect of particularity which Colwell clearly recognizes but does not explore to the same degree: that it is this Jesus who was crucified and who was raised from dead and ascended still bearing the marks of crucifixion. It is this particular humanity that is taken up into God's eternal life.

Yet this particularity has been pictured in different ways. We might exemplify this more literally in two paintings from the seventeenth century by Caravaggio and Rembrandt.[17] Both are depicting the encounter with Thomas described in John 20. Whereas Caravaggio offers a shocking realism to both Jesus and Thomas—with no halo but with dirty fingernails—in which Jesus's soon to be ascended body is undoubtedly human, Rembrandt depicts Jesus in a more traditional ethereal way in which Jesus's whole wounded body already glows with a heavenly glory. These two paintings offer strikingly different visual portrays of Jesus's wounded yet resurrected body.

Gerrit Dawson seems to offer a theology much more in keeping with Rembrandt. He finds in the patristic witness a range of views: from Justin's insistence that Jesus continues to bear the marks of his humiliation, arriving at the gates of heaven in the ascension with "uncomely and dishonoured appearance, and inglorious"[18] to Ambrose's account in which Jesus's ascension is described in the most glorious terms.[19] Yet Dawson introduces Justin's

---

15. There is an argument advanced by Barth and pursued by Colwell that we can never talk of the *Logos asarkos* but there is an "openness" to incarnation in God from all eternity. See Colwell, "In the Beginning Was the Word," 51–53, and Colwell, *Rhythm of Doctrine*, 34.

16. Colwell, *Rhythm of Doctrine*, 81–83.

17. Caravaggio, *Incredulity of Thomas* (1602); Rembrandt, *Incredulity of Thomas* (1634).

18. Dawson, *Jesus Ascended*, 61, quoting Justin Martyr, *Dialogue of Justin*, in Ante-Nicene Fathers, 1:36.

19. Dawson, *Jesus Ascended*, 66, quoting Ambrose, *Exposition of the Christian Faith*,

theology as "speculation" while no such caveat is offered about Ambrose. Although he recognizes that the foolishness and disgrace of the cross has become the wisdom and triumph of God, and recounts Henri Nouwen's interpretation of the prodigal son as also narrating the saving journey of Jesus himself, who returns home "ragged from his sojourn with us,"[20] Dawson is cautious about using the wounded resurrected Christ as the basis for theology, lest the ascension be understood in anything but strongly triumphant terms.

The challenge to the tradition exemplified in Ambrose, Rembrandt, and Dawson is that it begins with too human an understanding of glorification, which is then applied to the ascended Christ, rather than allowing the reality of Christ's resurrection and ascension to shape the meaning of glory. Given the way that John, in his Gospel, reworks concepts of glory to be focused on the cross, it would seem quite natural that the encounter of the disciples with the risen Christ who still bears the scars is not marginal but a significant image of the Gospel narrative and central to the theological exploration of resurrection and ascension the Gospels offer.

One modern challenge to such anthropocentric theology has come from those wrestling with issues of disability. Disability theology has been defined as

> the attempt by disabled and non-disabled Christians to understand and interpret the gospel of Jesus Christ, God and humanity, against the backdrop of the historical and contemporary experiences of people with disabilities.[21]

It seeks to "open up new theological space by allowing fresh questions that emerge from the human experience of disability."[22] One of the spaces opened up by such experience has been the deep sense of identification and connection between those who have experienced disability and the "disabled" Jesus on the cross.[23]

Yet the ascension, the declaration that the humanity of the risen crucified Christ is eternally taken into God, offers a different but equally profound point of departure for anthropology. It reveals "the setting of man once and for all, within the open horizons of the Trinitarian life and love,

---

in *Nicene and Post-Nicene Fathers* 10, 4.1.5–7.
    20. Dawson, *Jesus Ascended*, 62, drawing on Nouwen, *Return of the Prodigal*, 55–58.
    21. Swinton, "Disability Theology," 140–41.
    22. Swinton, "From Inclusion to Belonging," 172.
    23. Perhaps the most significant example of this is Eiesland, *Disabled God*.

where he may flourish and be fruitful in perpetuity."[24] Yet the ascension reveals this to be a future in which, while the pain of crucifixion has passed, the physical marks remain, and are given the most ultimate value by being taken eternally into God. Humiliation and disability are not things to be forgotten. Drawing on Chalcedon's insistence on the one, same Jesus Christ, we might equally insist that we encounter the same Jesus through the continuing incarnation in the ascension. In other words, Jesus does not become someone different, but the particular crucified and risen Christ ascends to God, offering an eschatological perspective to our anthropology.

The consequence for an eschatological anthropology is that we too remain the same but are transformed. What it means to remain the same person may, through the lens of disability theology, challenge assumptions about such transformation that will have implications for a wider anthropology, as we all continue to carry the marks of this life in a way that is transformed. This asks significant questions of the meaning of terms such as beauty, perfection and glorification, and does so in such a way as to deeply challenge some of our own human images of human beauty and perfection and our desires for our own future.[25] To expect that those significantly disabled will simply be changed to be like others—in other words like us at our best as part of a "cult of normalcy"[26]—may require such change that who they are has simply been rubbed out and begun again.[27] Sally Nelson suggests that in the same way that sin is forgiven, not erased and Christ is risen but not "undead" "so we can perhaps believe that disabilities are transformed and not eliminated and that in this new community it will be alright."[28]

This offers new insight into one traditional anthropological approach which has been to draw on the Aristotelian distinction between essence and accidence. Thomas Brooks, for example, a seventeenth-century Puritan theologian, represents the Reformed tradition's application of this as an ongoing interpretation of the Chalcedonian formula. Christ must have had those properties essential to being human—he was *homoousios* with us— but not those aspects that are only accidental. Drawing further on the Reformed tradition Dawson offers hunger, fatigue, passibility, and mortality as

---

24. Farrow, *Ascension Theology*, 36.
25. Swinton, "From Inclusion," 179, recognizes this but does not explore it further.
26. Reynolds, *Vulnerable Communion*, 201.
27. Here, as a father of a daughter with some significant, genetic-based learning difficulties, I have particular interests and struggles.
28. Nelson, *A Thousand Crucifixions*, 8.

examples of accidental properties that Jesus need not have owned.[29] Brooks himself suggests that the stamps of dishonor are retained partly for the confirmation of Christ's apostles and partly as an encouragement to us to accept suffering for him.[30] This would suggest that the continuing wounds of Christ are simply an accommodation to the disciples and to us rather than being intrinsic to the nature of who Jesus is and continues to be; as such they could simply be removed in the ascension.

The marks of crucifixion are clearly the result of the particularity of the incarnation, but as integral to the resurrected and ascended Jesus they may point to an aspect of anthropology that is more than merely accidental. Disability theology begins not with "autonomous self-sufficiency" but suggests that "our own human vulnerability is a starting point for discovering what we truly share in our differences."[31] Such an understanding of vulnerability as an essential human property finds its christological basis in the incarnation. Thomas Reynolds sees Jesus as fully and truly human not just in being, but as the one who fulfils the covenantal intention of God found in the history of Israel and does this by embodying God's solidarity with humanity in its incapacity, vulnerability and brokenness. Thus Jesus reveals true humanity by both being vulnerable and by sharing with the vulnerable.[32] But it is also significantly developed in the ascension: the wounds of crucifixion point to the essential nature of vulnerability behind them. Here is the basis for challenging an eschatological anthropology that simply finds human life in our hopes for a particular kind of perfection and glorification, but instead finds a reshaped glorification that transforms but does not lose the vulnerability of human life.

One of the desires of those wrestling with disability theology has not simply been to rethink how those with disabilities can be included, for example, but to challenge and rethink our whole understanding of human life, for those limitations, vulnerabilities and weaknesses, revealed more clearly in those who are disabled, are true of all human beings.[33] For this the incarnation and the cross are significant theological resources.[34] Yet if Jesus provides for us an eschatological shaped anthropology that reveals human

---

29. Dawson, *Jesus Ascended*, 44. The Reformed and Lutheran debates focussed on whether Jesus's humanity was circumscribed and localized or ubiquitous rather than exploring anthropological concerns.

30. Brooks, *Works of Thomas Brooks*, 5:169.

31. Reynolds, *Vulnerable Communion*, 4.

32. Reynolds, *Vulnerable Communion*, 200.

33. See Moltmann, "Liberate Yourself by Accepting One Another," 110.

34. Reynolds, *Vulnerable Communion*, 202–9, draws on incarnation, cross, and resurrection, but not ascension.

life as it is meant to be, then the unique contribution of the ascension is that truly human life never loses its sense of vulnerability and weakness—it does not need to. The suffering of the cross is past, there is no more mourning or crying or pain, but the vulnerability of human life remains. These essential elements of humanity are not obliterated in the future but transformed and held within the grace of God. The eschatological future is not one in which we become the self-sufficient autonomous individuals we may at times strive to be, but rather one in which our weakness and vulnerability will fit perfectly within the sufficient strength and grace of God.[35] So whereas experiences of suffering can certainly, and hopefully, be occasions for divine grace, this eschatological perspective suggests we should positively welcome vulnerability and weakness, in a way we do not welcome suffering itself, as such opportunities for grace.

TRULY DIVINE

As we indicated earlier, Chalcedon insisted that Jesus was perfectly and truly divine as well as being perfectly and truly human. The incarnation, of course, offers the fundamental challenge with which Chalcedon was wrestling, but in the ascension of Jesus God takes humanity into his eternal life. Incarnation is no temporary sojourn but eternally part of God's life as Trinity. Following on from the Chalcedonian definition, the humanity and divinity of Jesus are normally connected together by an "and"—truly God *and* truly human. This tends to lead to a picture of the two natures of Jesus as separate things that are joined together—the debate then being about the nature of the union.

In his book *The Rhythm of Doctrine*, Colwell offers a subtle but profound change to that language suggesting Jesus is "truly God *as* truly human and truly human *as* truly God."[36] The language of "as" instead of "and" offers an alternative way of framing the problem Chalcedon tackles while avoiding some of the positions Chalcedon rejects. There is no sense here that the divine "nature" needs to change to take on humanity or equally that human "nature" needs to change in the ascension. "Christ is . . . no less truly and fully human in the resurrection, ascension and reign. The one who prays for us continually and eternally remains truly and fully human."[37] The

---

35. Colwell writes movingly of his own experience of human weakness and divine grace in *Why Have You Forsaken Me?*

36. Colwell, *Rhythm of Doctrine*, 76, italics mine.

37. Colwell, *Rhythm of Doctrine*, 76.

humanity of Jesus, then, is a proper mode of being of the divinity of Jesus. This takes us back to what Karl Barth has called "the humanity of God."

The essay of that title was written and given first as a lecture in 1956, and is a self-conscious attempt both to affirm and rework his own radical new beginnings earlier in the century. For Barth, the fundamental significance of that term seems to be in its affirmation of God's choice of humankind as a covenant partner. So, "His free affirmation of man, His free concern for him, His free substitution of him—this is God's humanity."[38] This then is part of Barth's wider insistence that there is no second move for God in which he creates and then saves human beings; God's choice not to be God without us is fundamental to God's will to be God. But alongside this there is a further aspect in which he begins to explore the very nature of God. Barth suggests that "God's deity is thus no prison in which he can exist only in and for himself"; rather it is the freedom to be "with us and for us" which is also "to assert but also to sacrifice himself, to be wholly exalted but also completely humble . . . he who *does* and manifestly *can* do all that, He and no other is the living God."[39]

Written in a familiar rhetorical style that pairs together what appear to be opposites, Barth probes not simply God's will to include us in the everlasting covenant but the nature of God revealed in Jesus Christ. Barth's stress always seems to be to return to God's choice of humankind but more implicit in what he writes is the commitment that this choice reveals, perhaps constitutes, God's eternal nature.[40] Thus, we might affirm that in Jesus God is truly human *as* truly divine, and that both humanity and this particular human life is an appropriate, and elected, expression of God's divinity.

It is not only the first half of each of Barth's rhetorical pairings that are true of divinity: asserting, being wholly exalted, almighty, Lord and judge; rather in sacrifice, humility, mercy, service and in being judged God is also being truly divine. Central to any doctrine of the eternal election of humankind must be an understanding that divinity, as revealed in Jesus, encompasses those aspects normally associated with humanity—this is the humanity of God. To weep with those who weep, as Jesus does with Mary and Martha, is truly divine as well as being truly and perfectly human.

We may ask, again, what it is particularly about the ascension which adds to this understanding; not simply the commitment to humanity more generally but the inclusion of this particular human life, crucified, risen

---

38. Barth, *Humanity of God*, 51.
39. Barth, *Humanity of God*, 49.
40. "In the mirror of this humanity of Jesus Christ the humanity of God enclosed in His deity reveals himself." Barth, *Humanity of God*, 51.

and still bearing the wounds in God's Trinitarian life. First, in this image of the ascended Jesus, it is clear that what has happened in the incarnation has not simply been erased but even that the most painful aspect of Jesus's life is in some way taken up into the life of God. One way that this can be expressed is with the language of remembering. The past is not forgotten, nor does heavenly joy obliterate the pain that had been crucifixion. God remembers.[41]

Although this may appear to be a weak notion it appears in Scripture in a significant and profound way. God remembered Noah and Abraham and Rachel;[42] he remembered the covenants he had made with his people; Samson, Solomon, Nehemiah all prayed that God would remember them;[43] and the concept of remembering is deeply intertwined with God's redemption.[44] For God to remember is a profound and redemptive act, deeply contrasted through Scripture with the human tendency to forget. The ascension suggests, then, that God remembers God's own history, and the particularity of incarnation and crucifixion and that such remembering is part of God's divine nature. As we affirm God as, in Barth, the one who loves in freedom, so we affirm God as the one who remembers. That our past will not be obliterated and forgotten, even with its former pain, that our histories and the history of creation, will be given ultimate value is grounded in the nature of God as the one who remembers, for God remembers his own history with us.

Second, drawing again on disability theology, the visible and glorified wounds of Christ point to a God whose very nature is one of vulnerability, Reynolds, for example, describing Jesus as the "ikon of the vulnerable God."[45] Colwell, drawing on Barth's concept of theology as a "thinking after" God's self-revelation in Christ comes to a similar conclusion, although draws more on the language of an eternal "openness" in God. Rejecting the ideas on much modern theology on divine change, Colwell argues that

> the cross of Christ, the entire Gospel story, the entirety of God's story with his people narrated in Scripture, is simply the

---

41. For an earlier discussion of this concept, see my *Cry in the Darkness*, 245–46. This explores remembering in the context of theodicy.

42. Gen 8:1; 9:16; 19:29; 30:22.

43. Judg 16:28; 2 Chr 6:42; Neh 5:19.

44. Exodus 2:24; Num 10:9; Ps 98:3.

45. Reynolds, *Vulnerable Communion*, 198. See my *Cry in the Darkness*, 215–26, for an attempt to outline a doctrine of divine vulnerability.

outworking in our time and space of this eternal covenantal nature of the Triune God: who he is in this story he is eternally.[46]

Colwell's aim here is follow Barth in rethinking the nature of God, while upholding a more traditional belief in God's immutability.[47] While sympathetic to Colwell's (and Barth's) fundamental concern, that the eternal nature of God is truly revealed in Jesus Christ, the ascension, as well as the incarnation and cross, does suggest that there is theological space for both an affirmation of God's eternal nature as well as a carefully defined concept of change. The ascended Christ takes with him the marks of the cross, so that this particular humanity with these particular experiences are part of the eternal life of God. However we are to understand John's phrase about "the Lamb slain from the creation of the world"[48] it cannot suggest an eternal suffering outside of creation. Rather the God, who is revealed in Christ as vulnerable from all eternity, encounters the "no" of humankind which is transformed in resurrection and remembered in ascension. The particular humanity of the ascended Jesus, with the uniqueness and so newness of that particularity, is taken up into the life of the vulnerable God, whose nature remains unchanged. This suggests there is room in God's eternal future for the same valuing of the "new" that we bring to God, which Moltmann also described as the openness of the Trinity to creation.[49]

CONCLUSION

The references back to the ascension in the liturgies of the Order for Baptist Ministers draw helpfully and profoundly on the image of the wounded Jesus. If there is to be a fuller liturgy for Ascension Day, then expanding this image in prayers and readings would be a particularly helpful development. To be brought back again and again to these fundamental questions of who God is in Jesus Christ, and so who we are called to be, is part of the essential formative work of worship. Here some of our tendencies to glorify ourselves and rework God in our own fallen image are challenged by the gospel picture of Christ, crucified, risen, and ascended. Here vulnerability

---

46. Colwell, *Why Have You Forsaken Me?*, 122. Colwell in particular aims his criticism at Moltmann, who, from a Barthian perspective, he feels is not radical enough.

47. There does seem to be some ambiguity in Colwell's account here. He suggests that suffering is "an outworking of God's eternal nature in our time and space, in the context of our sinfulness and creation's fallenness," *Why Have You Forsaken Me?*, 122.

48. And however we translate the Greek, which could, as in the NRSV, be read that the names have been written from the creation of the world.

49. Moltmann, *Church in the Power of the Spirit*, 55–56.

as an attribute of true divinity and true humanity is celebrated and grace is offered for our ongoing and essential human weakness.

John Colwell in his theological work has sought faithfully, and at times bravely, to reflect on God's revelation in Christ in the context of his own named human weakness and vulnerability. We should be grateful to him for the example he has been of pursuing theology.

I end, daring to suggest a revision of the Order for Baptist Ministry liturgy, that might find a place in an Ascension Day text,

> *In your passion you reveal what it is to be God;*
> *in your resurrection*
> *what it is to be human;*
> *in your ascension,*
> *how our humanity is remembered and transformed;*
> *Come to us afresh, dear Lord Christ.*

15

Pentecost
The Rhythm of God on Monday

PAUL S. FIDDES

> Living Spirit,
> present in creation,
> present in Christ,
> present with us now.[1]

GOD ON MONDAY. This title of a book from some while ago[2] invokes the secular rhythm of the week, when the everyday world of work returns after the relief of a weekend, and it promises that God can be met even in the midst of that downbeat reality. The Daily Office for the Order for Baptist Ministry (OBM) enriches that promise with the energy of a new rhythm. Each week Christians celebrate Sunday as the day of the resurrection of Christ; so if we compress the rhythm of the Christian year into just one week, as the Office does for the "ordinary time" of the church year,[3]

---

1. OBM Daily Office—Monday and Pentecost—Living Spirit.
2. Phipps, *God on Monday*.
3. "Ordinary time" is the period outside the time of the great Christian festivals. In the OBM Office, the daily office for a particular day of the week during ordinary time is used extensively throughout the days of the festival to which it refers; so the office for

Monday becomes Pentecost with the reminder that daily life can be lived in the power of the Spirit. It is customary in Christian liturgy to repeat in each week of "ordinary" time the canticles and prayers that belong to each of the Christian seasons, but the OBM Office has made a closer parallel between the sequences of the year and the week than has been usual. So I want to ask what difference it makes to identify "God on Monday" as the Holy Spirit, to speak the word "Spirit" rather than simply "God." We surely encounter the whole triune God—Father, Son, and Holy Spirit—on Monday as on any day of the week, so what might it contribute to invoke the Holy Spirit, to pray *Veni Creator Spiritus* in our thinking, living and worshipping on Monday?

In answering my question I aim to honour the achievement in making theology by my good friend John Colwell, who has structured a systematic theology on the rhythm of the church's liturgical year, calling his book *The Rhythm of Doctrine*. I intend to be in particular conversation with chapter 6 of that book, entitled "The One Who Indwells and Transforms," where Colwell reflects on the doctrine of the Holy Spirit. Since he begins with Advent and "the One who comes," his rhythmic approach is not exactly synchronized with the daily rhythm of the OBM Office (to the creation of which he contributed), but allowing his insights to interact with the prayers and canticles of the OBM daily office for Monday will enable us to ask what it means to participate in the rhythm of God which is distinctively the rhythm of the Spirit.

In exploring this rhythm I will at times take a somewhat different path from John, and this will not surprise him, after many good talks together. But through all that follows I pay tribute to him as a teacher of Christian doctrine who has shown in a remarkable way how rigorous thinking about God can be combined with a sensitivity to liturgy, deep appreciation of the sacraments, rich pastoral experience and faithfulness to the Baptist heritage within the wider catholic church. In short, he is an expert practitioner of the coherent and harmonious living within "the purposefulness of life" that he names as prudence, and which is learned as a habit of mind by "listening to the whisperings of the Spirit through the created order."[4]

SPIRIT: THE METAPHORS

Each day of the week users of the OBM Daily Office are invited to light a candle. But only on Monday, celebrating Pentecost, are characteristics of the candle taken up into one of the opening prayers—burning, flame, and light

Monday is used on every day of the week following Pentecost.

4. Colwell, *Rhythm of Doctrine*, 105.

are associated with the Holy Spirit. The alternative opening prayer invokes God "whose power is known / through wind, fire, / and still small voice" and asks that our hearts may "burn within us" as we pray.[5] A more accurate translation of the Hebrew phrase "still small voice" (1 Kgs 19:12) is "the sound of low breathing," and so we have in the opening prayer two kinds of movement of air, both fierce and gentle—wind and breath—along with the movement of fire which both warms and burns. The liturgy ends with the recollection that the "God of Wind and Fire" has poured out the Spirit on disciples past and present. These metaphors make clear that when we want to speak of our experience of the Holy Spirit we have to go beyond the human, familial images of "Father" and "Son." Scripture offers all the images of fire, breath, wind, and water and adds other images for movement of the Spirit as well—the beating and hovering of wings, the trickling of oil ("anoint us with your Spirit" we pray as we bring our concerns to God in this liturgy), and notably the pouring of water (which is hinted at in the final prayer).

Writing this part of the paper in a reflective period spent on the east bank of the Jordan river, on the site where it is most likely that Jesus was baptized,[6] I am especially reminded of the metaphors used for the presence of the Spirit by the Evangelists as they tell the story of the baptism. Centre place is taken by the beating of wings like that of a dove, but standing by the river we are also aware of the flow of water which embraces Jesus, and the stirring of wind through the reeds along the riverside (according to the Evangelists Jesus describes John as a "reed, shaken by the wind"[7]).

I am not suggesting that these images indicate that the Holy Spirit is less "personal" than the identities in the Trinity that we name "Father" and "Son." No talk about God is literal. God is the supreme Mystery of love; as the only self-existent Reality there is, owing Being to nothing else than God's self, God cannot be known as created objects are known. God is unique, unclassifiable; indeed, through the prophet Isaiah of Babylon God asks, "To what can you compare me?" (Isa 45:6) Since God is strictly incomparable, all images and analogies we use to speak about God must correct and modify each other. They cannot describe God in any literal way, but as we gather them from Scripture and the tradition of the church they can be more or less "appropriate" in referring to God, and God uses them to lead us into the truth of what God is really like in God's own self. Images of the

---

5. OBM Daily Office, Monday and Pentecost, Living Spirit.

6. I was enjoying the hospitality of Prince Ghazi bin Muhammad bin Talal of Jordan, who has created an ecumenical "Baptismal Park" in this area, site of ancient Christian pilgrimages.

7. Matt 1:7; Luke 7:24.

human family—Father and Son—need then to be complemented by images taken from elsewhere in creation in order to begin to grasp and express the immensity of God, and this is what images of the Spirit offer us. Experience of the Spirit is like being caught up in a driving wind, or bathed in water, or soothed with oil, or breathed into, or warmed by fire, or nurtured by covering wings. These natural things are images of Spirit, but since God is "Creator Spirit" they are also occasions to encounter the Spirit anew.

It is not that we invent such metaphors. Central to the life and ministry of Jesus, who fully reveals God to us, we find a "Son" praying to God as "Father," so we can never do without the language of Father and Son. It is not an option to be discarded. But our experience of God will constrain us to use further metaphors to express our relation to God, including feminine ones like "mother" and "daughter," and we ought never to make the mistake of supposing that God is literally of either the male or female gender. In this kaleidoscope of language, the other indispensable image is "Spirit" or life-giving "breath" (whether breath stirring deep in the body or breath blowing through the world as wind) and this in turn diversifies into other images of fire, oil, water and beating wings.

These very images make clear that the Spirit cannot be gendered as either exclusively male or female, although the noun "spirit" and its accompanying metaphors may take different genders in different languages. The Spirit is certainly not the token female on an otherwise male divine committee. The impossibility of fixing breath or fire or water in gender should alert us to fact that the same is true of "Father" and "Son," and these words too refer to a reality that transcends gender and so need other-gendered words to express them. Further, just as language of "spirit" prompts us to realize that "Father" and "Son" are neither literal nor gendered, so it also helps us to see that the "persons" of the Trinity cannot be understood as individual beings or even individualized agents. We cannot think of Spirit, the wind that blows where it wills (John 3:8), in this modern sense of "person," and since the Spirit is coequal with the other "persons," we cannot think of any of the persons of the Trinity in this way either. In any case, this would be to turn God into an object that we could examine, even in thought. It should be stressed that when the church fathers used the Greek word *hypostasis* in speaking of the Trinity as "three hypostases in one substance (*ousia*)" they did not mean a centre of consciousness in the modern psychological sense, and certainly not an individual, but something like "a reality with distinct identity" which they envisaged as always characterized by relationships with others.

Now when we think of our experience of "Spirit," we are thinking of being caught up into a flow of life and love, immersed into a refreshing stream, or filled with energizing breath. We are participating in a movement that we can only say is like entering a relationship between persons. In one of the canticles chosen for the OBM liturgy, St. Paul expresses his experience of being "led" by the Spirit, and finding that when he cried "Abba" (Father) to God he was sharing in a "bearing of witness" that he was a child of God. This experience of Spirit guides us, I suggest, into understanding the word "person" of the Trinity as nothing more and nothing less than a relationship.[8] As we search for appropriate words to talk about God, we can say that the "persons" of the triune God are not individuals or subjects who "have" relationships, but movements of relationship themselves. As God encounters us, we find that we are sharing in relationships which are like a father sending out a son on mission into the world, a son responding to the commission of a father with obedience and love, and a Spirit being breathed out. In the end it is not a decisive matter whether we confess that the Spirit is breathed by the Father *through* the Son (Eastern church) or *by* the Father and the Son (Western church), although the first is more appropriate: what matters is that we are being breathed into.

I am not suggesting that in God there is nothing beyond the relations we know; in God there is always *more*. We cry in prayer to "Father, Son, and Spirit," but we cannot describe the destination of our prayer; we only know that as we invoke these names given to us in Scripture we find ourselves sharing in movements of life and love. God, as Karl Barth tells us, "happens" and the final word about God is that God is "event."[9] The word "person" refers to the event of relation, as Augustine tells us ("the words Father and Son . . . refer to the relation"),[10] and Aquinas was to give this philosophical weight by describing the persons as "subsistent relations"[11]—relationships that are just as real in their existence as any individuals who might have relations. We are not claiming to observe a God who "happens" in relations, but we bear witness to participating in God. What the *particular* character is

---

8. See further, Fiddes, *Participating in God*, 34–55; Fiddes, "Relational Trinity," 159–69.

9. Barth, *Church Dogmatics*, II/1, 263.

10. Augustine, *De Trinitate*, 5:6.

11. Aquinas, *Summa Theologiae* 1a, 29:4.

of participating in the relation that is the Spirit breathed into us I will leave for the next section.

We respect the mystery of God when we equate "person" with "relation" in God. For anything more, we have to remain silent. But we are also affirming that we can only know the relations in God through our relations as created beings, with each other and with the whole nonhuman created order. As John the Elder puts it, "No one has seen God at any time. If we love one another, then God lives in us and his love is made perfect in us." (1 John 4:12). We only know the "Spirit-relation" through relations with others, first because of God's transcendence ("no one has seen God"), and second, because God has made material things like bodies as a means of knowing God, using them to mediate the presence of the triune God. While Colwell does not go along with me in understanding "persons" as relations, all his work stresses that we know God, and here in particular the Holy Spirit, through bodies in the world to which God has committed God's self. This is true of the sacraments, especially bread and wine, and it is also true of the bodies of other people. So he writes of the acts of the Spirit recorded in the Acts of the Apostles, that all that the Spirit effects "is simultaneously mediated through the instrumentality of the Apostles and the host of other men and women who are caught up in the service of the gospel."[12]

THE MEDIATING SPIRIT

If the words Father, Son, and Spirit all refer to relational movements of life and love in which we share, the question arises as to what is distinctive about the "breathing" of the Spirit that causes us to celebrate "God on Monday." Traditionally, the particular working of the Spirit has been described as "mediation," and the Anglican missionary-theologian John Taylor has impressed this on the popular Christian imagination with his description of the Holy Spirit as the "Go-between God." In this way of thinking, the Spirit mediates between ("goes between") the other two persons of the Trinity, between God and the world, and also between created beings in the world as the medium of communication between them.[13] These different levels of mediation are linked up into an overall picture of the Spirit's activity, each kind of mediation implying the other; it is coherent, it is urged, for the One who bridges the gap between God and the world to bridge the gap between events of past and present (especially Scripture and today), to bridge gulfs of

---

12. Colwell, *Rhythm of Doctrine*, 93.
13. Taylor, *Go-Between God*, 5–23.

misunderstanding and hostility between persons in the world, and even to bring Father and Son into a communion of love in the Trinity.

I have made it a theme of my own Trinitarian theology to oppose this understanding of mediation,[14] and here I fear that I must respectfully part company with Colwell who—without reference to Taylor—presents his own extensive picture of the Spirit as the "Go-between God." I do *begin*—gratefully—with John in his affirmation of the material world as the medium for knowing God, or as a "means of grace." Bodies of people, other creatures and inanimate physical objects are all used by God to mediate God's own presence in the world; they can all become meeting places with God, places where we can engage more deeply in the fellowship of the triune God. For example, reflecting on the narrative in Exodus 3, Colwell writes that "God mediates his presence to Moses through the burning bush."[15] There is, then, no unmediated presence of God, and Colwell helpfully emphasizes the difference between the agency of mediation and the means or instrument of mediation, or between efficient cause and instrumental cause of divine presence.[16] It is God who freely, without constraint, makes God's self present *through* physical objects in the world. Colwell thus brings a welcome clarity to sacramental theology: Christ makes *himself* present through the bread and wine; the elements do not make him present.[17]

I gladly affirm with Colwell that the Spirit, in this sense, is a mediating agency, enabling the physical world to be a means of God's presence.[18] What remains, of course, is to identify the particular way in which the Spirit mediates, since the Father and the Son within the Trinity must also be involved in this "presencing" in the world. Here I cannot construct any kind of metaphysical ladder of mediation, such as that offered in the influential account by Colin Gunton. His theory is that the Son and the Spirit are the two agents of mediation between God the Father and the world, overcoming a gap of difference in Being (an ontological gulf) between the creator and creation. Thus, God mediates God's self through the physical world against the cosmic background that the Son and the Spirit are anyway mediating God's presence and activity to creation. Gunton proposes that the Son mediates divine presence in giving rationality and aim to the world, orientating it towards a new creation. The Spirit relates particular things in the world to

---

14. Most recently in Fiddes, *Seeing the World and Knowing God*, 207–12, 271–75.
15. Colwell, *Promise and Presence*, 56–57.
16. Colwell, *Promise and Presence*, 60.
17. Colwell, *Promise and Presence*, 28–30.
18. Colwell, *Rhythm of Doctrine*, 93–94.

this aim of the Son, so that the Spirit mediates between all created beings and God the Father through mediating between them and the Son.[19]

Gunton further proposes that by relating created beings to the Son, the Spirit maintains their particularity and distinctiveness, allowing them to be what they are. This is rooted in turn in an idea about the Trinity, that the Spirit is the agent of mediation between the Father and the Son in the eternal being of God and in this way maintains the distinctiveness of the divine persons themselves.[20]

For myself, I resist this total picture of mediation, which has been popular among a number of theologians. I do not think that the mediating activity of the Spirit—in enabling the physical world to be the place of God's presence—needs to be based in a mediation between divine and human spheres of being, and in a mediation within God's own eternal self. In short, I urge *participation* as the basic principle, not mediation. There is no gap to be bridged between God and the world, because all created reality is already existing and participating in God. Creation means that God freely, and with overwhelming generosity, opens up room within the fellowship of the divine life for created beings to dwell and to flourish. If God is all in all, creation cannot be anywhere except in the space that God makes for it within the interweaving relations of the Trinity.[21] Everything is participating in God, though not everything in the same way. Some may be participating with an attitude of rejection, "resisting the Spirit." But as Hans Urs von Balthasar affirms, the only place where human beings can say "no" to God is within the "yes" that the Son is speaking to the Father.[22] Refusal to follow God's purposes can only happen within the stream of communication already existing in God.

The alternative picture of two agents of mediation coming and going between God and the world derives from a Platonic worldview, in which there are two separate worlds (being and becoming) and some kind of bridging principle between them. The early church, though not the New Testament, tended to adopt this picture, which inevitably implied that God the Father was absent from the world in himself, and relied on mediation. The New Testament affirmation that Christ is a personal "mediator" in the sense of healing a broken relationship between human beings and God[23]

---

19. Gunton, *Triune Creator*, 43–64. So Colwell, *Promise and Presence*, 46–48; Colwell, *Rhythm of Doctrine*, 99–101, cf. 93–95.
20. Gunton, *Triune Creator*, 123, 180–209. So Colwell, *Promise and Presence*, 47–48.
21. See Fiddes, *Seeing the World and Knowing God*, 254–65.
22. Balthasar, *Theo-Drama*, 4:22–30.
23. 1 Tim 2:15; Heb 8:6.

was turned into the cosmic mediation of *Logos* according to the philosophy of the time. Nor do the movements of love in God which we can only say are like a father and a son need mediation between themselves. Father and Son are themselves names for relationship, as is the Spirit. We find ourselves engaged in a network of mutual giving and receiving in love. To suppose that only one "person" (the Spirit) relates the others to each other undermines the vision of Realities which are distinct by the particular way they relate—which includes relation to us. There is no need for one divine person alone to be a "go-between," or a "personal mediator of that love between the Father and the Son."[24] The fatherly relation is eternally "going between," like a relation between father and son; the filial relation is "going between," like a relation between a son and a father. And the distinct *way* that the Spirit "goes between" we shall explore in a moment.

The OBM daily office for Pentecost follows the same pattern as the liturgy for other days of the week.[25] The first two sections are headed "Becoming Present to God" and "Celebrating the Presence of God." The contents of these sections on every day, we notice, assume that worshippers are living in a world where the triune God is present. There is no indication that the presence of one Person of the Trinity is mediated by another. The Pentecost liturgy declares:

> Living Spirit,
> Present in creation,
> Present in Christ,
> Present with us now,
> *We worship you.*

This twice-repeated prayer rightly recalls that Jesus of Nazareth was fully indwelt by the Holy Spirit, as an anticipation of the filling of all human beings by the transforming Spirit.[26] It does not imply that Christ is only present with us through the mediation of the Spirit. Again, in the shorter daily office, we pray to the "God of hope":

> For your self-giving love,
> your enabling power,
> your renewing presence,
> *we praise you.*[27]

---

24. Colwell, *Rhythm of Doctrine*, 95.
25. OBM Daily Office—Monday and Pentecost—Living Spirit.
26. So Colwell, *Rhythm of Doctrine*, 94, 96.
27. OBM Shorter Daily Office for Monday and Pentecost.

While this God is praised for sending the Son and breathing out the Spirit, no system of mediation of this "renewing presence" is hinted at. If it is not needed in worship, should it be needed in theology?

A vision of humankind and all other created beings as participating in the triune God, as sharing in God's own communion of love, does not mean that the infinite difference between God and the world is ignored. Those who hold to a hierarchy of mediation often accuse all forms of pan-en-theism ("everything in God") of confusing God with the world.[28] But the fact that created beings dwell in God does not remove the difference between the creator and the created. It does not undermine the "otherness" of the created world from God, its reality in its own right. What is created only exists in God by God's own loving invitation, not as a matter of necessity. There is only one Uncreated Reality which is self-existent; everything else owes its existence to God, "in whom we live and move and have our being."[29]

Further, the presence of God still remains an act of God, an event. God cannot be absent from the world, but this is due to God's own gracious will. God has determined from all eternity to use material reality as the means of God's presence to those who dwell in God. It is because of the faithfulness of a God who keeps promises[30] that this situation does not fail. All creation lives in the presence of a self-disclosing or self-manifesting God, who has made covenant with "every living thing."[31] The words of Jesus in John 16:13–16, that the Spirit "does not speak on his own account" but "witnesses" to the Father and the Son should not be turned into a Trinitarian dogma in which the Father and the Son are only present in the world through the Spirit. After all, alongside the promise of the coming of the Spirit as advocate, Jesus gives assurance to his disciples that "we [he and God his Father] will come to them" (John 14:23). In the period of experimental thinking in the early church, moreover, the Apostle Paul testifies to an overlap between the respective identities of "the Spirit" and "the Spirit of Christ," so that there is no simple mediation of one by the other.[32]

The Spirit enables the material world to be a means of encounter with the triune God. In *this* sense the Spirit mediates. Yet the movements of love

---

28. So Colwell, *Promise and Presence*, 55.

29. Acts 17:28. It is uncertain from which Greek writer this formulation is quoted.

30. Colwell, *Promise and Presence*, 54–55, opposes the notion of a "sacramental universe" on the grounds that a sacrament requires the promise of God to be present there; on the same grounds I affirm it.

31. Gen 9:12–16. On this inclusive covenant, see Baptist Old Testament scholar Mark Brett, *Political Trauma and Healing*, 96, 184.

32. See Dunn, *Jesus and the Spirit*, 318–26.

in God that we call "the Father" and "the Son" must also act in this way, as created beings are held in the whole divine fellowship. What, then, can we say is distinctive about the presence of the Spirit? Why celebrate the Holy Spirit as "God on Monday"?

THE SPIRIT OF OPENNESS

The profusion of impressionistic images that Scripture and tradition give us for the Holy Spirit contribute to the sense of the self-effacement of the Spirit. The Spirit as "wind" or "fire" does not have a high profile like "Father" or "Son." There is something anonymous about the Spirit, but this does not mean that the Spirit is mediating the Father and the Son to us; it comes from the experience of believers that the Spirit witnesses to God, and the awareness that the divine Spirit is so intimately present to the human spirit that we find it difficult to separate them. The orthodox theologian Vladimir Lossky even speaks about the self-effacement of the Spirit before human beings. He makes the daring suggestion that "the Holy Spirit effaces himself, as Person, before the created persons to whom he appropriates grace." Commenting on the text of Paul that the Spirit cries "Abba, Father" in our hearts (Rom 8:14), which the makers of the OBM Pentecost liturgy choose for the canticle, he concludes that "he mysteriously identifies himself with human persons while remaining incommunicable. He substitutes Himself, so to speak, for ourselves."[33] H. Wheeler Robinson had earlier made a similar suggestion by speaking of the "kenosis of the Spirit" in a humble accepting of human life as the medium of presence and activity.[34]

But the elusive images also have another effect: they constantly *open up* our sense of God, provoking us to go beyond images of God as an agent like human subjects (Father, Son) or beyond any fixing in gender. They awaken us not only to encounter with God but to the nature of God. It would thus correspond to our *experience* of Spirit that Holy Spirit should be the movement within God that is constantly opening up the relationship of Father and Son to new depths of personality and to new fulfilment in the future. *All* the relations in God are movements of being, but we may discern a distinct movement that is always opening up the others, so that another image for the Spirit might be "the disturber." The Spirit does not mediate within God—no mediation is needed in a network of relations—but the Spirit does open up the relations that are eternally there.

33. Lossky, *Mystical Theology*, 172.
34. Robinson, *Christian Experience of the Holy Spirit*, 83, 87.

This picture of the Spirit was offered by a writer who somewhat broke away from the Western tradition of the Spirit as the "bond" of love. Richard of St. Victor proposed that if God is love, there must be a plurality of persons in God for love to be actualized. But if there are only two, love will be self-enclosed. In the most fervent kind of love, observes Richard, you wish there to be another person who could be loved equally by the one whom you love supremely and by whom you are loved supremely. He writes that "when a third is loved concordantly and socially by two, the affection of the two flows together in the kindling of a third love."[35] Perhaps we might add the analogy of love between husband and wife which is opened up and fulfilled by love for a child. In our experience of the Christian life, the Holy Spirit is the One who comes in, who opens up relationships, who makes us look more deeply at ourselves, at others, and our society around us. When the Third Person comes, it is to disturb—and through disturbing, to make a new fellowship. Two are never complete without the Third. And if this is true of *our* experience of the Spirit, it must surely also correspond to the fellowship of the Spirit in the communion of God's life. The Spirit is the disturber, the opener, the third over against the two.

We might be confirmed in this understanding of the Spirit as "the opener" or "the disturber" by reflecting on another aspect of the difficulty we find in establishing the distinct identity and role of the Holy Spirit. It seems especially problematic to distinguish the "Holy Spirit" as a "*person*" (*hypostasis*) from the whole *being* of God as Spirit. When the Jesus of the Fourth Gospel affirms that "God is Spirit, and those who worship him must worship in spirit and in truth" (John 4:24), he is echoing the use of the *ruach* (breath) of God in the Hebrew Scriptures. When the church doctrine of the Trinity develops the incipient diversity in God represented by the personification of divine Spirit, it seems that the word "Spirit" is now being used in an ambiguous way. *God* is Spirit, yet the Holy Spirit proceeds from the Father.

When we speak of the "Spirit of God," or "God as Spirit," we mean the whole being of God in communion, the divine essence, the mutual relating of persons. The Spirit is the fire of love glowing through the divine movements of love that we usually name "Father" and "Son," uniting them in their difference and shining forth from them. But when we use the name "Holy Spirit," we mean that through the initiative of the Father, this common life now stands over against Father and Son as a disturbing element, a movement of being that is always opening up the relationships of Father

---

35. Richard of St. Victor, *De Trinitate*, 3:11, 19; translated in Fortman, *Triune God*, 193.

and Son to new depths and a new future. This is the same life and love, but constantly renewing itself. In the words of Wolfhart Pannenberg, "The Spirit comes forth as a separate hypostasis as he comes over against the Son and the Father."[36]

The OBM daily office for Pentecost offers a hint of this disturbing, unexpected, and surprising activity of the Holy Spirit, opening up new possibilities. We pray that we might "tremble" in the presence of the Holy One, like the trembling candle flame; we give praise for every place that has made us "wonder" and for every moment when "time has stood still"; we make the petition for the Spirit to "enlarge our dreams, and enthuse our minds." The opening up of the future means liberation from the constraints of the present, and following the words of the canticle that "the creation will be set free from its bondage to decay," the prayers of concern remember those "who yearn to break out of their prisons." The OBM shorter office for Pentecost takes up the theme of the liberation that the Spirit brings even more extensively: the canticle affirms that "the Lord is the Spirit, and where the Spirit of the Lord is there is freedom," the prayers of concern are for "those who long for a way through their struggle," and the liturgy ends with plea for the Spirit "to lead us and all creation into your liberty."

If we envisage the Spirit as the One who "opens things up," it becomes clear why "fellowship" is appropriated to the Holy Spirit in the threefold blessing of the Grace (2 Cor 13:14). The making of fellowship (*koinonia*) cannot be restricted to the Spirit, any more than love can be confined to the Father or grace to Jesus Christ. There is no basis in this text for regarding the Spirit alone as a mediator who binds Father, Son, and all Christian disciples in relationship. But *koinonia* must constantly be opened up within itself and opened out to those who do not yet share it, and this is the distinctive movement of the Spirit. To speak of Spirit as the movement of love in God that opens up the future presumes, of course, that there is a future for God. It contests the theology of a static God, existing in a simultaneity of time and knowledge. It celebrates a God who, in freely willing to create, has committed God's self to the path of time and history. Out of God's own desire, the self-presencing of God in a material world will lead to new things that will be formed by God, not alone but in partnership with created beings, and so to a real future. This is no necessity forced on God, but springs from God's own loving decisions.

---

36. Pannenberg, *Systematic Theology*, 1:429.

THE SPIRIT AS WISDOM

In his study *The Rhythm of Doctrine*, Colwell observes that in the early days of the church the Spirit was associated with wisdom, in view of the Spirit's work of a "providential presence and ordering" in the universe. For Colwell (like Gunton), this act of guidance belongs to the Spirit's work in mediating between the Christ who embodies the goal of creation on the one hand, and particular entities within creation on the other.[37] He notes that in the Antiochene tradition the Spirit is thus identified with that "wisdom" of God who appears personified as a woman in Old Testament texts. On balance he prefers this to the Alexandrian tradition in which wisdom is identified with Christ, the Son and Word (*logos*) of God. It was the latter identification which was to win out, however, as the masculine *logos* tended to suppress a feminine *sophia*.

While preferring the characterization of wisdom as the Spirit, Colwell admits a difficulty. The identification with Spirit, he thinks, has a tendency to obscure the fact that the Spirit is only *witnessing* to the Son who, "rather than the Spirit," is the content and object of true wisdom. The Antiochene approach tends to make the Spirit not only the "agent" but the "content" of wisdom. In fact, urges Colwell, the Spirit is the agent for the Son who *is* the wisdom of God. For all that, he thinks it is a "more rounded" Trinitarian theology to name the Spirit as wisdom, preventing the simple assumption of the Spirit into the Son.[38]

My own response to this perplexity is to suggest that the problem comes from a theology of mediation, in which the Spirit has to be a mediating agent of the Son, who himself is a mediating agent of the Father. In this way of thinking, the "content" of wisdom (the Son) has to be distinguished from the "agent" (the Spirit). If we think instead of created beings as participating in God, then there is no need to distinguish between content and agent. We share in a triune fellowship in which we experience all three Persons *as* wisdom, though in different ways, just as all create and all redeem, but in different ways. The way in which the Spirit is wisdom must be in accord with the Spirit as "opening" and "disturbing," though this will need a little more explanation.

A key feature of wisdom is in fact very well expressed by Colwell, when he writes that "[the Spirit] witnesses to the goal of creation and of human life which is Jesus Christ. A life *coherently* and consistently ordered to this

---

37. Colwell, *Rhythm of Doctrine*, 101–2.
38. Colwell, *Rhythm of Doctrine*, 103–4.

goal is lived as true wisdom."[39] We may add that the figure of the divine Wisdom in Jewish literature expresses this coherence, an integrating and making whole of what is "many" and complex in the world. According to the author of the intertestamental Wisdom of Solomon, who equates wisdom with "Spirit":[40]

> Though she is only one she can do everything;
> and abiding in herself she can do all things;
> generation by generation she enters into holy souls
> and renders them friends of God and the prophets. (7:27)[41]

Wisdom is both one and many ("only one, she can do everything"), echoing the previous ascription "unique in her kind yet manifold" (v. 22, *monogenes, polymeres*). The point being made by our author here is not a Platonic one, as if wisdom were a mediator who provides a way for the many to return to the unmoving One from which they have unfortunately fallen away. Rather, wisdom as an image of the goodness of God provides a means for her disciples or "friends" to explore the many aspects of the world; this is a *positive* celebration of the many wonders of creation, a relishing of its variety and multiplicity.

Wisdom shares in the generous creativity of God, giving rise to endless delights of diversity. She does not offer a flight from the many to the alone, but a journey into the manifold aspects of the world which she knows intimately. Thus the author, assuming the identity of "Solomon," claims to have received through her an encyclopaedic knowledge of the world, in all its facets: cosmology, time, astronomy, zoology, meteorology, psychology, botany, and pharmacy (Wis 7:17–21). "I learnt it all," he declares, "hidden and manifest, for I was taught by her whose skill made all things." As in the Hebrew poems in Proverbs 8 and the Wisdom of Ben Sira 24 the availability of wisdom, walking out on the open road, stands alongside the sense of the wise that much about the world remains hidden to them. In face of the endlessness and elusiveness of the world, the personification of wisdom is a way of inviting human beings into a personal relationship with a divine wisdom which can enable them to live coherently in a complex situation.

Reflection on the Hebrew personification of wisdom should prompt us to make the paradigm change from the idea of mediation to that of participation. We might say that wisdom flows forth from God so that human beings can participate in that same flowing movement. While I am not

---

39. Colwell, *Rhythm of Doctrine*, 105.
40. See Perdue, *Wisdom and Creation*, 305–6.
41. My translation.

presuming to impose any cryptic Trinity upon Judaism, similar insights into movements of personal life within and from God, inviting human participation, are later to be expressed in the Christian concept of Trinity. The Son or *logos* comes forth from the Father, as does the Spirit, not to link a remote God with the world as in the mediation model, but so that the world can share in the movements of self-giving within God, participating in the flowing movement of love between the Father and the Son in the ever-surprising newness of the Spirit.[42]

The gifts of this Spirit are not possessions to be owned by disciples of Christ as a source of self-esteem. They are not faculties but events, movements of "giving" by the Spirit in which we participate as we live in God.[43] Reflecting on these gifts of the Spirit, Colwell observes that Paul heads a list of them in 1 Corinthians 12:7–11 with the title "the message of wisdom." He continues:

> The coming of the Spirit upon the Church at Pentecost is marked by remarkable signs, ecstatic utterances, spiritual elation, miraculous healings, but perhaps the most eminent and persuasive mark of the Spirit's coming and presence is the coherence of living which is true wisdom.[44]

Perceptively, he aligns this ability to bring life together in to an ordered whole with the cardinal virtue of "prudence" (practical wisdom) as discerned by Thomas Aquinas.

Wisdom, according to the Wisdom of Solomon, holds together the many things of the world. Christ, we may say, is the wisdom of God in the way that he brings the "many" into one in his body, embodying coherence: "in him all things hold together" (Col 1:17). The distinctive role of the Spirit as the wisdom of God is to show a particular aspect of "the many in one": that is, as we engage in the flow of the Spirit's self-giving we discover a *surprising* coherence. Sharing in the One who "opens up" and disturbs, we find connections between things and people that we did not expect, and which deeply challenge our long-accepted views. This is surely why the gift of prophetic utterance is ascribed to the Spirit, "forth-telling" in the way that cuts beneath the surface appearance of society around us, and "fore-telling" in a way that warns of shocking consequences of our actions. We may expect to find this surprising wholeness, and to discover surprising links between things, as we share in the "God on Monday."

42. Cf. Bonhoeffer, "There are not two realities, but only one reality, and that is God's reality revealed in Christ in the reality of the world," *Ethics*, 58.

43. So Dunn, *Jesus and the Spirit*, 201–5.

44. Colwell, *Rhythm of Doctrine*, 105.

In the OBM liturgy for Pentecost we find, as we would expect, explicit references to the wisdom that comes from the Spirit. We offer thanks "for each word that has spoken truth," and pray for "those who seek for truth and wisdom / and those who have given up the search." But more pervasively, there is a sense that fragments of experience need to be brought together and patterns found. It is significant that we give thanks "for each life that has touched ours, / every chance to show your love." In the context of a canticle in which we acknowledge that the universe has been "subjected to futility" (Rom 8:20) we confess a humanity in which we lack "peace"—a biblical word with the sense of "wholeness" (*shalom*)—and recall that Christ gives this peace as he breathes out the Spirit on his disciples.

In this chapter I have been allowing insights from John's book *The Rhythm of Doctrine* to interact with the OBM liturgy for Pentecost, as well as developing my own account of the presence and work of the Holy Spirit in dialogue with both him and the liturgy. I have diverged at times from his own approach, as he will be only too aware. But this has always been with admiration for his careful theological thinking which warns us—if we are to take another path—to be as rigorous and responsible before God as he is. His own liturgical proposal is that the period of "ordinary time" in the church year following Pentecost Sunday should be regarded as an "extended period of Pentecost," since it is the Spirit who "shapes us in coherence with . . . the Christ who is the goal of all creation."[45] This, in effect, makes every day a Monday, or at least a day when we can meet the Pentecostal "God on Monday."

---

45. Colwell, *Rhythm of Doctrine*, 105.

16

Trinity

The Blessing of Almighty God . . .

Ruth Gouldbourne

In the name of the Father and of the Son and of the Holy Spirit

Triune God: community of creative and outpoured love . . .
Blessing God—maker of all . . .
Redeeming God: mysterious, invisible One.[1]

"Please write a chapter," they said. "Well . . . ," I said. "It's for John Colwell," they said. "Then certainly," I said. "We want you to write on the Trinity," they said. ". . . ?? . . . ??" I said.

But there it was; an essay on the Trinity for a festschrift for John Colwell; my assignment, should I wish to accept it. So, I went and read books and looked at my notes from classes I had taken, and classes I had taught—and thought "but surely everything that can be said has been said," and "even if not, then I am not nearly good enough at this to write anything worthwhile."

But then I looked again at the books that inspired me—I read John himself and Colin Gunton, and Steve Holmes and Paul Fiddes, and Robin

---

1. OBM Daily Office—Saturday and Creation—Creating God.

Parry, and David Cunningham, and I dipped into Moltmann and (even!) Barth.[2] I browsed Augustine, and wrestled with Thomas (in translation and paraphrase), and I began to remember what had set me alight in studying theology in the first place. I remembered the youth ministry student who had attended a day I taught on the development of the doctrine of the Trinity who ended the day with a huge smile and eyes alight with joy and the immortal phrase "God is so big!" It was borne in on me again just how exciting this doctrine is, how much life and energy it gives when it is placed centrally in our study of theology—and I was even more daunted by the task.

Many have written of the need to reflect Trinitarian theology in our preaching and worship; the dangers of monism, or Unitarianism or various other forms of heresy that can emerge very easily when we do not reflect effectively theologically on what we are doing in our worship—especially in singing or in praying. This material needs to be taken very seriously. The discussion of Trinitarian theology is hard, and is not comfortably covered in most preaching. All too often, it is implied rather than addressed directly—and when it is, the images and illustrations can lead to deeper confusion rather than elucidation. The scene in the film *Nuns on the Run* remembering that the shamrock illustrates the Trinity, and so asserting that "God is like a shamrock; small, green and split three ways," is scarily accurate to how many of us in the pews can find ourselves taught and remembering what we have been taught about this doctrine of doctrines.

So, I have taken myself back to remembering what I have gained most from John's own writings—and while there has been more than can easily be covered in an essay of this kind, one of the most significant and enduring things he has taught me is that theology must be placed firmly in a doxological context.

And while it is true that there are those brave, skilled and much-to-be-honoured preachers who will teach directly on the Trinity, there are even more of us who will imply, assume that everybody understands, and perhaps just skirt round it, and hope nobody notices. And the result is that all too many people miss the chance of the wide-eyed wonder of my student, to celebrate how "big" God is—with all the possible worship, wonder, delight, and transformation that that brings.

But even where many of us avoid preaching or teaching anything more than passing references, one place where we do regularly invoke Trinity is in blessing; we say The Grace together, we end services with the prayer "may

---

2. Specifically, Colwell, *Promise and Presence*; Colwell, *Rhythm of Doctrine*; Gunton, *Promise of Trinitarian Theology*; Holmes, *Holy Trinity*; Fiddes, *Participating in God*; Cunningham, *These Three Are One*; Parry, *Worshipping Trinity*; Moltmann, *Trinity and the Kingdom*.

the Blessing of God, Father, Son, and Holy Spirit be with us and remain with us." When we name God for people in blessing and invocation, Trinity is assumed and spoken of directly. If we take John's insistence on the place of theology within doxology, then here is material for consideration—and if we also listen to Chris Ellis's assertion that we will know what we believe when we examine how we worship,[3] then here is a way into the consideration of this central doctrine, starting not from the kind of philosophical position that frightens or loses many, or from the mathematical assertions that are nonsense in this context, but from the lived experience and the sought faith of the people of God.

It is a particularly suitable place to begin a consideration of Trinity, since, of course, this is how the language of Trinity first emerges in the church's life; as people of faith sought to articulate their faith and experience as they worshiped God, in the presence and through the mediation of the Risen Son, and by the power, with the inspiration and empowering of the Holy Spirit.

There is here material for much more than one chapter, and much of it has been well explored and discussed in many learned works. In the interests of actually saying something worthwhile, I will spend the rest of this essay reflecting on two specific places in our services where we regularly name the Triune God—blessing and baptism. The reasons for concentrating on these events is that they are some of the few places where many of us regularly use "set words" which include the Trinitarian name, and which do not, so far as I am aware, often provoke direct attention and teaching. We will bless or share the (Trinitarian) grace, but not often explore just what we are doing and why the language matters. We will teach about the meaning of baptism and discipleship, the nature of the church, even the distinctive of being Baptist, but not, often in my experience on the Name into which we are baptized.[4] Yet, these are places where the doctrine of Trinity is regularly invoked and evoked among us, and therefore places where knowing what we are saying could be considered important.

---

3. Ellis, *Gathering*, 1.

4. The Baptist Union publication *Making a Splash*, by Nick Lear, does have a short section on the triune name in a section on exploring faith, 8–11. Cf. Warner, *Baptism and You*, 58–73. Earlier books by Baptists did not, see Winward, *Your Baptism*, and Gaukroger, *Being Baptized*.

BLESSING

A blessing at the end of a gathering for worship—either a sharing of the grace invoking "the grace of our Lord, Jesus Christ, the blessing of God and the fellowship of the Holy Spirit" or a prayer for the congregation requesting "the Blessing of God, Father, Son, and Holy Spirit" is a frequent ending to our time together. It is a way of signalling that we are moving from one activity to another, often that we are moving from concentrating on worship to being in the world in service and faith—("Go in peace to love and serve the Lord, and may the blessing . . ."), or/and a way of praying for one another "may the grace . . ." I have not found many contexts in which we reflect on this practice, rather than simply treating it as a formal way of saying "this bit is over, let's get to the next bit" or "goodbye." However, it is, I suggest, one of the few regular places where as congregations we use this way of speaking of and to God. It has been, if not contested, at least debated in recent years, not least in discussions about inclusive language. Regularly at the end of our services in my previous church my colleague would pray the blessing of the Triune God for our congregation; "may the blessing of God, Creator, Redeemer and Sanctifier be with us all." It is a powerful prayer, made all the more powerful by his careful attention to language. I have grown to love this phrasing, and I would listen out for it very carefully when he was leading that part of the service. It is inclusive and powerful and leads us into the presence of, and sends us out expecting to meet God.

But on the occasions when I am praying the blessing, I find myself using the terms Father, Son, and Holy Spirit. As a matter of conviction and discipline, I work hard to make my language, about and to God, and about and to people, inclusive. This is a matter of deep personal commitment. When I am leading public prayer, I never use Father, unless in concert with Mother; in preaching, I am more likely to refer to the "Only-Begotten One" than to "the Son." I labor not to have to use a pronoun in referring to the Holy Spirit. Because of this, and because I valued what my colleague did so much, this has become a matter of reflection; if what we pray shows us what we truly believe, then what is it that my prayer of blessing is demonstrating. And if for many of the congregation, their "training" in Trinitarian theology is going to occur through the prayers offered by the ministers, then what am I doing using these terms, and is it what I want to do?

John himself, of course, has a very cogent and helpful exploration of why he chooses the use of the traditional terms in *Promise and Presence*[5]— and it is an argument with which I find myself in sympathy. To continue

---

5. Colwell, *Promise and Presence*, 17–20.

to be part of the ongoing tradition matters. In a contemporary context in which we run the risk of losing our roots and severing ourselves from our tradition, there is a depth and discipline in consciously using the strangeness of the tradition to keep us alive to the continuity of our life in God. But there is more.

In naming the Three as "Creator, Redeemer, and Sanctifier" we are invoking, and relating to the Divine as Divine Doing. God is named, differentiated and God's unity affirmed in terms of what God does; God creates, God redeems, and God sanctifies. All of this is, of course, true. It is without doubt right that all three actions should be named as we invoke the Three, since no action is the sole prerogative of One Person. But, there is also the strong tradition that the differentiation within God aligns each Person with an action; traditionally the Father with creation, the Son with redemption and the Holy Spirit with sanctification. However, as Colwell himself points out, this understanding must be handled carefully:

> God is "simple" and, in some respects, the entire tradition of attribution can be misconstrued and misappropriated: God is not divided. And God is "a se," utterly sufficient in eternal Triune relatedness: divine mission like divine mercy is a form God's single and self-sufficient nature takes in relation to that which is other than God.[6]

Thus, we must also say that creation is though the Son,[7] that redemption is the action of the Spirit[8] and that sanctification is the gift of the Father.[9] To invoke one is always to invoke all, for there is no separation of action. Indeed, that is, in itself, part of the blessing; that our whole being is bound up in the action and gift of the Divine, in the divine Complex Simplicity.

The blessing in the name of the Creator, the Redeemer, and the Sanctifier maps well onto our traditional language but with the added benefit that it is gender inclusive and moves us beyond the unhappy inference that God is fundamentally male (with its concomitant possibility that therefore to be male is to be more in the image of God).

Thus, my colleague's words of blessing make a significant statement; that in the wholeness of the being of God, understood through the wholeness of the action of God towards the reconciliation and fulfilment of

---

6. Colwell "Mission as Ontology," 8.

7. "All things came into being through him," John 1:3.

8. "He saved us . . . through the water of rebirth and the renewal by the Holy Spirit," Titus 3:5.

9. "Father, the hour has come . . . sanctify them in the truth," John 17:1, 17.

creation in blessing, we are blessed, renewed, transformed—and when this is used at the close of worship—sent out to live that into being in the world.

But there is more.

If the blessing of God is invoked through the Divine Doing, if God in Complex Simplicity is identified with activity, and this then becomes the predominant way in which the identity of God is spoken of in our worship, then we are at least by implication privileging the activity over the being of God. Just as we have become rightly aware of the danger of exclusively male language for God, with its implied privileging of masculine over feminine, so we run the danger of privileging doing over being, with the consequent damage to our understanding of ourselves as those blessed by God.

It is a truism to remind us that we are human beings, not human doings. It is a commonplace to remark that on first meeting somebody, in our culture, it is unhealthy that one of the earliest questions we ask is "what do you do"? It is a well-known and probably overstated fact that at retirement or some other cessation of employment, people lose a sense of purpose and worth, and even self, because so much of those are tied up with having our activity recognized.

However these are truisms, commonplaces, and well-known facts precisely because they say something true about who we are and how our worldview and culture operates. There is value in activity, there is self-worth in doing what is worthwhile and is recognized by others as such, there is a right and proper place for the expression of our selves, our gifts and our energy through creativity, making things happen, interaction and productivity.

So, when we invoke God as Doer, we are telling the truth but not all the truth. Of course, we can never tell all the truth about God—especially when we are trying to find language to speak of Complex Simplicity. Clearly, it is not untrue to say that God is Creator, Redeemer, and Sanctifier. Not only is it not untrue, it is good thing to say. It is an appropriate blessing to pray for; to know ourselves as created, to experience ourselves as redeemed, to discover the ever-deepening sanctification of the life of faith is blessing indeed. It moves us to praise when we are called to celebrate what God does, through having it named for us in blessing. We are brought to thankfulness as the blessing of God's activity is named for us. The blessing is a doxological act, evoking wonder and worship, and naming the activity of God does that.

And such worship also shapes what we do. Named as those created in the image of God, and hearing God invoked as Doing blesses and sanctifies our doing when it is sustained by and expressive of the Doing of God. But do we only "image" God in doing? Might we also in "being" be the image(s) of the Triune? Is there also blessing to be found in knowing ourselves simply to "be"?

If we are considering the liturgical reality of blessing, and the naming of the Three in that context, might it be that we need to think further. When the writer of Genesis tells us of the creation of humanity, there is blessing given by God to them in their activity of caring for the created order. And then there is also a blessing of the seventh day as the day of rest, when God rejoices in what has been made, and its goodness.

In a context where so much of our worth, our value and even our identity is defined by our activity and our contribution, which we might parallel to the first Genesis blessing, might there also be place for the invocation of the second blessing—the blessing of being, without needing to do, to produce or create? Sabbath is grounded in the story that God, having been active then rested and enjoyed it. It is the call to not be productive or active or energetic, but to be—to be together, to be loved and loving, to be in the presence of God as the highest good.

This is the blessing that is called up in the Old Testament by the image of sitting under the fig tree. It is the blessing invoked in the Letter to the Hebrews, with the promised rest explored in chapter 4, as the fulfilment of creation and promise. It is the background of the city imagined in Revelation 21–22, in which there is only "being" in the presence of God—where there is no need to produce light, drink, food—all is provided because God is in the midst, and all that is, "is" in the presence of God, without needing to "do" anything more.

To be, to be together, and to be in the divine presence is the blessing to which we are pointed, and for which, the whole arc of Scripture suggests, we are made.

But there is more.

One of the major places where we read of blessing in the gospels is in the beatitudes, where there is a description of what it is to be blessed—it is to be hungry, poor, mourning, meek, etc., it is to be outside of the normal and accepted pattern of happy and fortunate living. It is to be part of a kingdom that is the wrong way round, whose values are incomprehensible from the outside. And, crucially for the sake of this discussion, according to Jesus's descriptions, it is to be in a state of being rather than doing. We are not to make ourselves hungry or mourning, rather, we are to recognize the position we are in, and discover the action and presence of God—indeed, the blessing, the gift of God in and through that. When we invoke the blessing of the Triune who Is, rather than who does, we are in this territory, I suggest. This is a blessing that is transformative because it is a blessing that meets us in those places where we are powerless, where we "suffer" life and cannot make it otherwise, where it happens to us—where we mourn, where we know the lack of righteousness, where we are persecuted. The Triune God who Is meets us where we are and brings blessing. In contexts where all that we do has no effect and where all we can do is be what we are—mourning, poor, hungry—a blessing that is in the name of Being is to be treasured. For, by invoking blessing in the Name of the Triune One who Is, we discover the blessedness of the Presence that, simply by being present transforms and makes life possible.

At the heart of this, of course, is relationship. This is not coincidental, since our attempt to name the Divine Complex Simplicity is in terms of relation. The terms that we use for this Being of God are, of course, just as limited as the terms we use for God as Doer. None of our language will stretch far enough, but with the terms Father, Son, and Spirit, we are speaking primarily not of self-sufficient identities who exist alongside one another, but of "Being-in-Relationship"; the Father is the Father of the Son, and must first be spoken of that way, the Son the Son of the Father, the Spirit the one who processes from the Father (and the Son?). To begin this discussion is to move into the depths and complexities of the current (and historic) debates about Trinity, and I do not intend, in the confines of this essay, to attempt to cover such complexities. I am concerned rather to reflect on the liturgical and therefore pastoral implications of naming God as Being and particularly as Being-in-Relationship rather than as Doing. To name relation as present and blessing in our need and powerlessness is clearly significant; Presence who can be "with us," when we can do nothing to claim, to please, to serve, is one of the great truths of our faith.

But there is more.

In a context which we are regularly told is shaped by increasing individualism, there is clearly a value in naming ultimate reality as relational rather than isolationist; not only because there is then an affirmation about "God with us," but also because it insists that our capacity for relationship is part of our "imaging" God.

Nonetheless, it is not sufficient to name God as relation and then simplistically to read off "and therefore we should be relational too." After all, Augustine was able to map the relationality of God onto the individual being of mind, memory and will. An even more significant objection is that the interpenetration of the perichoretic Godhead is not something that is open to a human identity; we may live in and through relationship but we also inhabit the inside of our own lives in ways that we cannot share with another, no matter how intimate the relationship. We are not capable of the identity of Identity that is the nature of the Triune.

Therefore, there has to be something else in the blessing in the name of Being-in-Relationship that shapes us. This will take us in a moment into a consideration of baptism, but I want to stay with blessing at the moment.

Not all the relationships in which we are involved are those of blessing. Relationship as a state of being is not, per se, blessed. Therefore, if we are being blessed in the Name of "Being-in-Relationship," it is not the relationship-ness that is significant, but the Complex Simplicity who is the "Being-in-Relationship." And whatever else is said about the nature of the relationship, what is always said is that it is love. This is a foundational reason for speaking of God as Complex Simplicity; for the statement "God is love" to make sense without implying that God is dependent on creation in order for there to be a beloved, there must be the capacity both to love and to be loved within the being of God. This, therefore leads to differentiation, and to simplicity; love is absolute, there is no shadow in it, and there is nothing more to God than loving—thus, simplicity. And there is "loving" and "belovedness" within God—thus complexity.

To be blessed, therefore, in the name of the Divine Being is to be placed within love, and to have our fundamental identity affirmed as those who are, before all things and above all things, those who are loved. The question of what we do is not raised. There is no requirement to do in order to be loved, nor even any need to love. The relationships within the Complex Simplicity do not require our participation, for love to have a response. To be blessed in the Triune Name, named as Being-in-Relationship, is to be blessed by being loved prior to and as a foundation of anything that we may do or offer.

BAPTISM

This "Being-Blessed" identity is the identity that we are incorporated into by baptism. The other regular place where we name the Triune as Father, Son, and Spirit, that is, as Being-in-Relationship is when we baptize and are baptized in(to) the Name of the Father, Son, and the Holy Spirit. While as Baptists we have a tradition of regarding baptism as a human practice in which we invoke God, rather than an action of God in which we participate, still there is a strand, explored and developed most recently by Anthony R. Cross, which argues that baptism is, in Beasley Murray's term, a trysting place, which human action and God's action come together.[10] And we name that action as being in or into the Name of the Father, Son, and Spirit—we link the identity of the baptismal candidate with the identity of the Triune God, and more than that; we witness to the incorporation of the baptizand

---

10. Cross, *Recovering the Evangelical Sacrament*, 143.

into the body of Christ that is the church. Action may flow from this—indeed, action must flow from this if the life of discipleship is to have form in the world. But action is consequent on being—we do what we are. We are part of the body of Christ by our baptism, and therefore we live and do and act and minister and all the rest of it. But the invocation of the Name of the Triune in terms of identity and relationship, and therefore our identity in that Name is prior to that.

Bonhoeffer insisted that we relate as Christians in Christ; that is, that between me and the other person is Christ, and it is in that "space" that identity, and so our encounter takes place and is realized. Colwell has written in depth about the mediated encounter with God, and the way in which we mediate that encounter for each other. We cannot recreate the depth of relationship between ourselves that subsists within God—but the relationships within God, precisely because God is love are not exclusive or closed. In the practice of baptism, we are called to, and indeed, brought into the life of the Triune. The movement of the relationship that is the being of the Triune is open and inclusive and in baptism we are named into it. This is not primarily to do or to be done to, but to be—to be caught up, into the love and mutuality that is the perichoretic being. Hazel Sherman writes of this when she discusses both the attractiveness of the model of being involved in the relationship of mutual giving and receiving that is at the heart of the Godhead—and the despair as we acknowledge that we cannot do it.

She continues:

> Therefore we must find new ways of remembering that in baptism we are not simply presented with a model to copy, we are immersed in the ongoing life of God in the world, who has covenanted with us, not to make life easy, but to bring us to life.
>
> There is no real imitation without participation. We are not simply in the business of copying a model. The baptismal formula is dynamic, for we are baptized into *the name* of Father Son and Holy Spirit . . . into the very life of God.[11]

The relationality of the Complex Simplicity is love—and in baptism we are taken into that love as our known and owned (by us) identity. We are caught up into and redefined by the loving life of the Triune. We cannot recreate the relational life of God between us as humans, but among those who are baptized in(to) the Name of the Triune, such a relationship is the defining feature.

But there is more.

---

11. Sherman "Baptized—'in the Name of the Father, Son and Spirit,'" 110.

The relationships in the Triune are also those of issuing and therefore going; the Father sends the Son, the Spirit proceeds from the Father (and the Son?) and as such there is direction—a direction of the *missio Dei*—the movement of the Triune into the world for saving and renewing. Being baptised in(to) the Name and therefore the Being is then, consequently, to be involved in this sending. The life of the disciple is being sent out into the world to be part of the *missio Dei*, for the blessing and renewal of the world, until all is caught up into the loving dance. What is significant here is the "being sent"; the identity that this is.

Colwell has argued passionately for understanding mission as "being sentness"—and therefore primarily as a matter of ontology rather than function—of *being* prior to *doing*. Clearly there is doing; there are tasks and activities for the church. But the being of the church, he argues, is not constituted by what it does, nor dependent on achieving or succeeding. It is constituted by "being-sentness"—the passive experience of being and being done to, rather than of doing:

> The Church's mission is constituted simply and solely by its being sent into the world; it is a matter of identity before ever it is a matter of activity.[12]

It does matter that with a concentration on being we do not lose sight of doing. God is absolute being in Complex Simplicity, and as that Being is also Act; action rooted in, moving from and ending as love. To be baptized in(to) that Name is to be drawn into the loving and therefore the acting, being involved in the sending; if we neglect this, then we are in danger of shutting down that which is open and constantly creating (or at least, trying to shut down, since we can never frustrate the action of God). While we may be frustrated or irritated when our being is conflated with our action, or in danger of losing our selves in the constant drivenness of activity for the sake of creating an identity, for the Complex Simplicity of the Divine, Being and Act are one and the same; to be is to do is to be. Thus being loved and being sent are not two different things though we may interpret them and experience them in different ways. Our being loved is our being sent, and our being sent is our being loved; both are our being blessed and being named, and both are done to us, prior to anything we do. When we own and express and trust this in the offering of blessing and naming in baptism, we will own and trust and express a richness of Trinitarian theology that emerges from our worship, and in turn deepens our worship.

---

12. Colwell, "Mission as Ontology," 10.

It has been a cry of theologians that not enough attention is paid to the Trinity. It has been a complaint of congregations that attention to Trinity is abstruse and incomprehensible. It is one of the gifts that John has given us that theology should be rooted in doxology, I suggest that by looking directly at "the" doxology, and reflecting on our practice of such prayers and blessings, we may find ways of communicating the delight, and joy of being baptized and blessed in the Triune Name that may deepen and broaden the life of faith among us for our surprise and the blessing of many.
And there is more. Always, there is more!

By taking further naming the Divine Complex Simplicity—as, for example, practiced in the OBM Daily Offices, with its introductory invocation "in the Name of the Father, the Son and the Holy Spirit" before anything else is said—as the context for our life, our prayer, our being, our service, we own and affirm that all that we are, all that we do is within and through this Being-in-Action and Acting-by-Being. And we discover then that there is always more—and more and more.

For here, surely, is the crucial point; just as my wide-eyed student discovered "God is so big" when Trinity was explored and reflected on, when we take seriously the words that we use in blessing and in baptism, we are above all things, expressing wonder, praise, delight, amazement, joy, worship; we are being doxologically theological and theologically doxological—to the glory of God, Father, Son, and Holy Spirit. Amen.

17

Creation
Participation and Goal

Helen Paynter

> Redeeming God:
> mysterious, invisible One,
> revealed and imaged in beloved Son . . .
> freeing and drawing all things together,
> working all things together for good.[1]

ALL OF LIFE IS worship. But in some parts of life, the worship feels more focused than at other times. Standing on top of a mountain is more awe-inspiring than standing in the supermarket queue. My experience of reading the work of John Colwell on creation, and in preparing this offering for his festschrift, has felt like a mountain-top experience. In his writing, and the Scripture that he has refreshed my appreciation for, I have reencountered an awe and worship for my Savior and Creator. This chapter is tendered as a humble *homage* to the theologian and as an offering of love to our Lord.

In his work on creation, Colwell richly sets out the theological thickness of the act of creation. I have chosen to focus on three themes to

---

1. *Order for Baptist Ministry*, Saturday.

direct my exploration: eschatological directedness, Trinitarian action, and participation.

First, if creation establishes a trajectory to which redemption will restore us, it is an upward one, not a horizontal one. The new will exceed the old:

> The work of redemption . . . is not intended merely to restore Creation and humankind to that initial but unperfected state by undoing this corruption and its effects; the work of redemption rather is intended both to undo this corruption *and* to bring Creation and humankind to that perfection that was originally intended.[2]

Second and third, Colwell stresses the involvement of all persons of the Trinity in creation, and humankind's invitation to participate in his purposes:

> The eternal intimacy of the Father, Son and Spirit . . . is reiterated in the unnecessitated but essentially coherent creative love of God for that which is other than himself . . . a love that freely invites and destines that which is other than himself to participate in his glory.[3]

In this chapter I am going to try to explore how this creative act by the Triune God, acting in loving concert, catches us into its narrative and goal. I will set out three themes, approximating (*only* approximating) to the roles and goals in creation of the three persons of the Trinity. Each theme begins in the garden, as described in Genesis 1, but reaches forward through both Testaments, straining to the eschatological goal which Colwell has reminded us, after Irenaeus, is the purpose of creation.

First, an apologia. I am a biblical scholar, not a theologian. As such, I feel towards theologians rather as—I imagine—a stone-dresser feels towards the designer of a cathedral—a sense of awe at the edifice which has been constructed out of the raw materials s/he has provided. My intention in this chapter is not to attempt another cathedral—that would be invidious. My aim, rather, is to lay a few dressed stones in order, and make a few humble suggestions as to how the cathedral-builders might proceed with them. So, to work—and worship.

---

2. Colwell, *Living the Christian Story*, 193, emphasis original.
3. Colwell, *Rhythm of Doctrine*, 38.

THE GLORY OF GOD TO THE ENDS OF THE EARTH

"Give us grace to work and live, play and dance on earth today as grateful and joyful daughters and sons of God."[4]

At the heart of the creation account in Genesis 1 lies what is commonly known as the *creation mandate*; the instruction by God to the man and the woman to "be fruitful and multiply, and fill the earth and subdue it" (Gen 1:28). A great deal of theological freight is contained within these six Hebrew words, but I would like to explore them with regard to the twin themes identified: eschatological directedness and participation.

The idea of "filling the earth" rapidly gains traction in the biblical account. In Genesis 3, the judgments against the woman and the man (pain of parturition and agricultural struggle)[5] are represented in terms of challenge to the fulfilment of the mandate. Following the flood, the mandate is reiterated twice to Noah.[6] Resistance to the mandate is the principle sin of Babel ("otherwise we shall be scattered abroad upon the face of the whole earth"),[7] which causes God to take matters into his own hands, "the Lord scattered them abroad . . . the Lord scattered them abroad."[8] The mandate finds its echoes in the promise to Abraham, "In you all the families of the earth shall be blessed."[9] Conversely, the Pharaoh's attempt to contain and sterilise the Hebrew slaves[10] should be understood in terms of opposition to this purpose of God.

Stephen Dempster has shown that the "image" language of Genesis 1, the vice-regency of Adam and Eve, and the multiplication and filling of the earth are multiple facets of the directedness of creation:

> Human beings are created as rulers of the earth, representing the mighty name of God throughout the world. They are the recipients of blessing, which includes not only their status, but also the ability to transmit the image of God by creating life . . . With the use of these terms, the writer makes the goal of Creation anthropological and thus doxological.[11]

---

4. OBM Daily Office—Saturday and Creation—Creating God.
5. Gen 3:16–19.
6. Gen 9:1, 7.
7. Gen 11:4.
8. Gen 11:8, 9.
9. Gen 12:3. Even if the alternate translation of the *niphal* "shall bless themselves" is preferred, the point that through Abraham the families of earth will come under the blessing of God is still strongly related to the theme.
10. Exod 1–2.
11. Dempster, *Dominion and Dynasty*, 61–62.

Similarly, Gregory Beale writes that Adam was "to spread God's luminescent presence," because "God's ultimate goal in Creation was to magnify his glory throughout the earth by means of his faithful image-bearers."[12] In other words, the crowning duty of humankind is to take the glory of God to the ends of the earth; this is an eschatological goal.

The language of "fruitfulness" and "filling the earth" provides theological vocabulary for the prophetic writings. Isaiah in particular uses the motif in both positive and negative ways on many occasions.[13] The frequent reference to untamable wild beasts (in at least seventeen different oracles) can be understood as a reversal or failure of the dominion given to humanity.[14] Conversely, Isaiah's expansive vision of the renewed creation frequently uses creation mandate language to describe its restoration. Thus the great vision of creational restoration of Isaiah 11 has images of wild beasts under the peaceful dominion of humanity, while the glory of the Lord has finally enveloped the whole world:

> The wolf shall live with the lamb,
> the leopard shall lie down with the kid,
> the calf and the lion and the fatling together,
> and a little child shall lead them . . .
> for the earth will be full of the knowledge of the Lord
> as the waters cover the sea.[15]

Or consider Isaiah 27. This oracle, which begins with the eschatological overtones of the slaying of Leviathan, uses the images of fruitfulness and filling of the earth:

> In days to come Jacob shall take root,
> Israel shall blossom and put forth shoots,
> and fill the whole world with fruit.[16]

Moving into the New Testament, Thomas Philips has argued that the beginning of Acts constitutes a retelling of the first chapters of Genesis. In particular, he suggests that Jesus is correcting his disciples' misapprehension about the nature of the kingdom of God by directing their attention to the

---

12. Beale, *The Temple and the Church's Mission*, 82.

13. This should not be viewed as a comment on the authorship question relating to the book of Isaiah, but reflects a decision to treat it as a literary unity. Intertextuality between Genesis and Isaiah has been identified by several authors, including Seitz, *Isaiah 1–39*, and Goldingay *Isaiah*.

14. Wenkel, "Wild Beasts in the Prophecy of Isaiah," 251–64.

15. Isa 11:6–9. Cf. Hab 2:14.

16. Isa 27:6. Cf. similar imagery in Hos 14:4–8.

"new people of God" who are tasked with continuing the commission of Abraham (and hence of Adam). "The people of God being created through the apostles, like the people of God created through Abraham, were charged with a universal mission, to spread God's message and blessing to the entire earth."[17]

Jesus's words to his disciples certainly seem to indicate an expanding series of rings: "You will be my witnesses in Jerusalem, in all Judea and Samaria, and to the ends of the earth."[18] Indeed, Luke appears to use these words as the framework for his book, with the focus being on Jerusalem until chapter 8 verse 1, on Judea and Samaria between chapter 8 verse 2 and chapter 9 verse 31, and the gospel going "to the ends of the earth"—symbolized by the arrival of Paul in Rome—in the remainder of the book.

A similar view that the mission of the church belongs within this paradigm is seen in the Pauline corpus. For example, the book of Colossians appears to draw on both the MT and LXX versions of the creation mandate in its opening paragraphs, and also may bear reference to the passages quoted above from Isaiah:[19]

MT	LXX.[A]	Colossians 1:6–10
Genesis 1:28 Be fruitful and multiply, and fill the earth and subdue it . . . **Isaiah 11:9** . . . for the earth will be full of the knowledge of the LORD as the waters cover the sea. **Isaiah 27:6** Israel shall blossom and put forth shoots, and fill the whole world with fruit	**Genesis 1:28** Increase [αὐξάνω] and multiply, and fill [πληρόω] the earth [γῆ] and subdue it . . . **Isaiah 11:9** . . . the whole [ἡ σύμπασα] is filled [ἐμπίπλημι] with the knowledge [γινώσκω] of the Lord, as much water covers the seas. **Isaiah 27:6** Israel shall bud and blossom, and the world [ἡ οἰκουμένη] shall be filled [ἐμπίπλημι] with his fruit [καρπός].	Just as [the gospel] is bearing fruit [καρποφορέω] and growing [αὐξάνω] in the whole world [κόσμος], so it has been bearing fruit [καρποφορέω] among yourselves . . . since the day we heard it, we have not ceased praying for you and asking that you may be filled [πληρόω] with the knowledge [ἐπίγνωσις] of God's will . . . as you **bear fruit [καρποφορέω]** in every good work and as you grow [αὐξάνω] in the knowledge [ἐπίγνωσις] of God.

A. Brenton, *Septuagint Version of the Old Testament*.

17. Philips, "Creation, Sin and Its Curse, and the People of God."

18. Acts 1:8.

19. The connections between Genesis and Colossians shown in this table are described in Beale, "Colossians," 842.

So we too must understand the church's mission in this way, as part of a great movement of the glory of God from creation to eschaton. This story begins with two people in a garden and spreads out initially before collapsing; it restarts with a family emerging from the chaos of flood, but soon collapses again; it restarts with one man called out of Ur, grows for a few centuries but then collapses. But then it restarts, definitively, with a baby in a stable; then spills out to a cluster of scared disciples in an upstairs room; next there are three thousand new converts. And it is still pressing onward, sweeping outward, is spilling into cities and surging along valleys, is growing and multiplying, teeming and burgeoning. Remembering this will help us grasp the purpose of our little, local missionary endeavors within the eternal purposes of God.

THE SON AS END-TIMES ADAM

> "Redeeming God, mysterious, invisible One,
> revealed and imaged in beloved Son."[20]

In *The Rhythm of Doctrine*, Colwell helpfully reminds us of the preexistence of the Son ontologically, though not temporally with regard to his incarnation,[21] a notion he expresses elsewhere in this way, "It is not . . . that Christ is made in the likeness of Adam, it is rather that Adam was created in the likeness of Christ."[22] This statement invites us to reflect upon the "likeness" imagery in Old and New Testaments, the first instance of which, of course, is the quadruple statement in Genesis 1:26–27 that humanity is created in the image/likeness of God. As we shall see, this forms an important theological background to some of the key christological texts of the New Testament.

The preexistence of the Son as the image of God is made clear in Colossians 1, where we read:

> He is the image of the invisible God, the firstborn of all Creation; for in him all things in heaven and on earth were created, things visible and invisible, whether thrones or dominions or rulers or powers—all things have been created through him and for him. He himself is before all things, and in him all things hold together. He is the head of the body, the church; he is the beginning. (Col 1:15–20)

---

20. OBM Daily Office—Saturday and Creation—Creating God.
21. Colwell, *Rhythm of Doctrine*, 35.
22. Colwell, *Living the Christian Story*, 193.

The Adamic language in this passage is evident. Beale points out that these three accounts of Christ—image of God, firstborn, before all things—are all representations which refer to Christ as an end-time Adam, due to their usage in the Hebrew Bible and intertestamental literature to refer to Adam or Adam-like creatures.[23] Further, the "image" language has both functional (revealing of the Father) and ontological (preexistence) meaning.[24] This ancient hymn, then, reaches both backwards to Adam and behind him to the preexistent Christ, and forwards to the eschatological kingdom. To summarize one small piece of this rich theological theme rather crudely, we might put it like this: The preexistent Christ bears the image of God; Adam is created in his image but fails in his vocation; the incarnate Christ takes on Adam's (physical) image and vocation.

This last point, not very apparent in the Colossians hymn, is writ large in Philippians 2:

> Christ Jesus, though he was in the form of God,
> did not regard equality with God
> as something to be exploited,
> but emptied himself,
> taking the form of a slave,
> being born in human likeness.
> And being found in human form,
> he humbled himself
> and became obedient to the point of death—
> even death on a cross. (Phil 2:5–8)

Like Colossians 1, this hymn goes on to show the eschatological thrust of the Adamic Christology, "that at the name of Jesus every knee should bend" (v. 10), but additionally, the theme of Christ's vocation becomes clearer. The parallels with the Servant Song of Isaiah 52:13—53:12 have been well-described; notably the common themes of the servant,[25] who is poured out to death,[26] but becomes highly exalted.[27] Thus Isaiah establishes a paradigm that the faithful servant of God can suffer, and the Philippians hymn builds upon that pattern to demonstrate the faithfulness of Jesus as Adamic figure and servant of God.

---

23. Beale, "Colossians," 854.
24. Beale, "Colossians," 853.
25. Isa 52:13; 53:11; Phil 2:7.
26. Isa 53:12 (MT); Phil 2:7–8.
27. Isa 52:13; Phil 2:9. See, e.g., Hawthorne, *Philippians*, 119; Wright, *Climax of the Covenant*, 60.

This theme of Adam-Christ-servant is complex and rich and I cannot possibly do justice to it in this short chapter. However, it is impossible to understand it at all without expanding the study to the concepts of Israel-as-Adam and Christ-as-Israel. Thus, with particular attention to the reiteration of the creation mandate in the Pentateuch, N. T. Wright says,

> At key moments—Abraham's call, his circumcision, the offering of Isaac, the transitions from Abraham to Isaac and from Isaac to Jacob, and in the sojourn in Egypt—the narrative quietly makes the point that Abraham and his family inherit, in a measure, the role of Adam and Eve.[28]

And Wright goes on to state,

> For Paul, Jesus stands in the place of Israel. To him, and to his people, the glory of Adam now belongs in the new Age which has already dawned. But second, the fact of the cross compelled Paul to rethink the nature of God's people.[29]

So let us draw these strands together. Adam is created in the image of the preexistent Christ, but fails to live according to that image, and fails in his vocation. This story is recapitulated in the new Adam, Israel, who also fails to live according to the image, and fails in its vocation. The incarnate Christ recapitulates the story of Israel,[30] accepts and fulfils Adam's vocation and is the true image of the invisible God. And with regard to the eschatological directedness of all of this, Colwell says,

> It is only in and through Christ that Creation, and humanity within Creation, reaches its goal and perfection ... the perfected humanity of Christ is ever the only means of the fulfilment of Creation's perfection; Creation comes to its goal here.[31]

What, then, is our role, as participants in God's eschatologically directed plans? First, we note that in Romans, Paul moves from discussing the Adamic role of Christ[32] to our own baptism into him and ethical call to live accordingly,[33] and then climaxes this argument in chapter 8 with the famous words, "Those whom he foreknew he also predestined *to be conformed to*

---

28. Wright, *Climax of the Covenant*, 22.
29. Wright, *Climax of the Covenant*, 40.
30. See, e.g., Wright, *New Testament and the People of God*, 400; Gundry, *Use of the Old Testament*, 210.
31. Colwell, *Rhythm of Doctrine*, 36.
32. Rom 5.
33. Rom 6.

the image of his Son, in order that he might be the firstborn within a large family."[34] We who are baptized into Christ are intended (like Adam) to conform to the image of the Son, that is, to the image of the Father.

The hymns of Colossians and Philippians contain further clues. We note the use of "body" language in Colossians, "He is the head of the body, the church." While the originality of "the church" in the phrase, has been disputed, Peter O'Brien has convincingly argued that this represents a development of thought from—but not discontinuity with—the "body" language in 1 Corinthians 12. In particular, he suggests that the Old Testament concept of corporate personality is in the background here in Colossians.[35] This would, of course, be entirely consonant with the expanding-contracting idea of Adam-Israel-Christ that we have been considering. Here, we begin to see hints that it is *the church* rather than—or perhaps as well as—individual believers who are to embody the new humanity which Jesus has exemplified.

What is the vocation towards which this new humanity is being summoned? What does conformity to the image of the Son look like? The hymn in Philippians gives us an idea. The Philippian church is called to have the same attitude as Christ Jesus; not simply in regard to regarding others better than themselves,[36] but, as Michael Gorman has shown, by being conformed to the cruciform model of willing suffering, in the pattern of Isaiah's suffering servant, in the pattern of the cross.[37]

The study of this biblical trajectory of Adam-Israel-Christ in anything but a cold academic exercise. It is, rather, an invitation to live according to our creational and baptismal vocation, to image our Savior and Creator, both individually and corporately.

THE SPIRIT AS BROODING POTENTIAL

"Fount of all Wisdom, and full of your Spirit."[38]

In *Promise and Presence*, Colwell describes the role of the Spirit as mediator of God's relatedness to creation. He draws our attention to the sacramentality of the tabernacle and temple, which form a physical and symbolic framework for the (sometimes unperceived) presence of God in the world, "in the light of God's specific promise to be present and active within these

34. Rom 8:29.
35. O'Brien, *Colossians*, 48–50.
36. Cf. Phil 2:3.
37. Gorman, *Cruciformity*.
38. OBM Daily Office—Saturday and Creation—Creating God.

sacramental signs."[39] Colwell is, of course, well aware that the very first temple—the cosmic temple—is shaped by God at creation, of which Eden is the microcosmic expression.[40] In fact, cosmos-Eden-tabernacle-temple imagery forms a rich vein in the Hebrew Bible and forwards into the New Testament. But the role of the Spirit in within this vein is sometimes overlooked.

The theological parallels between Eden/cosmos and tabernacle/temple are evidenced by two sets of semantic parallels in the text, relating to the role of humanity and of God. So the man is placed in the garden to "till it and keep it" (Gen 2:15), or to "work it and keep it" (ESV). This pair of verbs, ʿ bd and šmr, is found in three places to refer to the role of the Levites and priests (Num 3:7–8; 8:26; 18:5–6), although the translation used here (cf. ESV, which has "minister" and "guard") often obscures the correspondence.

While humanity is tasked to function in a priest-like capacity within Eden, the garden is for God a place to walk with his people (Gen 3:8), language that is used again later in the Pentateuch and beyond to describe his presence, mediated by the tabernacle, within the camp.[41]

These theological parallels are evidenced to the people with a number of physical similarities by which the symbolic tabernacles are shown to represent the cosmic/Edenic one. Of note is the construction of two cherubim to overshadow the ark[42] or to span the inner sanctuary of the temple[43] in imitation of the cherubim who were set by God to guard with flaming swords the way to the tree of life.[44] The use of onyx and gold in the tabernacle[45] and gold in the temple[46] reflect the presence of these precious materials in Eden.[47] The lampstands[48] represent the trees of the garden, perhaps the Tree of Life itself. Indeed the way that the tabernacle reflected the heavens and the earth was well-understood by Josephus, who sets out in his *Antiquities* a detailed description of the parallels, quite exceeding those explicit in Scripture.[49]

---

39. Colwell, *Promise and Presence*, 59.
40. See, e.g., Wenham, "Sanctuary Significance," 19–25.
41. Lev 26:12; Deut 23:14; 2 Sam 7:6–7.
42. Exod 25:18–22.
43. 1 Kgs 6:23–29.
44. Gen 3:24.
45. Exod 25.
46. E.g., 1 Chr 22, 29.
47. Gen 2:11–12.
48. Exod 25:31–35.
49. Josephus, "Antiquities," 179–87.

These features are all well-established in Old Testament scholarship. But what is not so commonly noticed is the imagery of the Spirit in relation to all three "temples," and how each temple's "creator" is described. At the beginning of Genesis 1, we are told that *rûaḥ ' ĕlōhîm* (the spirit of God) is over the waters. This expression *rûaḥ ' ĕlōhîm* is unusual in the Pentateuch, but is also found in Exodus 31:3, where Bezalel, the builder of the tabernacle, is filled with *rûaḥ ' ĕlōhîm* for the purpose of the project. In fact, as T. Desmond Alexander points out, there are close textual links between the building of the tabernacle, the building of the temple, and the descriptions of the act of creation given in Genesis and Proverbs.[50]

	Creation	Building of Tabernacle (Bezalel)	Building of Temple (Hiram)
rûaḥ ' ĕlōhîm the spirit of God	Gen 1:2	Exod 31:3 Exod 35:31	
ḥŏkmah wisdom	Prov 3:19	Exod 31:3 Exod 35:31 Exod 36:1	1 Kgs 7:14
tĕbûnāh understanding/skill	Prov 3:19	Exod 31:3 Exod 35:31 Exod 36:1	1 Kgs 7:14
daʿat knowledge	Prov 3:20	Exod 31:3 Exod 35:31	1 Kgs 7:14
kŏl-mĕlā' kāh all works	Gen 2:3	Exod 31:3 Exod 35:31	
	sevenfold work of creation in Gen 1:1–2:3.	seven distinct instructions to Moses about the tabernacle in Exod 25–31.[A]	sevenfold dedication speech by Solomon in 1 Kgs 8.[B]

A. Middleton, *Liberating Image*, 84.
B. Middleton, *Liberating Image*, 83.

Given this semantic overlap between these passages, and the background of the theological parallelism between the creation and the temple/tabernacle, Richard Middleton comments,

50. Alexander, *Exodus*, 607–8.

> Not only does the Tabernacle replicate in microcosm the macrocosmic sanctuary of the entire created order, but these verbal resonances suggest that Bezalel's discerning artistry in Tabernacle-building images God's own construction of the cosmos. Bezalel's Spirit-filled craftsmanship . . . images God's primordial wise design and construction of the cosmos.[51]

The importance of all this becomes more apparent when we trace the temple imagery through to the New Testament. The significance of the Spirit as the presence of God *within* each temple is well-described,[52] but the importance of the Spirit as creatively brooding over the construction of each of the temples is not so strongly emphasized among commentators. We will focus on just two key texts lying at opposite ends of Jesus's ministry: Luke 4:18–19 and John 20.

In rich and complex ways, the Isaiah 61 Jubilee pronouncement of Jesus in the Nazareth synagogue[53] connects to temple imagery. For it is following the act of atonement that the rams' horns of Jubilee would be blown; the whole event of Jubilee is predicated upon temple function. Jon Levenson says this: "The symbolic resonance established through one word [dĕrôr, release] in Isa 61:1 is resounding: Jubilee, Sabbath, Temple, enthronement, liberation, returning home, atonement."[54] So we can understand Jesus' inaugural speech to be—among many other things—a witness to the Spirit's role in empowering him as temple.

In commentaries on the Fourth Gospel, the themes of creation / new creation and of Jesus-as-temple are both well-understood; however, they are not often tied together. Jeannine Brown, for example, identifies many of the creational *motifs* in the Fourth Gospel, including the emphasis on "life," not simply as a privatized eschatological phenomenon, but as a reference to the renewing of creation.[55] At the resurrection account in John 20, clearly intended by the gospel writer to be reminding us of the creation (setting in a garden, Jesus-as-Adam imagery, double reference to the first day of the week), Jesus breathes the Holy Spirit into his disciples, paralleling Gen 2:7:

> When he had said this, he breathed (ἐμφυσάω) on them and said to them, "Receive the Holy Spirit. (John 20:22)

---

51. Alexander, *Exodus*, 87.

52. There are clear associations between the theophanies at the consecration of tabernacle and temple, and at Pentecost. See, e.g., Beale, "Descent of the Eschatological Temple."

53. Luke 4:18–19.

54. Levenson "The Temple and the World," 294.

55. Brown, "Creation's Renewal in the Gospel of John."

> The Lord God formed man from the dust of the ground, and breathed (LXX = ἐμφυσάω) into his nostrils the breath of life; and the man became a living being. (Gen 2:7)

Wright also emphasizes new creation here: "On Easter morning it is the first day of the week. Creation is complete; new Creation can now begin. The Spirit who brooded over the waters of Creation at the beginning broods now over God's world, ready to bring it to springtime life."[56]

On the other hand, as pointed out by Rowan Williams, the two angels in the empty tomb, one at the head and one at the foot, bear a striking resemblance to the cherubim guarding the atonement cover of the ark.[57] Just as creation and tabernacle language coexist in the prologue, so they do here. In the second half of the chapter, we note that immediately following the breathing of the Spirit upon the disciples is the declaration that they will fulfil a vital temple function; notably the forgiveness of sins. In the same way that the appropriation of this function to himself demonstrates Jesus' own temple function,[58] so the delegation of this task to the disciples reflects the church's own temple role, overseen by the bestowing of the Spirit.

So the Spirit whose brooding creativity oversaw the creation of the cosmic temple; who inspired Bezalel and Hiram to create its cultic models; who empowered the ministry of Jesus as true temple; this same Spirit broods over the birth of the church here in the resurrection account of John. Attention to the activity of the Spirit in Genesis and Exodus sensitises us to his role as brooding, creative, presence *over* each temple at its inauguration.

CONCLUSION: CAUGHT UP INTO THE CREATIVE REDEMPTIVE PURPOSE OF THE TRINITY

> Through the mediation of the Spirit we can be instrumental means through which Creation itself is moved towards its eschatological goal in the Son.[59]

Colwell's work on the theology of creation shows us Trinity acting in loving concert towards an eschatological purpose into which we are invited

---

56. Wright, *Challenge of Jesus*, 136.
57. Williams, *On Christian Theology*, 186.
58. Koester, *Dwelling of God*. Koester identifies three main functions of the tabernacle/temple, all of which are strongly present in the life of Jesus: revelation, atonement/forgiveness, and the dwelling of the presence of God in order to demonstrate his covenantal faithfulness.
59. Colwell, *Promise and Presence*, 61.

to participate. Allowing this to sensitize our reading of the creation accounts in Genesis highlights some vital themes which can shape our understanding of our vocation and purpose as church.

Perhaps we can rediscover ourselves as a temple created for the dwelling of God, and brooded over by the Spirit. Perhaps it is not too fanciful to suggest that we—like the temples of old—are being dreamed, *conceived* and in-spired by the Holy Spirit, and as such we are directed towards the eschatological temple, the new creation: foreshadowed in the Jubilee pronouncement of Jesus.

Perhaps we can rediscover our human vocation, which may (will?) involve suffering: because no servant is greater than his master; because in humility and self-giving we are most like our Savior; because his route to the kingdom is through the cross not the sword; because the end is better than the beginning; and because as a result of his sacrifice the eschatological Christ will be more glorious than Adam ever could have been.

And perhaps we can rediscover our trajectory to take the glory of God to the ends of the earth; which we are fulfilling even while we engage in our grassroots missional work of serving coffee to the lonely, running foo banks, or holding the hands of the dying. And perhaps we will remember that we are doing these things in order that the earth might be filled with the knowledge of the glory of God, as surely and utterly and overwhelmingly as the waters cover the sea.

18

All Saints'
Remembering, Learning, and Attending

Andy Goodliff

> For those who have formed us in faith
> and led us to Christ, sustained us and carried us in their heart,
> For all the saints who are now at rest,
> who await resurrection and worship on that farther shore,
> we praise and thank you.[1]

Belle Vue Baptist Church in Southend-on-Sea was founded in 1902 by the Reverend James McCleery, who was the minister of Avenue Baptist Church, also in Southend, and Mr. Colin Mackay and other interested friends.[2] A site was obtained in Belle Vue Avenue and an iron chapel was erected. The church was opened for worship on Sunday, November 2, 1902.[3] This would have been All Saints' Sunday. There is no indication that this was planned or that this new church would have even observed All Saints' Sunday. In terms of the latter, it was probably very unlikely. However, this

---

1. OBM Daily Office—All Saints'.
2. I have been minister of Belle Vue Baptist Church since 2010.
3. Bottoms, *Fifty Years of Faith*, 1–2.

237

happy coincidence has meant that whenever the church celebrates its anniversary on the first Sunday in November, quite often it lands on All Saints' Sunday. In my time as minister I have tried to make sure we mark All Saints' Day/Sunday. This feels appropriate because it reminds the present congregation that there is a history of saints who have worshiped at this church and so have made their own lives as a people named Belle Vue Church Baptist Church possible. Their witness, their ministry and mission, is the gift and story they give us. Furthermore, those earlier Christians who planted Belle Vue Baptist Church, some who were members of Avenue Baptist Church, also tell a story of how as a church we are part of a larger communion of saints, that there is a wider story of association, partnership and fellowship,[4] that goes back to 1612 and the first Baptist church on English soil, and to 597 and the arrival of Augustine to England, and right back to the gathering of the apostles in Jerusalem at that first Pentecost.

As a second way of introducing this chapter in 2011 the Baptist Missionary Society (BMS) encouraged churches to mark "Carey Sunday" on August 21, this being the closest Sunday to the 250th anniversary of William Carey's birth. In so doing Baptists were celebrating the life of one their most famous forebears. The BMS resources to go with the day sought to provide ways of remembering his life and its significance both for our Baptist story and as an ongoing example for us to emulate today.[5] This example shows how rare it is for Baptists to celebrate the life of someone from their history.[6] As Baptists we have no calendar of saints. There is no shared list of lives whose stories we tell. I have myself elsewhere offered a potential list,[7] but there has never been any denominational attempt to recognise those lives we might call significant, let alone saintly. Baptists are those who don't do saints, although we do have our heroes and even a few heroines.[8]

This lack of attention in the local church and as a Baptist Union of churches is reflected also by the omission of All Saints' Day from the two most recent worship books from the Baptist Union. Neither *Patterns and*

---

4. Wider help was given to the church at its beginnings by "a grant of £200 from the Baptist Union Twentieth Century Fund and a loan from the Baptist Building Fund" and in the early months services were led on some weeks by students from Regent's Park College (then in London) and Spurgeon's College, Bottoms, *Fifty Years of Faith*, 1–2.

5. http://www.bmsworldmission.org/resources/magazines/face/face-issue-17.

6. Personally I spent Autumn 2016 preaching a series on Baptist saints at Belle Vue Baptist Church featuring John Bunyan, Thomas Helwys, Dorothy Hazzard, Andrew Fuller, Violet Hedger, and Dan Taylor.

7. Goodliff, "Remembering Baptists."

8. The language of heroes and heroines is I suggest below unchristian.

Prayers (1991) nor *Gathering for Worship* (2005) include All Saints' Day,[9] although interestingly earlier worship books did provide prayers.[10] All of this goes to show that John Colwell is surely right when he says, "The celebration of All Saints' Day is rare amongst Baptists."[11] The lack of prayers for All Saints' is a big loss. It is a missed opportunity and points to an incompleteness in worship. It is a missed opportunity to remind the church that it is bigger than a local congregation, both in terms of space and also time. In addition, it is a missed opportunity as a means of enabling Christians to remember, give thanks and celebrate those who have died and are now with God. I suggest it points to an incompleteness in our worship because without it, we do not say anything about where those who have died have gone. The feast of Ascension celebrates that Christ is at right hand of the Father, the feast of Pentecost celebrates the gift of the Holy Spirit to the church on earth. What the feast of All Saints celebrates is precisely that those who have died are with Christ.

Having said that, three Baptists theologians have recently offered a book-length treatment of the communion of saints from the perspective of being Baptists.[12] Paul Fiddes, Brian Haymes, and Richard Kidd, in the appropriately titled *Baptists and the Communion of Saints*, argue that Baptists can, and must, take seriously the doctrine of the communion of saints and to ignore it is to impoverish our worship and life as churches. Their work is part of a wider conversation taking place at the time of writing amongst some Baptists around a theology and practice of celebrating saints.[13] A generation earlier, the American Baptist theologian James McClendon had already been reflecting on the lives of Christians as a way of doing theology in his *Biography as Theology*[14] and also *Ethics* (the first volume of his Systematic Theology).[15] In these works he looked at the lives of Dag Hammarskjold, Martin Luther King Jr., Clarence Jordan, Charles Ives, Sarah and

---

9. It is more surprising that *Gathering for Worship* does omit All Saints' Day when we consider its more ecumenical outlook. That it does, probably reflects it just takes over the same list of days in the year from *Patterns and Prayers*.

10. See Payne and Winward, *Orders and Prayers*, 124–25, and Gilmore, *Praise God*, 44–46.

11. Colwell, *Rhythm of Doctrine*, 107. This reflects a wider problem that Baptists do not give much attention either to Ascension, and arguably perhaps even Pentecost too. The high points of the Christian year for Baptists remain Christmas Day and Easter Sunday, with a nod to Pentecost, and probably still Harvest.

12. Fiddes et al., *Baptists and the Communion of Saints*.

13. The current project of the Baptist World Alliance Commission on Doctrine and Interchurch Co-operation is on Baptist saints. See Rees, "Search for Baptist Saints."

14. McClendon, *Biography as Theology*.

15. McClendon, *Ethics: Systematic Theology*.

Jonathan Edwards, Dietrich Bonhoeffer, and Dorothy Day.[16] In these lives, McClendon sees exemplars of the character of Christ, as saints, without being officially designated. If Baptists are to recover the celebration of All Saints' and even a more regular attention to particular saints, there are then already some places to look.[17]

What is lacking is any kind of (Baptist) liturgy that might aid our worship. Here the very recent introduction of a Daily Office by the Order of Baptist Ministry specifically for the season between All Saints' and the eve of Advent is to be welcomed. Connected to that are the suggestions found in the final chapter of *Baptists and the Communion of Saints* around including the lives of saints in the celebration of baptism and the Lord's Supper.[18]

I want to use the rest of this chapter to look at what one theologian says about saints and ask what we, as Baptists, might learn with regard to our theology and practice. The theologian is Stanley Hauerwas, to whom Colwell has said he owes "a great debt" and that reading Hauerwas "most radically changed my life."[19] Of course, many of us English Baptists owe John a great debt in introducing more of us to Hauerwas.[20]

Reading Hauerwas's most recent book, *Beginnings: Interrogating Hauerwas*, which is a set of conversations between Hauerwas and Brian Brock, I was introduced to a word I had not come across before: columbarium. For any, like me, who did not know what this word meant, a columbarium is a room where funeral urns are kept. Hauerwas says, "I think having a columbarium is useful. You get to remember who these people are. You get to touch these stones. They are all saints! On All Saints we read the name of every person that has died in our church, from the beginning!"[21] In this remark, we quickly pick up that the saints are important to Hauerwas because he thinks that they are important to the church. Sam Wells has even argued

---

16. Building on McClendon, Glen Stassen sees these lives and others as examples of "incarnational discipleship." See his *A Thicker Jesus*.

17. To this I might add my own short article "Towards a Baptist Sanctoral?"

18. See also the brief suggestions of Steven Harmon in *Towards Baptist Catholicity*, 170–71.

19. Colwell, *Rhythm of Doctrine*, 1.

20. The reception history of Hauerwas in the UK has been helped a lot by the work of Sam Wells, but many Baptists, especially those who had the privilege of being taught by John at Spurgeon's College, will have first read Hauerwas having first read John's *Living the Christian Story*. This was certainly my experience. I remember picking up *Living the Christian Story* one day in 2003 from my father's bookshelf, and then spent a lot of 2004 reading every book by Stanley I could. John and Stanley have certainly changed my life too!

21. Brock and Hauerwas, *Beginnings: Interrogating Hauerwas*, 99.

that the communion of saints is the key doctrine in Hauerwas's theology.[22] The church's witness, the church's interpretation of Scripture, the church's discipleship, all require for Hauerwas the existence of the saints. They are the church's elite.[23] Hauerwas's use of "elite" subverts its usual meaning, for the saints are not necessarily those who are the most powerful and best educated, but those who most "exemplify God's story better than others,"[24] which is a diverse and surprising bunch.[25] These recognized saints are elites, because their lives give them authority in the church as witnesses, interpreters of Scripture and as "paradigms of growth in the Christian life."[26]

Who are these saints? For Hauerwas the saints are not heroes or heroines.[27] The saints are not "eternally nice."[28] The saints do not set out to become saints, rather the pursuit is one of holiness.[29] Instead the saints are more likely to be difficult people. For example, Hauerwas points to the lives of St. Paul, St. Francis, or Dorothy Day.[30] What we find, Hauerwas believes, is that "our assumptions about what makes a saint a saint often fail to attend to the extraordinary diversity of people the church has named as saints."[31] For Hauerwas, saints are those whom God names, through the church.[32] Beyond that, Hauerwas does not provide definitions of sainthood, instead he gives examples. They are often "ordinary people caught up in the purposes of God."[33] So in *Resident Aliens*, Hauerwas and Willimon offer the witness of Dorothy and Gladys.[34] Saints, for Hauerwas, are both all those who are Christians (so the practice of the Church of Holy Family of naming everyone who has died on All Saints') and those whose witness the church has particularly recognized.[35]

---

22. Wells, *Transforming Fate into Destiny*, 83.
23. Hauerwas, *Work of Theology*, 106.
24. Hauerwas, *Peaceable Kingdom*, 71.
25. For instance think of the first disciples!
26. Hauerwas, "Ethics and the Ascetical Theology," 98.
27. Hauerwas, *Unleashing the Scripture*, 103. Following Hauerwas, Sam Wells has offered a helpful description on the differences between the saint and the hero. See his "Disarming Virtue of Stanley Hauerwas."
28. Hauerwas, *Unleashing the Scripture*, 100.
29. Hauerwas, "Homily on All Saints," 2.
30. Hauerwas, *Without Apology*, 24–25.
31. Hauerwas, *Without Apology*, 24.
32. Hauerwas, *Sanctify Them in the Truth*, 99.
33. Hauerwas and Willimon, *Resident Aliens*, 103.
34. Hauerwas and Willimon, *Resident Aliens*, 93, 102, 118–19, 121–23.
35. He does not seek to explain the church's rationale for naming saints, it is just accepted. In the homily he delivered in 2013, he begins by saying, "We know many of

From the beginning of Hauerwas's theological work, he argues that Christianity must produce lives that demonstrate the truthfulness of its convictions, of its story. These lives are those of the saints. He agrees with his friend James McClendon that "theology must be at least biography."[36] It takes Hauerwas until much later in his career to begin to offer theology through biography. His early point, that the convictions of Christians must "produce truthful lives"[37] if Christianity is true, is the same point he makes in his 2001 Gifford Lectures twenty-five years later, in which he argues for the necessity of witness.[38] At this juncture he offers two examples in the case of Pope John Paul II and John Howard Yoder,[39] and a brief referral to Dorothy Day.[40] His work has also pointed to others that he considers saints, like the already mentioned Dorothy and Gladys, but also Dietrich Bonhoeffer,[41] Mother Teresa,[42] and the still-living Jean Vanier.[43]

Hauerwas cannot imagine a church without saints (and the sacraments). At one point he defines the church as "the group of people capable of engendering and recognizing saints."[44] The way that Hauerwas does theology requires saints. They are a necessity for one who claims that the church does not have a social ethic, but is a social ethic.[45] If this is true it

their names . . . this list is long, but even if we named all who names we know, the list of those we do not know is longer," Hauerwas, "Homily on All Saints," 1.

36. McClendon, *Biography as Theology*, cited in Hauerwas, *Truthfulness and Tragedy*, 81.

37. Hauerwas, *Truthfulness and Tragedy*, 80.

38. Hauerwas, *With the Grain of the Universe*, 205–41.

39. The witness of John Howard Yoder has been made difficult, as we have come to know of his abuse of many women during the 1970s and '80s. For Hauerwas's own response, unsatisfactory for some, see *Hannah's Child*, 242–46; *Beginnings*, 184; and "In Defence of 'Our Respectable Culture': Trying to Make Sense of John Howard Yoder's Sexual Abuse," ABC Religion and Ethics, October 18, 2017.

40. Hauerwas, *With the Grain of the Universe*, 216–30. He also devotes a chapter to the importance of the witness of Karl Barth's *Church Dogmatics*, and so also to Barth.

41. See the first two chapters of Hauerwas, *Performing the Faith*, 33–72. He says of Bonhoeffer, "He is now part of God's exemplification given for our redemption," *Performing the Faith*, 54.

42. Hauerwas, *Prayers Plainly Spoken*, 123. Cf. Hauerwas, *Christian Existence Today*, 105–6.

43. Hauerwas has written on Jean Vanier and L'Arche in several places. Hauerwas, *Sanctify Them in the Truth*, 143–56; Hauerwas, "Politics of Gentleness," 77–99; and Hauerwas, *Learning to Speak Christian*, 73–78. Of Vanier he has said, along with Dorothy Day, that they are examples of "masters of the faith whose lives have been shaped by the grammar of Christ," Hauerwas, *State of the University*, 120.

44. Hauerwas, *Christian Existence Today*, 103.

45. Hauerwas first argues this in *Community of Character*.

suggests that the church is a body of people being transformed into the likeness of the one it proclaims as Lord. The church must produce saints and be able to recognize them as saints, otherwise it is not the church.

Outside of sermons, Hauerwas does not offer anywhere an extended reflection on the saints. Nearly all the references are only a sentence or two. This requires some assembly of what the saints mean to Hauerwas. Where he does reference them are in his wider arguments about the church as a community of memory and of witness. The church as a community that remembers reflects Hauerwas's apocalyptic theology.[46] He writes:

> Friendship is not only with those now present but with those who have gone before; we call this the communion of saints. That is why Christian communities live by memory. Our central feast is a feast of memory by which we are made part of God's very life in memory for the world. It therefore becomes crucial for Christianity to be about the formation of communities in which memory is not only a possibility but a necessity. Christianity can only be Christianity if we remember those who have gone before and made our faith possible.[47]

I say apocalyptic because, for Hauerwas, in Christ, God has done something decisive, of which the result is the church.[48] The church is God's new language, "God's memory for the world"[49] and it can only be such because "God produces the saints, and they are reproduced through us."[50] Without the saints, there would be no church. At the same time, Hauerwas is clear to say that "the saints make no sense apart from the life and death of Jesus of Nazareth."[51] Here, following Sam Wells, we see that Hauerwas shows the difference that Christ makes.[52] For "the memory of [the saints] derives its power from the memory of Him . . . the saints" faithfulness to this calling is

---

46. Hauerwas, "God's New Language," in *Christian Existence Today*, 47–65; "Creation as Apocalyptic," in *Dispatches from the Front*, 107–15; *Disrupting Time*, 1–9; *Cross-Shattered Church*, 44, 75, 135; "The End Is in the Beginning: Creation and Apocalyptic" and "The End of Sacrifice: An Apocalyptic Politics," in *Approaching the End*, 3–21, 22–36.

47. Hauerwas, *Better Hope*, 182. This paragraph comes from the chapter "Captured in Time," which Hauerwas cowrote with Laura Yordy.

48. So in the passage just quoted, Hauerwas writes, "We are *made* part of God's very life."

49. Hauerwas, *Better Hope*, 151.

50. Hauerwas, *Unleashing the Scripture*, 103.

51. Hauerwas and Pinches, *Christians among the Virtues*, 124.

52. See Wells, "Difference Christ Makes," 5–23.

concrete demonstration that by Jesus' resurrection a people is formed who can sustain the virtues necessary to remember His death."[53]

The saints are part of the church's memory, and they are part of the church's witness to the gospel of Christ. To speak of witness is of course to be reminded that the Greek word for "witness" is martyr. The importance of witness is central to Hauerwas's theology, seen most clearly in his Gifford Lectures, *With the Grain of the Universe: The Church's Witness and Natural Theology*. In a sermon called "Witness" he describes the saints as those witnesses whose lives have become part of the story of the gospel that the ongoing witness to the story of Jesus cannot avoid including the lives of the saints "if the story is to be truthfully told."[54] Some of these witnesses are martyrs in that their witness meant they died for the sake of the gospel. This link between the saints, martyrs, and witness is most explicit in another sermon "Saints," delivered on All Saints' Day in 2012, where Hauerwas says that sainthood is a "refusal to compromise with worldly powers."[55] This is what is demonstrated by the martyrs of the second century and the ascetics of the third and fourth centuries. The martyrs' witness is found in their lack of fear towards dying, because the meaning of their deaths is already "determined in baptism."[56] The martyrs are "courage exemplified,"[57] in which the glory of God is reflected[58] and "death is undone."[59] The memory and witness of the saints is found in the myriad of ways they imitate Christ faithfully in life and in death.

The saints do not just lie dormant in the memory of the church, but to remember and celebrate the saints is also, as Hauerwas points out, an example of the church's eschatological orientation.[60] We are made members and participants in the communion of saints through baptism and in the Eucharist.[61] Hauerwas has not said much about what it means to be part of that communion, nor the nature of that communion, outside of saying that "prayer is always in the communion of saints," which means we never pray

---

53. Hauerwas and Pinches, *Christians among the Virtues*, 124.

54. Hauerwas, *Cross-Shattered Church*, 47.

55. Hauerwas, *Without Apology*, 24.

56. Hauerwas, *Without Apology*, 26.

57. See the chapter of this name in Hauerwas and Pinches, *Christians among the Virtues*, 149–65.

58. Hauerwas, *Without Apology*, 15.

59. Hauerwas, *Cross-Shattered Church*, 81–87.

60. Willimon and Hauerwas, *Preaching to Strangers*, 76–77.

61. Hauerwas, *Without Apology*, 26; *Cross-Shattered Church*, 87; *Unleashing the Scripture*, 104.

alone.[62] Brock says that Hauerwas's emphasis on memory and remembering can appear "to deny the saints any agency,"[63] which I take to mean, they can be read as stuck in the past. This might also reflect Hauerwas's reticence to talk explicitly about the work of the Holy Spirit, for, as Colwell claims, it is the work of the Spirit that makes our communion with the saints, as they live with Christ, alive and real.[64] Brock goes on to offer this claim about the saints: "When we're talking about the stories of the saints we're not exclusively talking the past sense. Their stories are alive for us because in some sense they are alive, alive to us through the Holy Spirit."[65] Hauerwas finds that helpful. It is, I think, not only correct, but important, that we speak of the saints as being alive to us, especially as we gather at the Lord's Supper. And yet, at the same time, there is a sense that for us who live on earth, we cannot share fully in this communion—we experience only in part that which the saints experience in fuller measure.

If we were to compare Hauerwas with Colwell we see they share an emphasis on the sacraments. For Colwell, living the Christian story is an indwelling of the sacraments.[66] What Colwell has not developed or felt necessary to provide is an equal emphasis on the saints.[67] Hauerwas believes that "the salvation offered by the church . . . is to be found in sacrament and saints."[68] In a review of Colwell's *Living the Christian Story*, he points to the absence in Colwell's argument of "witnesses . . . actual lives, with all the ambiguity and equivocation that entails."[69] Colwell does not do theology as biography, he does not narrate particular lives which speak of the Christian gospel, apart, that is, from one paragraph in *The Rhythm of Doctrine*, where he writes:

> The example of Mother Theresa and Brother Roger alongside
> the example of Billy Graham and Martin Luther King; would

---

62. Willimon and Hauerwas, *Lord, Teach Us*, 29.

63. Brock and Hauerwas, *Beginnings: Interrogating Hauerwas*, 112.

64. Colwell, *Rhythm of Doctrine*, 110. More recently Hauerwas has begun to give more attention to the Holy Spirit, so see Hauerwas, *Work of Theology*, 32–52, and Hauerwas and Willimon, *Holy Spirit*.

65. Brock and Hauerwas, *Beginnings: Interrogating Hauerwas*, 113.

66. "It is through our indwelling of the gospel story, through our hearing it proclaimed, through our participation in it sacramentally, through our sharing in the living narrative of the Christian community that our identity as Christians is shaped by the Spirit," Colwell, *Living the Christian Story*, 168–69.

67. Colwell does say, "The stories of Church history should alert us to the sheer variety of forms that true saintliness can assume," Colwell, *Living the Christian Story*, 182.

68. Hauerwas, *Sanctify Them in the Truth*, 79.

69. Hauerwas and Sider, "Distinctiveness of Christian Ethics," 231.

respect the self-sacrifice of Francis Xavier just as they respect the self-sacrifice of William Carey; and would be impressed by the transparency and simplicity of Francis of Assisi or Catherine of Sienna . . . all are commended for the consistency of their Christian witness through historical testimony . . . all sought humbly to follow the example of Christ and, as such, all validly are examples to us—and the more we know of their lives, of their weaknesses and struggles as much as of their effectiveness and courage, the more poignant and powerful the example.[70]

The Rhythm of Doctrine is only a sketch of Christian doctrine and ethics. If Colwell was ever minded (and some of us pray he would be) to write a more expanded version, it would be interesting to see alongside his linking of doctrine to liturgy and to virtue to include those named above and others as saints who have embodied his presentation of Christian faith and faithfulness.

What is perhaps surprising is that Hauerwas has offered Colwell himself as an example of Christian witness. In the afterword to the paperback edition of *Hannah's Child*, Hauerwas discusses some of the reviews and responses to the book, one of which came from Gerald McKenny who asks the question whether Anne (Hauerwas's first wife), who suffered from bipolar illness, is "the surd that resists your story, refusing to be assimilated into it and therefore reminding you of the limits of any account of Christian discipleship, including yours?" Hauerwas, in reply, offers the "powerful witness of Kathryn Greene-McCreight, as well as John Colwell,"[71] as a means of showing how one can live with mental illness and live with Christ. Colwell becomes one who teaches us how to be Christian, and that to be Christian "is to avoid easy answers,"[72] such as "why do I suffer from depression?" Colwell and Greene-McCreight take responsibility, observes Hauerwas, for their mental illness, in such a way that it does not become determinative of their lives. More important for Colwell is his baptism and his continued sharing in the Lord's Supper.[73]

---

70. Colwell, *Rhythm of Doctrine*, 108–9. In one other place, Colwell offers a brief mention of some saints: "Only the gospel story as narrated in Scripture makes sense of the lives of Julian of Norwich, Francis Xavier, of John Wesley, of William Carey, of Mother Teresa—and through the witness of such lives the story that shaped them is accessed," Colwell, "Church as Ethical Community," 223.

71. Hauerwas, *Hannah's Child*, 303. Hauerwas is referring to Greene-McCreight's book *Darkness Is My Only Companion* and Colwell's *Why Have You Forsaken Me?*

72. Hauerwas, *Hannah's Child*, 305.

73. Colwell, *Why Have You Forsaken Me?*, 40–41.

What might Baptists learn from Hauerwas with regards to the saints? It might simply be: we cannot be church without them. Hauerwas has criticized Baptists for having "no catholic sensibilities" and "when all you have is the New Testament era and the 'now,' you are a bit short on resources to stand against the world."[74] I would hope this remark might now be revised in the light of the theological work of a number of Baptist theologians, including Colwell.[75] Having said that, his point might still continue to hold some truth amongst a large number of Baptist churches who have little knowledge of the lives that make their own possible. The Baptist Union's Declaration of Principle has, rightly in my view, a strong commitment to the authority of Christ,[76] but it includes what Colwell has called "a blatant denial of catholicity,"[77] offering instead, in Barrie White's words, "an assertion of unbridled independency."[78] What is missing is any recognition of the place of "the saints of the church [to] provide guidance in how to interpret and perform scripture."[79] We have already noted the lack of a Baptist calendar of saints or witnesses, which leaves us without a common "cloud of witnesses." We have thus a limited sense of the past and with that a little appreciation of what it has meant to be Baptist in terms of following Christ. This is especially the case in terms of what it meant to be dissenters, the cost of following Christ.[80] Colwell would probably argue that this stems from an impoverished Protestant doctrine of sanctification in which "the expectation that too often is instilled [in Christians] is that they will not change."[81] Saints become an impossibility and with that our understanding of what it might mean to follow Christ. We Baptists believe too often (along with

---

74. Hauerwas, *In Good Company*, 61. The article this comes from was originally published in 1991. By 1994 Curtis Freeman had written "A Confession for Catholic Baptists." We might note also that Hauerwas probably has in view Southern Baptists. For more on Hauerwas and Baptists, see the special edition of *Review & Expositor* 112.1 (February 2015).

75. See, e.g., the various monographs by Curtis Freeman, Steven Harmon, Elizabeth Newman, Paul Fiddes, Stephen Holmes, and John Colwell.

76. "That our Lord and Saviour Jesus Christ, God manifest in the flesh, is the sole and absolute authority in all matters pertaining to faith and practice, as revealed in the Holy Scriptures, and that each Church has liberty, under the guidance of the Holy Spirit, to interpret and administer His laws."

77. Colwell, "Catholicity and Confessionalism," 144.

78. White, "Practice of Association," 19, cited in Colwell, "Catholicity and Confessionalism," 143.

79. This is one of nine theses for interpreting Scripture that can be found in Hays and Davis, *Art of Reading Scripture*.

80. On this, see most recently Freeman, *Undomesticated Dissent*.

81. Colwell, *Living the Christian Story*, 48.

many other Protestants) that we "get to make Christianity up because what it means to be a Christian is to have a personal relationship with God."[82] The gift of the church that recognizes the saints is to see that we are made Christian, that "Christianity is to have one's body shaped, one's habits determined, in a manner that the worship of God is unavoidable."[83] For these reasons alone Baptists must retrieve the saints.[84] We must, as the Order for Baptist Ministry Daily Office offers, provide a litany of the saints, rehearse their names, learn their stories, attend to their lives. These saints will be both widely known and in some cases only known perhaps to a particular congregation.

As this chapter draws to its conclusion. I offer one final suggestion. We are in this collection of essays honoring the contribution that John has made to the work and task of theology. We write as those who have benefited from his writings. This is what festschrifts do. In an essay headed "All Saints" we might also recognize John as one who has been and is a saint amongst us. He would be one of those difficult saints, not straightforwardly recognized. He would be a peculiar saint for John is a recovering charismatic, a Baptist with strong Catholic tendencies, who has dared to offer a defence of Christendom[85] and questioned our obsession with doing mission.[86] John has lived all his adult life with recurring depression, and yet has sought to be a faithful minister and teacher of the gospel, and so we might see that God has made him a saint. And if we are to say John is a saint, we must surely say Rosie, his wife, is one too!

---

82. Hauerwas, *Work of Theology*, 105.

83. Hauerwas, *Sanctify Them in the Truth*, 79.

84. For a similar argument, see Banner, "On What We Lost When (or If) We Lost the Saints."

85. Colwell, "In Defence of Christendom."

86. Colwell, "Mission as Ontology."

Bibliography of the Writings of John E. Colwell

(In order of publication)

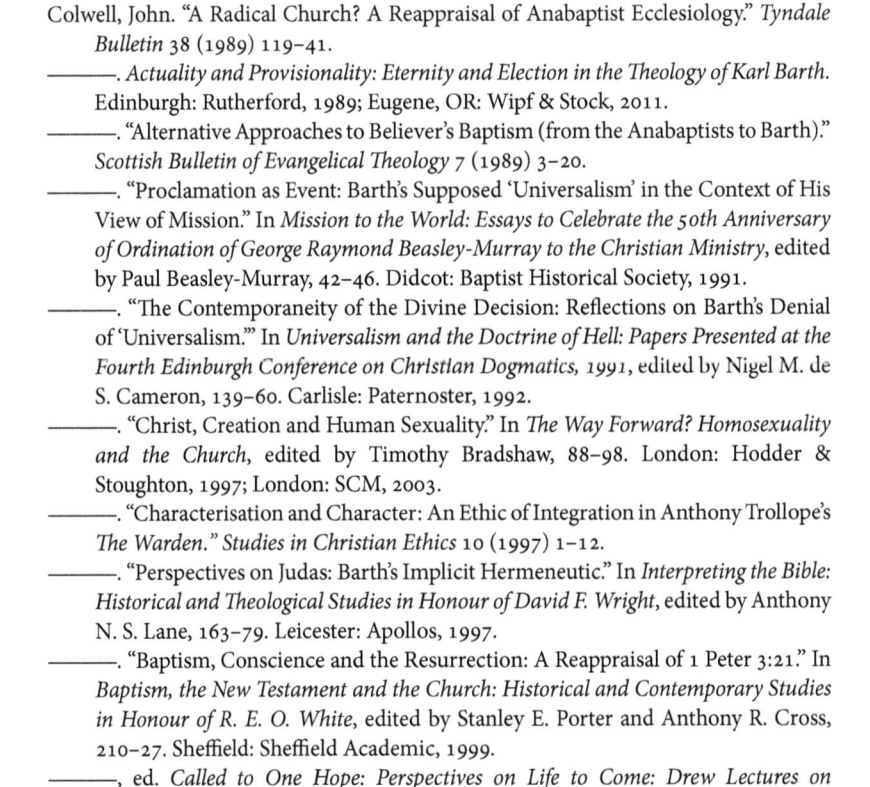

Colwell, John. "A Radical Church? A Reappraisal of Anabaptist Ecclesiology." *Tyndale Bulletin* 38 (1989) 119-41.

———. *Actuality and Provisionality: Eternity and Election in the Theology of Karl Barth*. Edinburgh: Rutherford, 1989; Eugene, OR: Wipf & Stock, 2011.

———. "Alternative Approaches to Believer's Baptism (from the Anabaptists to Barth)." *Scottish Bulletin of Evangelical Theology* 7 (1989) 3-20.

———. "Proclamation as Event: Barth's Supposed 'Universalism' in the Context of His View of Mission." In *Mission to the World: Essays to Celebrate the 50th Anniversary of Ordination of George Raymond Beasley-Murray to the Christian Ministry*, edited by Paul Beasley-Murray, 42-46. Didcot: Baptist Historical Society, 1991.

———. "The Contemporaneity of the Divine Decision: Reflections on Barth's Denial of 'Universalism.'" In *Universalism and the Doctrine of Hell: Papers Presented at the Fourth Edinburgh Conference on Christian Dogmatics, 1991*, edited by Nigel M. de S. Cameron, 139-60. Carlisle: Paternoster, 1992.

———. "Christ, Creation and Human Sexuality." In *The Way Forward? Homosexuality and the Church*, edited by Timothy Bradshaw, 88-98. London: Hodder & Stoughton, 1997; London: SCM, 2003.

———. "Characterisation and Character: An Ethic of Integration in Anthony Trollope's *The Warden*." *Studies in Christian Ethics* 10 (1997) 1-12.

———. "Perspectives on Judas: Barth's Implicit Hermeneutic." In *Interpreting the Bible: Historical and Theological Studies in Honour of David F. Wright*, edited by Anthony N. S. Lane, 163-79. Leicester: Apollos, 1997.

———. "Baptism, Conscience and the Resurrection: A Reappraisal of 1 Peter 3:21." In *Baptism, the New Testament and the Church: Historical and Contemporary Studies in Honour of R. E. O. White*, edited by Stanley E. Porter and Anthony R. Cross, 210-27. Sheffield: Sheffield Academic, 1999.

———, ed. *Called to One Hope: Perspectives on Life to Come: Drew Lectures on Immortality*. Carlisle: Paternoster, 2000.

———. "'The Glory of God': Justice and the Glory of God's Grace; Contemporary Reflections on the Doctrine of Hell in the Teaching of Jonathan Edwards." In *Called to One Hope*, edited by John Colwell, 112-29. Carlisle: Paternoster, 2000.

———. *Living the Christian Story: The Distinctiveness of Christian Ethics*. Edinburgh: T. & T. Clark, 2001.

———. "Offending in Many Things: A Comparison of John Wesley and Thomas Aquinas on the Nature of Sin in the Believer." In *Wesley Papers: Papers Presented to the Wesley Fellowship Conference in 2000*, edited by Paul Taylor, 3–14. Ilkeston, UK: Wesley Fellowship, 2002.

———. "The Sacramental Nature of Ordination: An Attempt to Re-engage a Catholic Understanding and Practice." In *Baptist Sacramentalism*, edited by Anthony R. Cross and Philip E. Thompson, 228–46. Carlisle: Paternoster, 2003.

———. *Promise and Presence: An Exploration of Sacramental Theology*. Milton Keynes: Paternoster, 2005.

———. "The Church as Ethical Community." In *The Bible in Pastoral Practice: Readings in the Place and Function of Scripture in the Church*, edited by Paul Ballard and Stephen R. Holmes, 212–24. London: Darton, Longman & Todd, 2005.

———. "Making a Calvinist out of Wesley: Comparing John Calvin and John Wesley on the Lord's Supper." Unpublished paper presented to the Wesley Fellowship, April 23, 2005.

———. "Mission as Ontology: A Question of Theological Grammar." *Baptist Ministers' Journal* 295 (2006) 7–12.

———. "In Defence of Christendom." *Baptist Ministers' Journal* 298 (2007) 21–29.

———. *The Rhythm of Doctrine: A Liturgical Sketch of Christian Faith and Faithfulness*. Milton Keynes: Paternoster, 2007.

———. "Living for the Future: The End of Ethics." In *What Are We Waiting For? Christian Hope and Contemporary Culture*, edited by Stephen Holmes and Russell Rook, 189–99. Milton Keynes: Paternoster, 2008.

———. "The Church as Sacrament: A Mediating Presence." In *Baptist Sacramentalism 2*, edited by Anthony R. Cross and Philip E. Thompson, 48–60. Milton Keynes: Paternoster, 2008.

———. "Catholicity and Confessionalism: Responding to George Beasley-Murray on Unity and Distinctiveness." *Baptist Quarterly* 43 (2009) 4–23. Reprinted in *Truth That Never Dies*, edited by Nigel G. Wright, 131–51. Eugene, OR: Pickwick, 2014.

———. "The Coherence of Freedom: Can Church and State Ever Be Truly Free?" In *Challenging to Change: Dialogues with a Radical Baptist Theologian: Essays Presented to Dr Nigel G. Wright on His Sixtieth Birthday*, edited by Pieter J. Lalleman, 39–53. London: Spurgeon's College, 2009.

———. *Why Have You Forsaken Me? A Personal Reflection on the Experience of Desolation*. Milton Keynes: Paternoster, 2009.

———. "Provisionality and Promise: Avoiding Ecclesiastical Nestorianism?" In *The Theology of Colin Gunton*, edited by Lincoln Harvey, 100–105. London: T. & T. Clark, 2010.

———. "A Matter of Conscience: A Quest for Otherness." In *Questions of Identity: Essays in Honour of Brian Haymes*, edited by Anthony R. Cross and Ruth Gouldbourne, 141–54. Oxford: Centre for Baptist History & Heritage, 2011.

———. "The Word of His Grace: What's So Distinctive about Scripture?" In *The "Plainly Revealed" Word of God? Baptist Hermeneutics in Theory and Practice*, edited by Simon Woodman and Helen Dare, 191–210. Macon, GA: Mercer University Press, 2011.

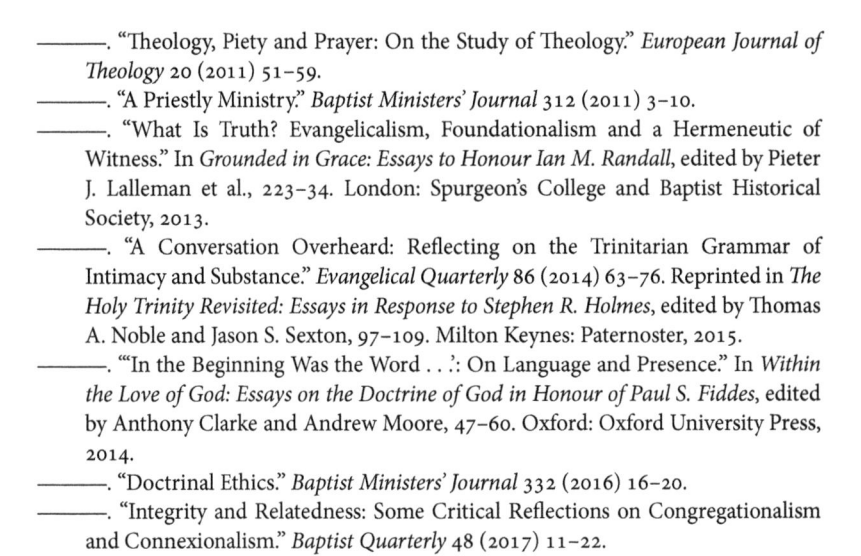

———. "Theology, Piety and Prayer: On the Study of Theology." *European Journal of Theology* 20 (2011) 51–59.

———. "A Priestly Ministry." *Baptist Ministers' Journal* 312 (2011) 3–10.

———. "What Is Truth? Evangelicalism, Foundationalism and a Hermeneutic of Witness." In *Grounded in Grace: Essays to Honour Ian M. Randall*, edited by Pieter J. Lalleman et al., 223–34. London: Spurgeon's College and Baptist Historical Society, 2013.

———. "A Conversation Overheard: Reflecting on the Trinitarian Grammar of Intimacy and Substance." *Evangelical Quarterly* 86 (2014) 63–76. Reprinted in *The Holy Trinity Revisited: Essays in Response to Stephen R. Holmes*, edited by Thomas A. Noble and Jason S. Sexton, 97–109. Milton Keynes: Paternoster, 2015.

———. "'In the Beginning Was the Word . . .': On Language and Presence." In *Within the Love of God: Essays on the Doctrine of God in Honour of Paul S. Fiddes*, edited by Anthony Clarke and Andrew Moore, 47–60. Oxford: Oxford University Press, 2014.

———. "Doctrinal Ethics." *Baptist Ministers' Journal* 332 (2016) 16–20.

———. "Integrity and Relatedness: Some Critical Reflections on Congregationalism and Connexionalism." *Baptist Quarterly* 48 (2017) 11–22.

General Bibliography

Ahl, Diane Cole. *Fra Angelico*. London: Phaidon, 2008.
Alexander, T. D. *Exodus*. London: SPCK, 2017.
Allison, Dale. *Resurrecting Jesus: The Earliest Christian Tradition and Its Interpreters*. London: T. & T. Clark, 2005.
Ante Nicene Fathers: Translations of the Writings of the Fathers Down to AD 325. Edited by Alexander Roberts and James Donaldson. 10 vols. Grand Rapids: Eerdmans, 1956.
Athanasius. *On the Incarnation of the Word*. Translated by Archibald Robertson. In *Christology of the Later Fathers*, edited by Edward Rochie Hardy, 55–110. Library of Christian Classics 3. London: SCM, 1954.
Atherstone, Andrew. *Confessing Our Sins*. Cambridge, UK: Grove, 2004.
Atkinson, David. *God So Loved the World: Towards a Missionary Theology*. London, SPCK, 1999.
Aubery, M. E., ed. *A Minister's Manual*. London: Kingsgate, 1927.
Augustine. *St. Augustine: Sermons for Christmas and Epiphany*. Translated by Thomas Comderford Lawler. Ancient Christian Writers 15. Westminster, MD: Newman, 1952.
Baillie, D. M. *God Was in Christ*. London: Faber, 1963.
Balthasar, Hans Urs von. *Theo-Drama: Theological Dramatic Theory*. Translated by Graham Harrison. 5 vols. San Francisco: Ignatius, 1988–98.
Banner, Michael. "On What We Lost When (or If) We Lost the Saints." In *The Freedom of the Christian Ethicist: The Future of a Reformation Legacy*, edited by Brian Brock and Michael Mawson, 175–90. London: T. & T. Clark, 2014.
The Baptist Church Hymnal. London: Psalms and Hymns Trust, 1900. Rev. ed., 1933.
The Baptist Hymn Book: With Music. London: Psalms and Hymns Trust, 1962.
Baptist Praise and Worship. Oxford: Oxford University Press, 1991.
Baptist Union of Great Britain. *Five Core Values for a Gospel People*. Didcot, UK: Baptist Union, 1998.
———. *Patterns and Prayers for Christian Worship: A Guidebook for Worship Leaders*. Oxford: Oxford University Press, 1991.
Barth, Karl. *Church Dogmatics*. Translated and edited by G. W. Bromiley and T. F. Torrance. 14 vols. Edinburgh: T. & T. Clark, 1936–77.
———. *The Christian Life: Lecture Fragments*. In *Church Dogmatics*, vol. 4, pt. 4, translated by Geoffrey W. Bromiley. Grand Rapids: Eerdmans, 1981.

———. *God Here and Now*. Translated by Paul M. van Buren. London: Routledge, 2003.
———. *The Humanity of God*. London: Collins, 1961.
———. *Wolfgang Amadeus Mozart*. Translated by Clarence K. Pott. Grand Rapids: Eerdmans, 1986.
Bass, Dorothy, ed. *Practicing Our Faith: A Way of Life for a Searching People*. San Francisco: Jossey-Bass, 1997.
Beale, Gregory K. "Colossians." In *Commentary on the New Testament Use of the Old Testament*, edited by G. K. Beale and D. A. Carson, 841–70. Grand Rapids: Baker Academic, 2007.
———. "The Descent of the Eschatological Temple in the Form of the Spirit at Pentecost. Part 2: Corroborating Evidence." *Tyndale Bulletin* 56 (2005) 63–90.
———. *The Temple and the Church's Mission: A Biblical Theology of the Dwelling Place of God*. Downers Grove: Apollos, 2004.
Bebbington, David. *Baptists through the Centuries: A History of a Global People*. Waco, TX: Baylor University Press, 2010.
Beeley, Christopher. *Gregory of Nazianzus on the Trinity and the Knowledge of God*. Oxford: Oxford University Press, 2008.
Begbie, Jeremy. *Resonant Truth: Christian Wisdom in the World of Music*. London: SPCK, 2007.
———. *Theology, Music and Time*. Cambridge: Cambridge University Press, 2000.
———. *Voicing Creation's Praise: Towards a Theology of the Arts*. Edinburgh: T. & T. Clark, 1991.
Bockmuehl, Markus. "Resurrection." In *The Cambridge Companion to Jesus*, edited by Markus Bockmuehl, 102–20. Cambridge: Cambridge University Press, 2001.
Bonhoeffer, Dietrich. *The Cost of Discipleship*. London, SCM, 1959.
———. *Ethics*. Dietrich Bonhoeffer Works 6. Translated by R. Krauss. Minneapolis: Fortress, 2005.
———. *Letters and Papers from Prison*. Dietrich Bonhoeffer Works 8. Translated by Isabel Best et al. Minneapolis: Fortress, 2010.
———. *Life Together*. Translated by John W. Doberstein. London: SCM, 1954.
Bottoms, Walter W. *Fifty Years of Faith and Works*. Southend-on-Sea, UK: Belle Vue Baptist Church, 1952.
Bower, Peter. *Handbook for the Revised Common Lectionary*. Louisville: Westminster John Knox, 1996.
Bradley, Ian. *Water: A Spiritual History*. London: Bloomsbury, 2012.
Bradshaw, Paul. *Daily Prayer in the Early Church: A Study of the Origin and Early Development of the Divine Office*. London: Alcuin Club & SPCK, 1981.
———. *The Search for the Origins of Christian Worship*. London: SPCK, 1992.
Bradshaw, Paul, and Maxwell Johnson. *The Origins of Feasts, Fasts and Seasons in Early Christianity*. London: SPCK, 2011.
Brand, Hilary, and Adrienne Chaplin. *Art & Soul: Signposts for Christians in the Arts*. Carlisle: Piquant, 2001.
Brenton, L. C. L. *The Septuagint Version of the Old Testament: English Translation*. London: Bagster, 1870.
Brett, Mark. *Political Trauma and Healing: Biblical Ethics for a Post-Colonial World*. Grand Rapids: Eerdmans, 2016.

Brock, Brian, and Stanley Hauerwas. *Beginnings: Interrogating Hauerwas*. London: T. & T. Clark, 2017.
Brock, Sebastian. "The Consecration of the Water in the Oldest Manuscripts of the Syrian Orthodox Baptismal Liturgy." *Orientalia Christiana Periodica* 37 (1971) 317–32.
———. *Fire from Heaven: Studies in Syriac Theology and Liturgy*. Aldershot: Ashgate, 2006.
———. *The Luminous Eye: The Spiritual World Vision of Saint Ephrem*. Kalamazoo: Cistercian, 1992.
———. "Studies in the Early History of the Syrian Orthodox Baptismal Liturgy." *Journal of Theological Studies* 23 (1972) 16–64.
Brooks, Thomas. *Works of Thomas Brooks*. Vol 5. Edinburgh: Nicol, 1866.
Brown, J. K. "Creation's Renewal in the Gospel of John." *Catholic Biblical Quarterly* 72 (2010) 275–90.
Brown, Raymond E. *The Birth of the Messiah*. New York: Doubleday, 1979.
Bulgakov, Sergius. *Churchly Joy: Orthodox Devotions for the Church Year*. Grand Rapids: Eerdmans, 2008.
Bunyan, John. *I Will Pray with the Spirit*. In *The Miscellaneous Works of John Bunyan*, vol. 2, edited by Roger Sharrock. Oxford: Oxford University Press, 1976.
Calvin, John. *Institutes of Christian Religion*. Edited by J. T. McNeil. 2 vols. Philadelphia: Westminster, 1960.
———. *Sermons on the Book of Micah*. Translated and edited by B. W. Farley. Phillipsburg, NJ: P & R, 2003.
Carnley, Peter. *The Structure of Resurrection Belief*. Oxford: Clarendon, 1987.
Casey, Maurice. *Jesus of Nazareth: An Independent Historian's Account of His Life and Teaching*. London: T. & T. Clark, 2010.
Catchpole, David. *Resurrection People: Studies in the Resurrection Narratives in the Gospels*. London: Darton, Longman & Todd, 2000.
Catechism of the Catholic Church. London: Chapman, 1994.
Celebrating Common Prayer: A Version of the Daily Office, SSF. London: Mowbray, 1992.
Clarke, Anthony. *A Cry in the Darkness: The Forsakenness of Jesus in Scripture, Theology and Experience*. Macon, GA: Smyth and Helwys, 2002.
Common Worship: Services and Prayers for the Church of England. London: Church House, 2000.
Cornwell John. *Powers of Darkness, Powers of Light: Travels in Search of the Miraculous and the Demonic*. London: Penguin, 1992.
Craig, William Lane. *Assessing the New Testament Evidence for the Historicity of the Resurrection*. Lewiston: Mellen, 1989.
Cross, Anthony R. *Baptism and the Baptists: Theology and Practice in Twentieth-Century Britain*. Carlisle: Paternoster, 2000.
———. *Recovering the Evangelical Sacrament: Baptisma Semper Reformandum*. Eugene, OR: Pickwick, 2013.
Crum, W. E., and Wilhelm Riedel, eds. *The Canons of Athanasius of Alexandria*. London: Williams and Norgate, 1904.
Cunningham, David S. *These Three Are One: The Practice of Trinitarian Theology*. Oxford: Blackwell, 1998.

Cyprian of Carthage. *De Oratione Dominica: Treatise 8*. In *Tertullian, Cyprian and Origen on the Lord's Prayer*, translated by A. Stewart-Sykes, 90–113. Crestwood, NY: St. Vladimir's Seminary Press, 2004.

Daley, Brian. *Gregory of Nazianzus*. London: Routledge, 2006.

Dalmais, Irénée Henri, et al. *Liturgy and Time*. Collegeville: Liturgical, 1986.

Dawson, Geritt Scott. *Jesus Ascended: The Meaning of Christ's Continuing Incarnation*. London: T. & T. Clark, 2004.

DeJonge, Michael P. "Bonhoeffer from the Perspective of Intellectual History." In *Interpreting Bonhoeffer: Historical Perspectives, Emerging Issues*, edited by Clifford J. Green and Guy C. Carter, 197–204. Minneapolis: Fortress, 2013.

———. *Bonhoeffer's Theological Formation: Berlin, Barth & Protestant Theology*. Oxford: Oxford University Press, 2012.

Dempsey, Michael T., ed. *Trinity and Election in Contemporary Theology*. Grand Rapids: Eerdmans, 2011.

Dempster, S. G. *Dominion and Dynasty: A Theology of the Hebrew Bible*. Downers Grove: Apollos, 2003.

Denysenko, Nicholas E. *The Blessing of Waters and Epiphany: The Eastern Liturgical Tradition*. Aldershot: Ashgate, 2012.

Detweiler, Craig. *Into the Dark: Seeing the Sacred in the Top Films of the 21st Century*. Grand Rapids: Baker Academic, 2008.

Dickinson, Emily. *Everyman's Poetry*. London: Dent, 1997.

Dillard, Annie. *Teaching a Stone to Talk: Expeditions and Encounters*. New York: HarperCollins, 1982.

Dillistone, F. W. *The Christian Understanding of Atonement*. 2nd ed. London: SCM, 1984.

Douglas, Mary. *Purity and Danger*. Abingdon: Routledge, 1966.

Drijvers, Jan Willem. *Cyril of Jerusalem: Bishop and City*. Leiden: Brill, 2004.

Dunn, James D. G. *Jesus and the Spirit*. London: SCM, 1975.

Edward VI. *The First and Second Prayer Books of Edward VI*. London: Dent, 1968.

Ehrman, Bart D. *Did Jesus Exist? The Historical Argument for Jesus of Nazareth*. New York: HarperCollins, 2012.

Eiesland, Nancy. *The Disabled God: Toward a Liberatory Theology of Disability*. Nashville: Abingdon, 1994.

Eliot, T. S. *Four Quartets*. In *The Poems of T. S. Eliot: The Annotated Text*, vol. 1. London: Faber and Faber, 2015.

Ellis, Christopher J. *Approaching God: A Guide for Worship Leaders and Worshippers*. Norwich: Canterbury, 2009.

———. *Gathering: A Theology and Spirituality of Worship in Free Church Tradition*. London: SCM, 2004.

Ellis, Christopher J., and Myra Blyth, eds. *Gathering for Worship: Patterns and Prayers for the Community of Disciples*. Norwich: Canterbury, 2005.

Evdokimov, Michel. *Light from the East*. New York: Paulist, 2004.

Everrett, Daniel. "From Threatened Languages to Threatened Lives." http://www.yourdictionary.com/elr/everett.html.

Fabricius, Kim. *Propositions on Christian Theology*. Durham: Carolina Academic, 2008.

Farago, Jason. "Why Museums Are the New Churches." BBC.com. July 16, 2015. http://www.bbc.com/culture/story/20150716-why-museums-are-the-new-churches.

Farrow, Douglas. *Ascension and Ecclesia: On the Significance of the Doctrine of the Ascension for Ecclesiology and Christian Cosmology.* Edinburgh: T. & T. Clark, 1999.

———. *Ascension Theology.* London: T. & T. Clark, 2011.

Fenwick John R. K., and Bryan D. Spinks. *Worship in Transition: The Twentieth Century Liturgical Movement.* Edinburgh: T. & T. Clark, 1995.

Ferguson, Everett. *Baptism in the Early Church: History, Theology, and Liturgy in the First Five Centuries.* Grand Rapids: Eerdmans, 2009.

———. "Preaching at Epiphany: Gregory of Nyssa and John Chrysostom on Baptism and the Church." *Church History* 66 (1997) 1–17.

Fiddes, Paul S. *The Creative Suffering of God.* Oxford: Clarendon, 1988.

———. "Ex Opere Operato: Re-thinking a Historic Baptist Objection." In *Baptist Sacramentalism,* edited by Anthony R. Cross and Philip E. Thompson, 2:219–38. Milton Keynes: Paternoster, 2008.

———. *Participating in God: A Pastoral Doctrine of the Trinity.* London: Darton, Longman & Todd, 2000.

———. *Past Event and Present Salvation.* London: Darton, Longman & Todd, 1989.

———. "Praying with Mary and All the Saints." In *Baptists and the Communion of Saints: A Theology of Covenanted Disciples,* by Paul Fiddes et al., 73–101. Waco, TX: Baylor University Press, 2014.

———. "Relational Trinity: Radical Perspective." In *Two Views on the Doctrine of the Trinity,* edited by Jason Sexton, 159–71. Grand Rapids: Zondervan, 2014.

———. *Seeing God and Knowing the World: Hebrew Wisdom and Christian Doctrine in a Late-Modern World.* Oxford: Oxford University Press, 2015.

———. "Spirituality as Attentiveness: Stillness and Journey." In *Under the Rule of Christ: Dimensions of Baptist Spirituality,* edited by Paul S. Fiddes, 25–57. Macon, GA: Smyth & Helwys, 2008.

———. *Tracks and Traces: Baptist Identity in Church and Theology.* Carlisle: Paternoster, 2003.

———. "'Walking Together': The Place of Covenant Theology in Baptist Life Yesterday and Today." In *Pilgrim Pathways: Essays in Baptist History in Honour of B. R. White,* edited by W. H. Brackney et al., 47–74. Macon, GA: Mercer University Press, 1999.

Fiddes, Paul S., et al. *Baptists and the Communion of Saints: A Theology of Covenanted Disciples.* Waco, TX: Baylor University Press, 2014.

Fortman, Edmund J. *The Triune God: A Historical Study of the Doctrine of the Trinity.* London: Hutchinson, 1972.

Foster, Richard. *Celebration of Discipline.* London: Hodder & Stoughton, 1980.

Frankl, Victor E. *Man's Search for Meaning.* New York: Pocket Books, 1984.

Freeman, Curtis W. "A Confession for Catholic Baptists." In *Ties That Bind,* edited by Garry A. Furr and Curtis W. Freeman, 83–97. Macon, GA: Smyth & Helwys, 1994.

———. *Contesting Catholicity: Theology for Other Baptists.* Waco, TX: Baylor University Press, 2014.

———. *Undomesticated Dissent: Democracy and the Public Virtue of Religious Nonconformity.* Waco, TX: Baylor University Press, 2017.

Foucauld, Charles de. *Meditations of a Hermit.* Translated by Charlotte Belfour. London: Burnes and Oates, 1981.

Friesen, Aileen. "Missionary Priests' Reports from Siberia." In *Orthodox Christianity in Imperial Russia: A Source Book on Lived Religion*, edited by Heather J. Coleman, 249–61. Bloomington: Indiana University Press, 2014.

Gathercole, Simon. "What Is the Historical Evidence That Jesus Christ Actually Lived and Died?" *Guardian*, April 14, 2017. https://www.theguardian.com/world/2017/apr/14/what-is-the-historical-evidence-that-jesus-christ-lived-and-died.

Gaukroger, Stephen. *Being Baptized*. London: Pickering, 1993.

Gennep, Arnold van. *The Rites of Passage*. Translated by Monika B. Vizedom and Gabrielle L. Caffee. Chicago: University of Chicago Press, 1960.

Getcha, Job. *The Typikon Decoded: An Explanation of Byzantine Liturgical Practice*. Crestwood, NY: St. Vladimir's Seminary Press, 2012.

Gillet, Lev. *Orthodox Spirituality: An Outline of the Orthodox Ascetical and Mystical Tradition*. 2nd ed. London: SPCK, 1978.

———. *The Year of Grace of the Lord: A Scriptural and Liturgical Commentary on the Calendar of the Orthodox Church, by a Monk of the Eastern Church*. Translated from French by Deborah Cowen. London: Mowbray, 1980.

Gillett, David K. *Trust and Obey: Explorations in Evangelical Spirituality*. London: Darton, Longman & Todd, 1993.

Gilmore, Alec, et al. *Praise God*. London: Baptist Union, 1980.

Goldingay, John. *Isaiah*. Peabody: Hendrickson, 2001.

Goodliff, Andy. "Remembering Baptists." *Baptist Minister's Journal* 331 (2016) 25–28.

———. "Towards a Baptist Sanctoral?" *Journal of European Baptist Studies* 13 (2013) 24–30.

Goodliff, Paul W. *Ministry, Sacrament and Representation*. Oxford: Regent's Park College, 2010.

———. *Shaped for Service: Ministerial Formation and Virtue Ethics*. Eugene, OR: Pickwick, 2017.

Gorman, Michael. *Becoming the Gospel*. Grand Rapids: Eerdmans, 2015.

———. *Cruciformity: Paul's Narrative Spirituality of the Cross*. Grand Rapids: Eerdmans, 2001.

Gray, Brett. *Jesus in the Theology of Rowan Williams*. London: Bloomsbury, 2016.

Green, Joel. *The Gospel of Luke*. NICNT. Grand Rapids: Eerdmans, 1997.

Greene-McCreight, Kathryn. *Darkness Is My Only Companion*. Grand Rapids: Brazos, 2006.

Grenfell, Joyce. "If I Should Go." https://www.poemhunter.com/poem/death-if-i-should-go/.

Guiver, George. *Company of Voices: Daily Prayer and the People of God*. London: SPCK, 1988.

Gundry, Robert. *The Use of the Old Testament in St. Matthew's Gospel*. Leiden: Brill, 1967.

Gunton, Colin E. *The Triune Creator: A Historical and Systematic Study*. Grand Rapids: Eerdmans, 1998.

Guthrie, Stephen R. *Creator Spirit: The Holy Spirit and the Art of Becoming Human*. Grand Rapids: Baker Academic, 2011.

Guttierez, Gustavo. *A Theology of Liberation*. London: SCM, 1974.

Hales, Thomas. *On Being a Missionary*. Pasadena, CA: William Carey Library, 1995.

Hardison, O. B. *Christian Rite and Christian Drama in the Middle Ages: Essays on the Origin and Early History of Modern Drama*. Westport, CT: Greenwood, 1983.

Hargreaves, Sam, and Sara Hargreaves. *Whole Life Worship*. Leicester: InterVarsity, 2017.
Harmon, Steven. *Towards Baptist Catholicity*. Milton Keynes: Paternoster, 2006.
Hart, David Bentley. *Atheist Delusions*. London: Yale University Press, 2009.
Hart, Trevor. *Faith Thinking: The Dynamics of Christian Theology*. London: SPCK, 1995.
———. "Protestantism and Art." In *The Blackwell Companion to Protestantism*, edited by Alister E. McGrath and Darren C. Marks, 268–86. Oxford: Blackwell, 2004.
———. *Regarding Karl Barth: Essays toward a Reading of His Theology*. Carlisle: Paternoster, 1999.
Hauerwas, Stanley. *Approaching the End*. Grand Rapids: Eerdmans, 2013.
———. *A Better Hope*. Grand Rapids: Brazos, 2000.
———. *Christian Existence Today*. Grand Rapids: Brazos, 2001 [1988].
———. *A Community of Character*. Notre Dame: Notre Dame University Press, 1981.
———. *A Cross-Shattered Church*. Grand Rapids: Brazos, 2009.
———. *Dispatches from the Front*. Notre Dame: Notre Dame University Press, 1994.
———. *Disrupting Time*. Eugene, OR: Cascade, 2004.
———. "Ethics and the Ascetical Theology." *Anglican Theological Review* 16 (1979) 87–98.
———. *Hannah's Child: A Theologian's Memoir*. Grand Rapids: Eerdmans, 2012.
———. "A Homily on All Saints" In *The Difference Christ Makes*, edited by Charlie Collier, 1–3. Eugene, OR: Cascade, 2015.
———. *In Good Company*. Notre Dame: Notre Dame University Press, 1995.
———. *Learning to Speak Christian*. London: SCM, 2011.
———. *The Peaceable Kingdom*. 2nd ed. London: SCM, 2003 [1983].
———. *Performing the Faith*. London: SPCK, 2004.
———. "The Politics of Gentleness." In *Living Gently in a Violent World*, by Stanley Hauerwas and Jean Vanier, 77–99. Downers Grove: InterVarsity, 2008.
———. *Prayers Plainly Spoken*. Eugene, OR: Wipf & Stock, 2003 [1999].
———. *Sanctify Them in the Truth*. Edinburgh: T. & T. Clark, 1998.
———. *The State of the University*. Oxford: Blackwell, 2007.
———. *Truthfulness and Tragedy*. Notre Dame: Notre Dame University Press, 1977.
———. *Unleashing the Scripture*. Nashville: Abingdon, 1993.
———. *With the Grain of the Universe*. 2nd ed. Grand Rapids: Baker, 2013 [2001].
———. *Without Apology: Sermon's For Christ's Church*. New York: Seabury, 2013.
———. *The Work of Theology*. Grand Rapids: Eerdmans, 2015.
Hauerwas, Stanley, and Charles Pinches. *Christians among the Virtues*. Notre Dame: Notre Dame University Press, 1997.
Hauerwas, Stanley, and J. Alexander Sider. "The Distinctiveness of Christian Ethics: A Review Article on John E. Colwell, *Living the Christian Story*." *International Journal of Systematic Theology* 5 (2003) 225–33.
Hauerwas, Stanley, and William Willimon. *The Holy Spirit*. Nashville: Abingdon, 2015.
———. *Resident Aliens*. Nashville: Abingdon, 1989.
Haward, Joseph. *The Ghost of Perfection: Searching for Humanity*. Eugene, OR: Resource, 2017.
Hawthorne, G. F. *Philippians*. Dallas: Word, 2004.
Hays, Richard, and Ellen Davis, eds. *The Art of Reading Scripture*. Grand Rapids: Eerdmans, 2003.

Helwys, Thomas. *A Short Declaration of the Mistery of Iniquity*. Edited by Richard Groves. Macon, GA: Mercer, 1998.

Holberg, Jennifer L. "'The Courage to See It': Toward an Understanding of Glory." *Christianity and Literature* 59 (2010) 283–300.

Holmes, Stephen. *Baptist Theology*. London: T. & T. Clark, 2012.

———. *God of Grace, God of Glory*. Edinburgh: T. & T. Clark, 2000.

Hopkins, Gerard Manley. "God's Grandeur." In *Gerard Manley Hopkins: The Major Works*, edited by Catherine Phillips, 128. Oxford: Oxford University Press, 2002.

Hornby, Nick. *31 Songs*. London: Penguin, 2003.

Howlett, Greg. "Ending a Song on a IV Chord." Howlett's blog. March 27, 2012. https://greghowlett.com/blog/free-lessons/032712.aspx.

Hulst, Fulco van. "Abelard on Atonement: Through Love or through Penal Substitution? Reading Abelard from a Peace Church Perspective." *Baptistic Theologies* 6 (2014) 14–23.

Hunsinger, George Hunsinger. "Postcritical Scriptural Interpretation: Rudolf Smend on Karl Barth." In *Thy Word Is Truth: Barth on Scripture*, edited by George Hunsinger, 29–48. Grand Rapids: Eerdmans, 2012.

Ignatius of Loyola. *Spiritual Exercises*. Translated by Louis J. Puhl. Chicago: Loyola University Press, 1951.

Irvine, Christopher. *The Art of God: The Making of Christians and the Meaning of Worship*. London: SPCK, 2005.

Jantzen, Grace. *God's World God's Body*. London: Darton, Longman & Todd, 1984.

Jeanrond, Werner G. "Karl Barth's Hermeneutics." In *Reckoning with Barth: Essays in Commemoration of the Centenary of Karl Barth's Birth*, edited by Nigel Biggar, 80–97. London: Mowbray, 1988.

Johnson, Maxwell E. *The Rites of Christian Initiation: Their Evolution and Interpretation*. Collegeville: Liturgical, 1999.

———, ed. *Sacraments and Worship: The Sources of Christian Theology*. Louisville: Westminster John Knox, 2012.

Jones, Keith. "Lent." In *A Dictionary of European Baptist Life and Thought*, edited by John H. Y. Briggs, 299. Milton Keynes: Paternoster, 2009.

Jones, L. Gregory. *Embodying Forgiveness: A Theological Analysis*. Grand Rapids: Eerdmans, 1995.

Josephus. "Antiquities." In *The Works of Josephus*, translated by W. Whiston. Peabody: Hendrickson, 1987.

Kavanagh, Aidan. *On Liturgical Theology*. New York: Pueblo, 1984.

Koester, Craig R. *The Dwelling of God: The Tabernacle in the Old Testament, Intertestamental Jewish Literature, and the New Testament*. Washington: Catholic Biblical Association of America, 1989.

Kung, Hans. *Mozart*. London: SCM, 1992.

Ladd, G. Eldon. *I Believe in the Resurrection of Jesus*. London: Hodder & Stoughton, 1975.

Lampe, G. H. W. *God as Spirit*. Oxford: Clarendon, 1977.

Lane, Belden C. *The Solace of Fierce Landscapes: Exploring Desert and Mountain Spirituality*. Oxford: Oxford University Press, 1998.

Langley, Jonathan. "Music, Modern Art and Mystery." *Mission Catalyst* 4 (2012) 7–9.

Lathrop, Gordon. *Holy Things*. Minneapolis: Fortress, 1993.

Lear, Nick. *Making a Splash: A Guide for Baptism*. Didcot, UK: Baptist Union, 2015 [2007].
Ledwich, William. "Baptism, Sacrament of the Cross." In *The Sacrifice of Praise*, edited by Bryan D. Spinks, 199–211. Rome: Via Pompeo Magno, 1981.
Levenson, Jon. D. "The Temple and the World." *Journal of Religion* 64 (1984) 275–98.
Levine, Amy-Jill. *The Misunderstood Jew: The Church and the Scandal of the Jewish Jesus*. New York: HarperCollins, 2006.
Licona, Michael R. *The Resurrection of Jesus: A New Historiographical Approach*. Nottingham: Apollos, 2010.
Lorenzen, Thorwald. *Resurrection and Discipleship*. Maryknoll: Orbis, 1995.
Lossky, Vladimir. *The Mystical Theology of the Eastern Church*. Cambridge: Clarke, 1957.
Louth, Andrew. *Introducing Eastern Orthodox Theology*. London: SPCK, 2013.
———. *Modern Orthodox Thinkers*. London: SPCK, 2015.
Lumpkin, William L. *Baptist Confessions of Faith*. Rev. ed. Valley Forge, PA: Judson, 1969.
Luther, Martin. "'This Is My Son, the Beloved': Sermon on the Baptism of Jesus." *Word and World* 16 (1996) 7–10.
MacCulloch, Diarmaid. *A History of Christianity: The First Three Thousand Years*. London: Lane, 2009.
———. *Thomas Cranmer*. New Haven: Yale University Press, 1996.
Mackintosh, H. R. *The Christian Experience of Forgiveness*. London: Nisbet, 1927.
Macquarrie, John. *Twentieth-Century Religious Thought*. SCM: London, 1963.
Maddox, Randy L. "John Wesley and Eastern Orthodoxy: Influences, Convergences and Differences." *Asbury Theological Journal* 45 (1990) 29–53.
Marie, comité mixte Baptiste-Catholique en France. Documents Episcopat 10. Paris: Le Secrétariat Général de la Conférence des Évêques de France, 2009.
Marsh, Rob. "Looking at God Looking at You." *The Way* 43 (2004) 19–28.
———. "Praying through Film, Story, Song, Art." http://rmarsh.com/2014/06/03/praying-through-film-story-song-art.
Mathewes-Green, Frederica. *The Open Door: Entering the Sanctuary of Icons and Prayer*. Brewster, MA: Paraclete, 2008.
McClendon, James W., Jr. *Biography as Theology: How Life Stories Can Remake Today's Theology*. Rev. ed. Philadelphia: Trinity, 1990.
———. *Doctrine*. Vol. 2 of *Systematic Theology*. Nashville: Abingdon, 1994.
———. *Ethics*. Vol. 1 of *Systematic Theology*. Rev. ed. Nashville: Abingdon, 2002.
McDonald, Suzanne. Review of *The Rhythm of Doctrine*, by John E. Colwell. *Theology* 117 (2009) 225–26.
McDonnell, Kilian. "Jesus' Baptism in the Jordan." *Theological Studies* 56 (1995) 209–36.
McFague, Sallie. *The Body of God: An Ecological Theology*. London: SCM, 1993.
———. *Metaphorical Theology: Models of God in Religious Language*. Philadelphia: Fortress, 1982.
McGuckin, John. *St. Gregory of Nazianzus: An Intellectual Biography*. Crestwood, NY: St. Vladimir's Seminary Press, 2001.
McNamara, Beverly. *Fragile Lives: Death, Dying and Care*. Buckingham: Oxford University Press, 2001.
McVey, Kathleen E. *Ephrem the Syrian: Hymns*. New York: Paulist, 1989.

Merton, Thomas. *The Wisdom of the Desert*. New York: New Directions / Gethsemani, 1960.
Meyers, Ruth A. *Continuing the Reformation: Re-Visioning Baptism in the Episcopal Church*. New York: Church, 2000.
———. "Renewal of Baptismal Vows." In *New SCM Dictionary of Liturgy and Worship*, edited by Paul Bradshaw, 52–53. London: SCM, 2013.
Micklem, Caryl, ed. *Contemporary Prayers for Public Worship*. London: SCM, 1967.
Middleton, J. Richard. *The Liberating Image: The Imago Dei in Genesis 1*. Grand Rapids: Brazos, 2005.
Molnar, Paul. *Divine Freedom and the Doctrine of the Immanent Trinity*. 2nd ed. London: T. & T. Clark, 2017 [2002].
Moltmann, Jürgen. *The Church in the Power of the Spirit*. London: SCM, 1977.
———. "Liberate Yourself by Accepting One Another." In *Human Disability and the Service of God: Reassessing Religious Practice*, edited by Nancy Eiesland and Don E. Saliers, 105–22. Nashville: Abingdon, 1998.
———. *Theology of Hope*. Translated by James W. Leitch. London: SCM, 1967.
———. *The Trinity and the Kingdom of God: The Doctrine of God*. Translated by Margaret Kohl. London: SCM, 1981.
Morgan, Robert. *Then Sings my Soul*. Nashville: Nelson, 2003.
Nelson, Sally. *Confronting Meaningless Suffering*. PhD thesis, University of Manchester, 2011.
———. *A Thousand Crucifixions: The Materialist Subversion of the Church*. 2009 Whitley Lecture. Oxford: Whitley, 2009.
Nicene and Post Nicene Fathers. Edited by Philip Schaff and Henry Wace. Grand Rapids: Eerdmans, 1960.
Nilles, Nicolaus. *Kalendarium manuale utriusque ecclesiae orientalis et occidentalis*. 2 vols. Oeniponte: Rauch, 1896–97.
Nouwen, Henri. *The Return of the Prodigal: A Story of Homecoming*. New York: Doubleday, 1992.
O'Brien, P. T. *Colossians*. Dallas: Word, 1998.
Ohanjanyan, Anna. "Evangelical and Pentecostal Communities in Armenia." In *Armenian Christianity Today*, edited by Alexander Agadjanian, 91–121. London: Routledge, 2016.
Pannenberg, Wolfhart. *Systematic Theology*. Vol. 1. Translated by G. W. Bromiley. Grand Rapids: Eerdmans, 1991.
Parry, Robin. *Worshipping Trinity*. Milton Keynes: Paternoster, 2005.
Parsons, Michael. *Calvin's Preaching on the Prophet Micah: The 1550–1511 Sermons in Geneva*. Lewiston, NY: Mellen, 2006.
Paterson, Ross. *The Antioch Factor: The Hidden Message in the Book of Acts*. Tonbridge, UK: Sovereign World, 2000.
Payne, Ernest A., and Stephen Winward. *Orders and Prayers for Church Worship: A Manual for Ministers*. 4th ed. London: Baptist Union of Great Britain, 1967 [1960].
Perdue, Leo G. *Wisdom and Creation. The Theology of Wisdom Literature*. Eugene, OR: Wipf & Stock, 2007.
Perschbacher, W. J. *The New Analytical Greek Lexicon*. Peabody: Hendrickson, 1990.
Philips, T. E. "Creation, Sin and Its Curse, and the People of God." *Horizons in Biblical Theology* 25 (2003) 146–60.
Phipps, Simon. *God on Monday*. London: Hodder & Stoughton, 1966.

Pittenger, Norman, and David Pailin. *God and the Process of Reality*. London: Routledge, 1989.

Placher, William. *Narratives of a Vulnerable God*. Louisville: Westminster John Knox, 1994.

Pollock, David C., and Ruth E. Van Reken. *Third Culture Kids: Growing Up among Worlds*. Rev. ed. London: Brealey, 2009.

Pound, Marcus. *Theology, Psychoanalysis and Trauma*. London: SCM, 2007.

Prokhorov, Constantine. *Russian Baptists and Orthodoxy, 1960–1990*. Carlisle: Langham Monographs, 2013.

Puhl, Louis J. *The Spiritual Exercises of St. Ignatius*. Chicago: Jesuit Press, 1951.

Rahner, Karl. "Virginitas in Partu." In *Theological Investigations*, 4:134–62. London: Darton, Longman & Todd, 1966.

Rashdall, Hastings. *The Idea of the Atonement*. London: Macmillan, 1919.

Ratcliff, Edward. "The Old Syrian Baptismal Tradition and Its Resettlement under the Influence of Jerusalem in the Fourth Century." In *Liturgical Studies*, edited by Arthur Couratin and David Tripp, 135–54. London: SPCK, 1976.

Rees, Frank. "The Search for Baptist Saints." *Pacifica* 30 (2017) 284–99.

Regan, D. *Experience the Mystery: Pastoral Possibilities for Christian Mystagogy*. London: Chapman, 1994.

Reynolds, Thomas E. *Vulnerable Communion: A Theology of Disability and Hospitality*. Grand Rapids: Brazos, 2008.

Ricoeur, Paul. *The Rule of Metaphor*. Abingdon: Routledge, 2003.

Robinson, H. Wheeler, *The Christian Experience of the Holy Spirit*. London: Nisbet, 1928.

Robinson, Marilynne. "Dietrich Bonhoeffer." In *The Death of Adam: Essays on Modern Thought*, 108–25. New York: Picador, 1998.

———. *Gilead*. London: Virago, 2004.

Saliers, Don E. *Worship as Theology: Foretaste of Divine Glory*. Nashville: Abingdon, 1994.

Saliers, Don, and Emily Saliers. *A Song to Sing, A Life to Live*. San Francisco: Josey Bass, 2005.

Sander, E. P. *The Historical Figure of Jesus*. London: Lane, 1993.

Scaer, David. "Luther, Baptism and the Church Today." *Concordia Theological Quarterly* 62 (1998) 247–68.

Schmemann, Alexander. *Introduction to Liturgical Theology*. Translated by Asheleigh E. Moorehouse. Crestwood, NY: St. Vladimir's Seminary Press, 1975.

———. *Of Water and the Spirit: A Liturgical Study of Baptism*. London: SPCK, 1976.

———. "The Task and Method of Liturgical Theology." In *Primary Sources of Liturgical Theology: A Reader*, edited by Dwight W. Vogel, 54–62. Collegeville: Liturgical, 2016.

Seitz, Christopher. *Isaiah 1–39*. Interpretation. Louisville: John Knox, 1993.

Senn, Frank. *Christian Liturgy: Catholic and Evangelical*. Minneapolis: Fortress, 1997.

Sheldrake, Philip. *Spirituality: A Brief History*. Oxford: Wiley-Blackwell, 2013.

Sheppard, Lancelot. "The New Calendar." In *The New Liturgy*, edited by Lancelot Sheppard, 9–18. London: Darton, Longman & Todd, 1970.

Sherman, Hazel. "Baptized—'in the Name of the Father and of the Son and of the Holy Spirit.'" In *Reflections on the Water: Understanding God and the World through the*

Baptism of Believers, edited by Paul S. Fiddes, 101–16. Macon, GA: Smyth and Helwys, 1996.

Sölle, Dorothée. *The Inward Road and the Way Back: Texts and Reflections on Religious Experience*. Translated by David L. Scheidt. London: DLT, 1979.

Songulashvili, Malkhaz. *Evangelical Christian Baptists of Georgia*. Waco, TX: Baylor University Press, 2015.

Soskice, Janet M. "Trinity and Feminism." In *Cambridge Companion to Feminist Theology*, edited by Susan Frank Parsons, 135–50. Cambridge: Cambridge University Press, 2002.

Southall, David. *Rediscovering Righteousness in Romans*. Tübingen: Mohr Seibeck, 2008.

Spinks, Bryan. *Reformation and Modern Rituals and Theologies of Baptism: From Luther to Contemporary Practices*. Aldershot: Ashgate, 2006.

Spufford, Francis. *Unapologetic*. London: Faber and Faber, 2013.

Spurgeon, Charles H. *Lectures to My Students: A Selection of Addresses Delivered to the Students of the Pastors' College, Metropolitan Tabernacle, Lectures*. London: Passmore and Alabaster, 1906.

Stassen, Glen. *A Thicker Jesus: Incarnational Discipleship in a Secular Age*. Louisville: Westminster John Knox, 2012.

Stewart, Aubrey, ed. *Luloph von Suchem's Description of the Holy Land, and of the Way Thither*. Cambridge: Cambridge University Press, 2013.

Storr, Anthony. *Music and the Mind*. London: Collins, 1992.

Stott, John R. W. *The Radical Disciple*. Nottingham: InterVarsity, 2010.

Swinton, John. "Disability Theology." In *Cambridge Dictionary of Christian Theology*, edited by Ian McFarland et al., 140–41 Cambridge: Cambridge University Press, 2010.

———. "From Inclusion to Belonging." In *Theology and the Experience of Disability*, edited by Andrew Picard and Myk Habets, 171–81. Abingdon: Routledge, 2016.

Talley, Thomas. "Liturgical Time in the Ancient Church." In *Between Memory and Hope: Readings on the Liturgical Year*, edited by Maxwell E. Johnson, 25–46. Collegeville: Liturgical, 2000.

———. *The Origins of the Liturgical Year*. New York: Pueblo, 1986.

Taylor, John V. *The Go-Between God. The Holy Spirit and the Christian Mission*. London: SCM, 1974.

Thompson, Ross. *Spirituality in Season: Growing through the Christian Year*. Norwich: Canterbury, 2008.

Tillich, Paul. *Systematic Theology: Combined Volume*. James Nisbet: London, 1968.

Trexler, Richard. *The Journey of the Magi: Meanings in History of a Christian Story*. Princeton: Princeton University Press, 1997.

Trigg, Jonathan. *Baptism in the Theology of Martin Luther*. Leiden: Brill, 2001.

Tripp, David. *The Renewal of the Covenant in the Methodist Tradition*. London: Epworth, 1969.

Turner, Victor. *The Ritual Process: Structure and Anti-structure*. Harmondsworth, UK: Penguin, 1969.

Vanier, Jean. *Becoming Human*. Mahwah, NJ: Paulist, 1998.

———. "The Vision of Jesus." In *Living Gently in a Violent World: The Prophetic Witness of Weakness*, by Stanley Hauerwas and Jean Vanier, 59–76. Downers Grove: InterVarsity, 2008.

Voke, Christopher J. *Creation at Worship*. Milton Keynes: Paternoster, 2009.

Walker, Peter. *The Weekend That Changed the World: The Mystery of Jerusalem's Empty Tomb*. London: Marshall Pickering, 1999.

Ward, W. R., and R. P. Heitzenrater. *The Works of John Wesley, "Journals and Diaries IV."* Vol. 21. Nashville: Abingdon, 1992.

Ware, Kallistos, and Mother Mary, trans. *The Festal Menaion*. London: Faber & Faber, 1969.

Warner, Rob. *Baptism and You*. London: Hodder & Stoughton, 2000.

Watts, Isaac. *Hymns and Spiritual Songs*. London: Lawrence, 1707.

Weaver, J. Denny. *The Nonviolent Atonement*. Grand Rapids: Eerdmans, 2001.

Webber, Robert E. *Ancient-Future Worship: Proclaiming and Enacting God's Narrative*. Grand Rapids: Baker, 2008.

Webster, John. *The Cambridge Companion to Karl Barth*. Cambridge: Cambridge University Press, 2000.

———. *Holy Scripture: A Dogmatic Sketch*. Cambridge: Cambridge University Press, 2003.

Wells, Samuel. "The Difference Christ Makes." In *The Difference Christ Makes: Celebrating the Life, Work, and Friendship of Stanley Hauerwas*, edited by Charles M. Collier, 5–23. Eugene, OR: Cascade, 2015.

———. "The Disarming Virtue of Stanley Hauerwas." *Scottish Journal of Theology* 52 (1999) 82–88.

———. *The Nazareth Manifesto: Being with God*. Chichester: Wiley-Blackwell, 2015.

———. *Transforming Fate into Destiny*. Carlisle: Paternoster, 1998.

Wenham, Gordon. "Sanctuary Symbolism in the Garden of Eden Story." In *Proceedings of the World Congress of Jewish Studies*, 19–25. Jerusalem: World Union of Jewish Studies, 1985.

Wenham, John. *Easter Enigma*. Exeter: Paternoster, 1984.

Wenkel, D. H. "Wild Beasts in the Prophecy of Isaiah: The Loss of Dominion and Its Renewal through Israel as the New Humanity." *Journal of Theological Interpretation* 5 (2011) 251–64.

White, B. R. *The English Baptists of the Seventeenth Century*. Didcot, UK: Baptist Historical Society, 1996.

———. "The Practice of Association." In *A Perspective on Baptist Identity*, edited by David Slater, 19–29. Ilkley, UK: Mainstream, 1987.

White, James F., ed. *Documents of Christian Worship*. Edinburgh: T. & T. Clark, 1992.

———. *Protestant Worship: Traditions in Transition*. Louisville: Westminster John Knox, 1989.

Whitehead, Alfred North. *Process and Reality: An Essay in Cosmology*. New York: Macmillan, 1929.

Wilken, Robert. "The Interpretation of the Baptism of Jesus." *Studia Patristica* 11 (1972) 268–77.

William A. Barry, and William J. Connolly. *The Practice of Spiritual Direction*. New York: HarperCollins, 1982.

Williams, Howard. *The Song of the Devil*. London: Epworth, 1972.

Williams, Rowan. *On Christian Theology*. Oxford: Blackwell, 2000.

———. *Silence and Honey Cakes: The Wisdom of the Desert*. Oxford: Lion Hudson, 2003.

———. *The Truce of God*. Glasgow: Fount Original, 1983.

Williams, Thomas. "Sin, Grace, and Redemption." In *The Cambridge Companion to Abelard*, edited by Jeffrey E. Brower and Kevin Guilty, 258–78. Cambridge: Cambridge University Press, 2004.

Willimon, William H. *Conversations with Barth on Preaching*. Nashville: Abingdon, 2006.

Willimon, William H., and Stanley Hauerwas. *Lord, Teach Us: The Lord's Prayer and the Christian Life*. Nashville: Abingdon, 1996.

———. *Preaching to Strangers*. Nashville: Abingdon, 1993.

Winkler, Gabriele. "A Remarkable Shift in the 4th-Century Creeds: An Analysis of the Armenian, Syriac, and Greek Evidence." *Studia Patristica* 17 (1982) 1396–401.

Winter, Sean F. "Word and World: Dietrich Bonhoeffer and Biblical Interpretation." *Pacifica* 25 (2012) 137–50.

Winward, Stephen F. *Your Baptism*. London: Baptist Union, 1975 [1969].

Wood, Donald. *Barth's Theology of Interpretation*. Aldershot: Ashgate, 2007.

"The Word of God in the Life of the Church: A Report of International Conversations between the Catholic Church and the Baptist World Alliance, 2006–2010." *American Baptist Quarterly* 31 (2012) 28–122.

Wright, Nigel G. *The Real Godsend: Preaching the Birth Narratives in Matthew and Luke*. Abingdon: Bible Reading Fellowship, 2009.

Wright, N. T. *The Challenge of Jesus*. London: SPCK, 2000.

———. *The Climax of the Covenant*. Edinburgh: T. & T. Clark, 1991.

———. *John for Everyone*. Part 2. London: SPCK, 2002.

———. "Mind, Spirit, Soul and Body: All for One and One for All Reflections on Paul's Anthropology in his Complex Contexts." Society of Christian Philosophers: Regional Meeting, Fordham University, March 18, 2011. http://ntwrightpage.com/2016/07/12/mind-spirit-soul-and-body/.

———. *The New Testament and the People of God*. London: SPCK, 1992.

———. "Resurrection: From Theology to Music and Back Again." In *Sounding the Depths*, edited by Jeremy Begbie, 193–202. Canterbury: SCM, 2002.

———. *The Resurrection of the Son of God*. London: SPCK, 2003.

———. *Simply Christian*. London: SPCK, 2006.

———. *Surprised by Hope*. London: SPCK, 2007.

Zizioulas, John D. *Being as Communion*. London: Darton, Longman & Todd, 1984.